WrESTLiNgObserver

TRIBUTES II

REMEMBERING MORE OF THE
WORLD'S GREATEST
PROFESSIONAL WRESTLERS

DAVE MELTZER

FOREWORD BY
BRET HART

SP
SPORTS
PUBLISHING
L.L.C.

www.SportsPublishingLLC.com

ISBN: 1-58261-817-8

PUBLISHER: Peter L. Bannon
SENIOR MANAGING EDITOR: Susan M. Moyer
ACQUISITIONS EDITORS: Nick Obradovich and Scott Rauguth
DEVELOPMENTAL EDITOR: Dean Miller
ART DIRECTOR: K. Jeffrey Higgerson
BOOK DESIGN AND SENIOR PROJECT MANAGER: Jennifer L. Polson
DUST JACKET DESIGN: Ralph Roether III
IMAGING: Kerri Baker, Dustin Hubbart, Chris Mohrbacher and Heidi Norsen
PHOTO EDITOR: Erin Linden-Levy
VICE PRESIDENT OF SALES AND MARKETING: Kevin King
MEDIA AND PROMOTIONS MANAGERS: Nick Obradovich (regional),
Randy Fouts (national), Maurey Williamson (print)

Printed in the United States

Sports Publishing L.L.C.
804 North Neil Street
Champaign, IL 61820

Phone: 1-877-424-2665
Fax: 217-363-2073
Web site: www.SportsPublishingLLC.com

I would like to dedicate this book to my family, my parents, Herb and Marilyn Meltzer, my wife, Mary Anne, and son, Cody, for putting up with me for all these years and being such a great help in ways I don't think they themselves will ever fully realize. I'd also like to dedicate this book, like the first book, to the readers of the Wrestling Observer Newsletter.

Without them, nothing like this would have been possible.

Dr. Mike Lano

CONTENTS

I VAGUELY RECOLLECT A TIME many years ago, I'm guessing it was back in the mid- '80s, when I first met Dave Meltzer. I'd heard about him from my parents, who were avid readers of his fledgling *Wrestling Observer Newsletter*.

It was a time when old schoolers still went to great lengths to "protect the business," living our characters not just in the ring but whenever the public—the marks—were around. In fact, as late as the mid-'90s the storyline had Owen and I feuding, so for the sake of realism, as much as we would have enjoyed traveling together on the road, we instead avoided each other and wouldn't even sit together on numerous long plane rides back to Calgary.

We'd get on different lines going through customs, and the agents, who saw us come through on a regular basis, were more and more convinced that the heat between Owen and I was real. Finally, on this one occasion, I sort of passed by Owen and whispered something I needed him to know. Suddenly a customs agent came running out of some hidden room in which she'd caught a glimpse of it on a security monitor, and pointing at me, she

grinned, "Ah ha! I got ya! I knew you guys didn't really hate each other!"

Owen and I just couldn't help but burst out laughing! Busted fair and square! Especially being that Owen and I were second-generation wrestlers, kayfabe came naturally as a part of the only way of life we'd ever known. A way of life in which protecting the business was the cardinal rule.

So imagine how I was taken aback a decade earlier when I met Meltzer in a hotel hallway and he told me I was going to be turning face any day now, especially since I had no knowledge of it whatsoever! I dismissed it rather quickly, we chatted for a few minutes, and I was surprised by his knowledge of the innerworkings of the business. He was talking to me with a smile on his face, meanwhile I was thinking, who is this guy to make a living by exposing, and therefore jeopardizing, what I do for a living? Who is he to feed himself by taking food off the tables of all the wrestlers? And so, Dave Meltzer became the enemy—sort of.

The majority of the wrestlers of my era shared my contempt for him, while at the same time swarming like bees to honey if someone brought an issue of what the wrestlers came to call "the s—t sheet" into the dressing room. He was the enemy, but he was also the only accurate source of what was going on in the business, even for the people in it!

A few days after Meltzer told me I was turning face, I was on the phone with Vince McMahon, who notified me that I actually was!

From that point on I resented the truth being written in *The Observer* and I suppose it had a lot to do with the fact that this wet-behind-the-ears outsider often knew what I was doing before I did.

It's a credit to Meltzer that as time went by he educated himself about the business, gradually prying open doors that'd been welded shut for generations. His observations and analysis were increasingly detailed and insightful, and it became obvious that he was gradually compiling the only factual chronicle of pro wrestling, especially of my era, and that it was encyclopedic in scope. That kind of dedication and tenacity could only come from someone who genuinely loves the business, who, in his own way, lives and breathes it.

It'd be hard to hate Meltzer for that—and so he earned respect where there'd been contempt.

The business is an open book now, ironically, in large part because of the Montreal screw job. Prior to November 9, 1997, the number of wrestling fans who were smart to the business were only a single-digit percentage of all the fans watching on TV. After Montreal that changed overnight, because all the fans wanted to know what the heck had just happened—and it wasn't rocket science to know that Vince would immediately run damage control in an attempt to rewrite history, not just for the fans, but in the dressing room, too. So I found myself in the strange position of being a guy known by his peers for always protecting the business, but now, for the real truth to be known, I'd have to divulge its innerworkings to an unprecedented degree. I think Vince was counting on the fact that it just wasn't in me to do that.

I did. I believed, and I still do, that it was in the best interest of all the boys that the truth be told—if the biggest wrestling organization in the world can screw the world champion, then it was a powerful head's up to every wrestler in every dressing room everywhere.

Minutes after the Montreal screw job I was talking to my friend/office manager, Marcy, about getting the real truth out there, far and fast, through our vast network of contacts around the world. When it came to Meltzer, I wondered whether I could rely on my old nemesis to tell the truth in a situation so politically explosive that he'd run the risk of alienating himself from sources that he needed to make his living in the future. Marcy called Meltzer and asked him that very question and he was so disturbed by what had just happened, not just to me but to the business, that he wanted nothing more than to get at and print the truth!

So, one of the most unlikely phone conversations of all time took place. I gave Meltzer the whole intrepid account, and it was such a detailed and convoluted debacle that I was sure he wouldn't get it right. He did. I also told him to go ahead and try to disprove anything or everything I told him. There were no retractions. All I can say is that I have always been grateful to Dave for the integrity with which he handled that situation and for putting out the most accurate and detailed account of that time in my life, one that has stood the test of time.

I've lost many comrades over the years and have been moved by Dave's honest portrayals of their lives, not just as wrestling characters, but as people. I truly appreciated everything he wrote about Owen, and his profile of my complex father is the most moving and honest one that I've ever seen. I believe that all the wrestlers in this book would appreciate the fact that somebody has taken the time to portray them accurately and at last get it right.

Dave Meltzer has become a true friend of mine. He is a man who has dedicated his life to wrestling every bit as much as I have. All wrestlers should admire him for doing his utmost to find the truth, for all our sakes, to preserve the legacy of what we broke our bodies and spilled our blood for, for the love of wrestling.

Bret "Hitman" Hart
Calgary
August, 2004

INTRODUCTION

PRO WRESTLING IS A UNIQUE WORLD. Part dramatic performance. Part athletic performance. Part comedy. Part bad taste. It's a world that doesn't fit quite into any category. Its fans are millions, but its history, until recent years, is largely nonexistent.

In the past few years, many of the giants of that industry, from those who date back before there was even television, to stars of the modern era who were creatures of television, have passed away. They all lived colorful lives, some long, and many others far too short. They were all unique survivors in a very tough world, one with very little regard for the people who make it tick.

In this book are chronicled some of the biggest names in its history. They don't come any bigger than Lou Thesz, who many would say was the greatest the business ever had. He was the athlete and perennial world champion when pro wrestling hit network television in the late '40s. If it was baseball, he'd have been Joe DiMaggio or Ted Williams, or if it was boxing, he'd have been Joe Louis or Rocky Marciano. But he was a pro wrestler, and when his day was done, to his neighbors,

he was the fit, old grandfatherly Lou, and few of them even knew he was one of the biggest TV sports stars of the '50s, or that he was known as "The God of Wrestling" by an entire nation in Japan.

Two of his contemporaries were Stu Hart and Freddie Blassie. Hart, like Thesz, was an accomplished real wrestler. Thesz grew up as a fan of pro wrestling, and when young, learned from the best. In the case of Hart, he was more of a fan of amateur wrestling and learned from the best as well. But in Western Canada when he was growing up, the best was a man named Jack Taylor, who happened to be a pro wrestling star as well. Stu Hart was never a superstar pro wrestler, but he was a legend within pro wrestling. In hindsight, due to who he started and how many people came through Stampede Wrestling, he was among the most influential men ever in the profession. His son Bret, is Canada's most famous pro wrestling export. In this book, also profiled are his son Owen, who passed away in a tragic ring accident on a pay-per-view event in 1999; as well as his longtime son-in-law, Davey Boy Smith, the British

Bulldog, who is one of England's most famous pro wrestling exports. Both Owen Hart and Davey Boy Smith were prodigies of the business, among the best by their early 20s, who attained stardom in Japan and Canada for years before they were discovered by American fans. Hart was a tragedy of an accident. Smith was a tragedy of the excesses of the business. Smith used steroids to bulk up from 175 pounds to, at times, 270 pounds on a 5-10 frame. The unique moves and hard style he and partner Dynamite Kid, now confined to a wheelchair in England, developed, put a different kind of stress on his body. Soon, he was into drugs for back pain. As the years went by, his problems got worse. The last few years of his life saw him spiral out of control, before one day, predictably to those who knew him best, it was over.

Freddie Blassie, like Lou Thesz, came from St. Louis. The two were roughly the same age. But their careers hardly paralleled, although Blassie did take Thesz' spot in the early '60s as the biggest American drawing card in Japan. Blassie was no wrestler. He was an arrogant heel wrestler, like few others in history. There is a phrase in wrestling about having the ability to talk people into buying tickets to matches. Few were any better at it than Blassie. But it took a while. Thesz was a superstar in wrestling by the age of 21, when he won his first world title. Blassie started wrestling a few years earlier but was hardly an instant success. Few had even heard of him until television hit in the early '50s, and he became a star. In the early '60s, when Thesz was the grand old man of the game, Blassie was a current major superstar who was selling out the Olympic Auditorium in Los Angeles. Blassie was ahead of his time, as one of the first men in wrestling who understood what current wrestling promoters don't, about drawing a diverse audience. If you talk to Hispanic wrestlers, whether they be Pedro Morales, a Puerto Rican sensation in the '60s and '70s, or Ray Mendoza, one of Mexico's all-time legends, they'll credit their American stardom to Blassie, who stood up for them and booked them strong, and created an entirely new audience for matches.

If Freddie Blassie wasn't the greatest wrestling heel of all time, perhaps it was The Sheik. Born Ed Farhat, he created the persona of a Syrian madman who used pencils to cut his opponents and fire to blind them. He was responsible for inciting riots, and he was a worldwide sensation, who could get over immediately. While Blassie incited fans with his mouth, Sheik did it without ever saying a word. He played partially on stereotypes. It was easy to get North Americans to hate a rich foreigner, who always cheated, and in his heyday, almost never lost.

Andre the Giant was the most famous wrestler of the '70s. To wrestling fans, he was almost a creature out of a fairy tale, but his real life was very different. He lived fast. Some feel had he dedicated himself to a sport, with his natural size and strength, he could have excelled, but he fell in with wrestlers as a teenager and became bigger in that world than almost anyone who had preceded him. There have been men as big as he was, and far more agile, but none who had his charisma, or will be remembered at the same level.

Another giant, not of freakish size like Andre, was Gorilla Monsoon. He was a big star in the '60s, who in real life was a 6-4$^{1}/_{2}$ and 400-pound educated Ithaca College graduate, and was a star in wrestling and track. When he got into pro wrestling, he was bigger and more powerful than just about anyone in the business. But he gained more of his fame behind the scenes, as a television straight man for the likes of Bobby Heenan and Jesse Ventura. It was little known that he was a partial owner of the WWWF, when the company was known as Capitol Sports. But in later years, he suffered greatly, both because of declining health, and in particular, because of the death of his son, Joey Marella, a WWF referee, in an auto accident.

Even the most ardent wrestling fan wouldn't know the name George Woodin. When he was very young, he was given the nickname Tim and became a major college wrestling star. He started as a pro wrestler but was not a major star, until a promoter in Nebraska came up with the idea of a white-clad Mr. Wrestling. He was an immediate hit and became a legend when he left Nebraska and went to Georgia, where a booker decided to build the territory around him, and he became one of the biggest names of the early '70s.

You'll also read about Johnny Valentine and Wahoo McDaniel, two of the hardest hitters and biggest stars of their generation. The two were rivals in Texas and Florida and changed the face of wrestling in the Carolinas. McDaniel was a celebrity long before wrestling as a pro football player, better known for his name and craziness than for being a great player. Valentine was a strange man, with a sick sense of humor who scared a lot of wrestlers who didn't know if he was all there. But in the ring he had a style and he seemed to enjoy getting hit as hard as possible, and loved to reciprocate, with his goal making people believe what they were seeing was real. He was one of those characters even more legendary among wrestlers than he was among fans who saw him.

And we also look at the sad modern cases. Pro wrestling boomed in the 1980s. Like Davey Boy Smith, some of its biggest stars were Mr. Perfect, The Lovely Elizabeth, The Road Warriors and the Fabulous Freebirds. It was a lifestyle of people who grew up in a business where they suddenly, at a young age, were making tons of money, almost out of nowhere. They were hardly the only ones who dabbled in the '80s lifestyle of drinking and drugs, and working an insane travel schedule. But Curt Hennig, Elizabeth Hulette, Mike Hegstrand and Terry Gordy were some of its most famous victims. All were superstars as wrestling hit it big through national cable and syndication, and Hegstrand and Gordy were even more famous in Japan.

But behind the facade, these were all very different people. They wound up in a world that gave them euphoria as performers, and then, cruelly, in many cases, took it away. Their stories are all, at times, very successful. But ultimately, they are not stories, they are reality, and not all have a happy ending.

ACKNOWLEDGMENTS

I'D LIKE TO THANK THE CREW AT SPORTS Publishing, most notably Nick Obradovich and Dean Miller, for their support in this project. I'd also like to thank Ted Hobgood and Larry Weaver for the initial idea which resulted in the original *Tributes* book, as well as people like Gary Will, Steve Yohe, Mike Tenay, Larry Matysik, Koji Miyamoto, Ross Hart, Scott Teal, Koichi Yoshizawa, Bob Leonard, Fred Hornby and so many others who have been over the past decade able to uncover and preserve history of a unique business which had almost none to speak of. I'd also like to thank so many of the current and former wrestlers for their help in providing memories of their contemporaries.

I'd also like to thank Bryan Alvarez for all his help in doing a weekly radio show, Alex Marvez for being such a great friend and confidante, and again thank Mick Foley for all he has done in opening up the book publishing industry to give wrestling fans a chance to learn far more about the history and personalities of their industry than would have otherwise been possible had he not taken the chance and written a different-style first book.

DAVE MELTZER IS CONSIDERED THE PIONEER OF pro wrestling journalism. A lifelong fan, Meltzer began writing about pro wrestling at the age of ten, in various newsletters and fan club publications. His *California Wrestling Report* and *International Wrestling Gazette* in the '70s were considered two of the top underground wrest-ling publications. While attending San Jose State University and writing for the *Oakland Tribune*, Meltzer started the *Wrestling Observer Newsletter* in late 1982.

The *Observer* was the first publication covering pro wrestling that reported on it as it was, without pretending storylines and matches were not prearranged, and that it was a business, opening up a very different way to view what was going on. The *Observer* coined the phrase "athletic entertainment" to describe pro wrestling, years before Vince McMahon began using the term "sports entertainment."

Very quickly, the publication was read by virtually every major decision-maker in pro wrestling, as subscriptions went to almost every major wrestling office. Many of the biggest names in wrestling were early subscribers, some openly, and others trying to hide by using their wives' maiden names. However, the publication was also loathed in the '80s and even the '90s for breaking kayfabe—

the ancient pro wrestling code never to admit that even the most blatantly scripted scenarios were planned in advance, or that winners and losers of matches were predetermined.

The newsletter was a cult favorite among wrestling fans in the '80s, and gained great popularity in the '90s with Meltzer's weekly pro wrestling column in *The National*, and his appearances on dozens of television news shows, talk shows and documentaries. With Vince McMahon's admission years later that pro wrestling was scripted entertainment, virtually all wrestling fans today accept it and embrace it as such, given pro wrestling's greater popularity than nonscripted fighting sports.

Through the *Observer*, Meltzer was responsible for educating a generation of fans and future wrestlers about what the industry was really all about, as well as opening the doors to the American audience to wrestling in places like Japan and Mexico, which helped open up the U.S. style.

The *Observer* has remained the publication of record in the industry to this day. Its annual awards issue has been covered by major daily newspapers around the world as the most prestigious wrestling awards on a world-wide basis and its Hall of Fame, with voting among the top historians, writers, wrestlers and front office people, is considered the most respected of any of its kind. After 23 years, Meltzer still writes literally half a book worth of news material, covering all the current news as well as looks at history, on a weekly basis, read by readers in more than 30 countries. He self-published several books in the '80s, and his original *Tributes* book in 2001 was the best-selling pro wrestling book for several months. Through the years, it has been ranked in the newsletter field as one of the best and most successful newsletters of any kind in the United States, and Meltzer has been rated in several lists by wrestling historians as one of the most influential people in the 100-plus year history of the industry.

Meltzer grew up in San Jose, California, and graduated with a journalism degree from San Jose State University. He worked for several newspapers from 1981 to 1987 before making writing about pro wrestling a full-time endeavor. He has been quoted as the leading outside authority on pro wrestling in virtually every form of media, including the *New York Times*, *Los Angles Times*, *Sports Illustrated* and *TV Guide*. He was featured in the two most widely acclaimed documentaries on the inside of the pro wrestling business, *Hitman Hart: Wrestling with Shadows* and *Beyond the Mat*. Since 1999, he has done a pro wrestling radio show, which for two years was the most popular internet-generated talk show on the air, and currently is syndicated nationally on the Sports Byline radio network.

TRIBUTES II

REMEMBERING MORE OF THE
WORLD'S GREATEST
PROFESSIONAL WRESTLERS

CHAPTER 1

OWEN HART

OWEN HART WAS BORN May 7, 1965. You know the place. You know the house. You've even seen what it looks like on the inside. He was the youngest of a family of eight boys and four girls. All eight boys became wrestlers. All four girls married them. It's definitely not what their mother had in mind.

He was always around wrestling. It was his father's life. All his brothers did it. Older wrestlers who were superstars of the early '70s tell stories about five-year-old Owen running barefoot in the snow. Or eight-year-old Owen helping older brother Bruce write the wrestling programs. Or 14-year-old Owen, accompanying big brothers Bruce and Keith to a big show in Honolulu where they played heel against a huge, untalented Samoan tag team in a building with inadequate security and rabid Samoan fans. The brothers, used to playing face at home, were a little too effective playing heel, and a riot broke out. A few attacked Bruce and Keith, who were doing a decent job holding them off. A large adult Samoan fan threw a chair at Keith. Owen, totally undersized, jumped right in the fray and wound up with a black eye.

As a child, he shared a room with three of his brothers, Ross, who was five years older, Bret, who was eight years older, and Dean, who was ten years older. But the biggest influence on him was

OPPOSITE: Scott Hall, in his Razor Ramon days, works over the wrist of Owen Hart. (Dr. Mike Lano)

Bruce, 15 years his senior, who taught him the world of practical jokes that among wrestlers he became probably more famous for than even for his considerable ability inside the ring. All his brothers tried wrestling with varying degrees of success. Keith and Bruce went to college first and got their teaching credentials, but wound up working in their father's wrestling business.

Bret, who at first never wanted to be a wrestler, one day wound up in the ring and turned out to be pretty good and never stopped. Ross, who probably wanted to be a great wrestler and loved being on the road with the boys more than any of the brothers, but didn't have the athletic ability of his more famous brothers, wound up working more backstage and occasionally wrestling. Owen, growing up, was the best athlete of all the boys, and thus, became Stu's favorite.

He would goof around the ring as a teenager, and picked everything up quickly. He never did gymnastics, but one day he decided to do a backflip off the turnbuckles to set up a hip-toss spot. He tried it with a spotter once, hit the move perfectly, and never needed a spotter again. It was like that with every move. He grew up seeing legends like the Funk Brothers and Harley Race come through Stampede Wrestling as touring NWA world champions, and all the great British professional wrestlers from Billy Robinson to the Dynamite Kid and young Japanese stars as well, and learned to mix all the various styles and even threw in some Lucha Libre

at a time when nobody in wrestling learned any style other than what was done in their own local territory. As early as the age of 16, under a mask in small towns in the middle of nowhere, since it had to be kept secret to maintain his amateur wrestling eligibility, he'd fill in on shows, and his brothers remember him as being a natural. He played varsity baseball, football and wrestled at Ernest Manning High School, becoming City and Alberta Provincial high school champion in 1983 at 165 pounds. By this point he was also watching a lot of Japanese wrestling videotapes that his family would get, since Bret by this time was a major junior heavyweight star there, and Dynamite Kid, the greatest worker in the promotion and possibly the world at the time, was becoming legendary in the Orient.

After graduating high school in 1983, he accompanied brother Ross on a wrestling tour of Europe. Ross was going there as a wrestler. Owen was going there because he had a chance to spend the summer after graduation in Europe. Just before leaving, there was an injury in the crew and Owen, in two small towns in the middle of nowhere, and under a mask to protect both kayfabe and his amateur eligibility, formed a tag team with Dynamite Kid against older brother Bret and Gary Eichenhauser. By the time they went to England for Joint Promotions, Owen was wrestling under his real name, since wrestling news from England was hardly in danger of making its way to the collegiate authorities in Canada. He was an immediate star after wrestling a classic 40-minute television match against Marty Jones and also feuding with a veteran star named David "Fit" Finlay.

"Nobody pushed him into it," remembered Ross. "We all knew from the start he was a natural talent. He was never that anxious to make it a career. He just wanted to do it to see how it was. I never had the talent of a skilled wrestler like Owen and Bret, but he always encouraged me and made me feel good. But I was so happy to see him follow Bruce, Bret and Keith."

HART RETURNED HOME for his freshman year at the University of Calgary. He was studying for his teaching credential, following in the footsteps of brothers Bruce and Keith, both of whom at the time were wrestling for Stampede. He was a very good college wrestler, and in fact was never once pinned in three years of collegiate varsity competition, although he lost a few matches, mostly via close decisions. As a sophomore, Owen went to the CIAU (Canadian collegiate amateurs) nationals and placed third at 177 pounds. When he considered going into pro wrestling, his father strongly discouraged it. Stu loved pro wrestling, but as a great amateur himself and a two-time national champion in the late '30s, he was a total aficionado for what was real and wanted one of his sons to achieve the goal he never did, wrestle in the Olympics.

Bret gave up amateur wrestling after high school. Owen would be the last son. During his junior year, he placed second in the CIAU nationals at 177 pounds in 1986, but after that season, it had already been decreed that the University of Calgary was shutting down its wrestling program and Owen would be off scholarship. A few weeks later, Owen Hart, without a mask, under his own name, and in his home town of Calgary, made his pro debut, and was an instant success.

Owen and Bruce were supposed to become the headline tag team for Stampede. As it turned out, Bruce blew out his knee and needed major surgery and was out for ten months. A brother-in-law, Ben Bassarab, filled in and formed a team with Owen and they quickly became the International tag-team champions, forming a still legendary feud against the masked Viet Cong Express. The teams were having the best matches in North America, and Hart was within a few weeks of his debut, already the biggest star in the company.

"He was sensational from day one," recalled Bruce. "He had all the moves, and the timing and psychology. We had a great crew in here. ...It all started clicking."

The two teams fought many lengthy matches over the tag-team titles, which later led to Hart vs. Hase under a mask as a feud that was reprised in New Japan the next year when Hase returned to Japan as the top junior heavyweight in the promotion and brought in Hart as his favorite opponent for several tours, including a brief period when Hart held the IWGP junior heavyweight title, the first foreigner ever to hold it (and one of only three,

ABOVE: Owen Hart and Mick Foley. (Dr. Mike Lano)

the others being Chris Benoit and Sabu in history ever to hold it). Hart had only been a pro for a few months, but his reputation as already one of the most spectacular wrestlers in the business began spreading. The WWF offered him a deal, and the money was tempting, but he turned it down, wanting to spend the weekends with his girlfriend.

Eventually, upon prodding from Bret, Davey, Dynamite and Jim Neidhart, Owen changed his mind and went to the WWF as a masked high flier, patterned after Tiger Mask. Vince called him The American Eagle, The Blue Angel, The Blue Demon, The Blue Lazer and finally settled on the Blue Blazer, which later became joked on the inside with him being known as the Blue Sports Coat.

Although he got over very strong initially with his spectacular work, particularly with young children, the company didn't have eyes for a guy who was 5-9 and 210 pounds. He got no push, and eventually fans caught on that he wasn't a star. Many times he came close to quitting, both because he wanted to spend more time with his girlfriend at home, because he felt his development as a wrestler was going backwards and because he didn't like how he was being used. His father would always tell him to stick it out. Eventually he suffered a serious testicle injury after being head-butted when Greg Valentine didn't duck low enough on a leap-frog spot at the Survivor Series on November 24, 1988 in Richfield, Ohio. When he returned, his slowed-down push was stopped. At the time he was rooming on the road with Ultimate Warrior. The two came in at about the same time and Jim Hellwig, with the monster push and limited ability, got over amazingly strong in the era of steroids. Hart finally decided to quit. At the time Hellwig was also wanting to quit as well and work full time in Japan as Hart was talking about doing. Hart figured that between the money he'd save since the promotion pays for hotels and travel was taken care of in Japan and he'd have more time off the road, he'd actually come out of the year with the same money for less days away from home, and he'd have more fun having good matches in the process.

But Hart convinced Hellwig that Japan isn't for everyone and he'd be better off staying put. Hart at this point wrestled his way around the world and became, along with Chris Benoit, perhaps the only expert at every style of wrestling, with stops back home in Stampede in between tours of Germany and Austria for Otto Wanz, New Japan and also Mexico for the UWA where he arrived as the Blue Blazer and made a big in-ring hit before losing his mask at El Toreo in Naucalpan to Canek. He had classic matches, both in this incarnation and the

previous one with the top New Japan junior heavyweights like Hase, Jushin Liger, Shiro Koshinaka, Nobuhiko Takada, Wild Pegasus (Chris Benoit) and Kuniaki Kobayashi. In August of 1989, after Davey Boy Smith, Chris Benoit, Jason the Terrible and Ross Hart were injured in an auto accident, Owen took Smith's place in the company's headline feud against Dynamite Kid, in what are remembered as Kid's last great singles matches.

WCW finally brought him in for a few weeks in 1991. After a few weeks, he was offered a contract to form a tag team called Wings with Pillman, but he didn't feel that the style suited him, and he saw through the cliques and didn't see where he'd have a spot, so he turned down the offer and went back to Germany.

Owen grew up ribbing. It wasn't something learned while being a pro wrestler. He learned from Bruce, and maybe from hanging around with the older wrestlers when he was still a kid. He was already pulling ribs on everyone when he was a college wrestler, and the generally harmless pranks continued throughout his pro career. Pillman, who started his career a few months later after getting cut from the Stampeders football team after suffering an ankle injury, and wound up teaming with Bruce when he recovered as Badd Company, was also a notorious ribber. The stories of both in their early Calgary days are almost legendary in that part of the country. Pillman used to make life miserable for a lot of the younger, more naive guys, none more so than the one-time real-life strongest man in the world, Bill Kazmaier, who Pillman used to call "Quagmire," a name that stuck among all the boys.

But a few times Owen got the better of Pillman.

They were working a little town in the middle of nowhere. Pillman, a notorious playboy, had a date with some hot babe in Kelowna, where the crew was headquartered for two days. Kelowna was the nearest city, about one hour from the town they were wrestling in. When he got to the house show, Owen told Bob Johnson, a company road agent, to tell Pillman the company had him booked to do a "Say No to Drugs" speech and the address he was given was a local senior citizens center. Pillman came to do his guest appearance at about 10:30 p.m., at a time when lights were out at the rest home and everyone was sleeping. Somehow Johnson and the Harts convinced them to let them in to give their speech because the elderly people all watched wrestling. Pillman, furious on the inside, was telling a group of elderly people in their 70s and 80s to stay away from crack while it was long past their bed time. Owen and Bruce snuck out and drove to Kelowna without him, forcing him to hitchhike his way back to his hotel room. They got into Pillman's hotel room first, and gimmicked it up to the max, right out of a bad movie scene. They put a dog in his bed, grabbed his Badd Company wrestling attire and dressed the dog up in it.

They put the proverbial bucket of water on top of the bathroom door and unscrewed all the light bulbs in his room.

Pillman came to the room furious, as it was past last call and his date, thinking he stood her up, was gone. He kept flipping light switches, stumbled around, got doused with the water when he opened the bathroom door, jumped on the dog which in the dark room he may have felt was the girl he was going to meet, who freaked out and ran off. There was a joke the next several months whenever they came to Kelowna they would look on the side of the road for a dog running around in Badd Company attire.

Owen used to do imitations, and one of his favorite ribs was to imitate a famous wrestler or celebrity and call his dad up from the road. After five or six minutes into the conversation, he'd crack up and Stu would start yelling at him. At the late March television tapings at the Meadowlands, Hart locked the WWF computer techs in their room.

In late 1991, Owen returned to the WWF just as Bret was becoming a major star, and quickly was wearing suspenders and baggy clown pants forming a tag team with Koko Ware called "High Energy." Going back to the WWF was not his first choice of a lifestyle. He had gotten married to Martha on July 1, 1989, and bought his first home. The two went together on lengthy German tours, which they loved, because it was so many days straight playing in the same city, so during the day it was almost like being on vacation, and the job had very little stress, and Otto Wanz treated him very well. He tried to get into

OPPOSITE: Famous Calgary TV personality and wrestling announcer Ed Whalen interviews Owen Hart. (Dr. Mike Lano)

the Calgary Fire Department, with the idea that would be his steady job since Stampede Wrestling was closing down, and he'd continue to do Japanese tours, but he couldn't get on. So he went back to the WWF.

A few years earlier at a television taping at the Cow Palace in San Francisco, they had attempted to put the two together as a team when Hart was still the Blue Blazer, an idea that was quickly dropped, although Hart felt totally embarrassed in the ring with his Blue Blazer outfit on, flapping his arms and dancing after the match to a song called "Bird, bird, bird." That team went nowhere the second time as well. Owen was stuck in openers, except for a period where they put him with Jim Neidhart as the New Hart Foundation with a medium push, since Bret had long since outgrown being a tag-team wrestler and was being groomed for a top singles slot with the company.

Eventually Bret agreed to do the family feud angle, starting at a Survivor Series match where Keith and Bruce were brought in, and Stu was put at ringside, to team with Bret and Owen against Shawn Michaels and three masked wrestlers (Jeff Gaylord, Barry Horowitz, and Greg Valentine). Owen lost the only fall for his team, and ended up turning on the entire family. For months they teased a break-up with Bret refusing to wrestle him, and teased being put back together, to set up their first meeting with Bret putting Owen over at Wrestlemania X on March 20, 1994 in Madison Square Garden in

the opening match on the show— a show that later ended with Bret winning the WWF title from Yokozuna. Bret vs. Owen was the big summer feud in the WWF. WWF business was in the toilet, but the Bret vs. Owen house show run after Wrestlemania for the title was the biggest run of business the company did since the bottom fell out in 1992.

To further push him as Bret's top contender, he won the King of the Ring on June 16, 1994, in Baltimore with wins over Tatanka, 1-2-3 Kid and Razor Ramon. The big blow-off was a cage match that went 32:17 that was the best cage match the company ever presented on PPV until the famous Shawn Michaels-Undertaker match, with Bret winning. The feud was somewhat kept alive when Owen talked mother Helen into throwing in the towel for Bret, costing him the WWF title at Survivor Series on November 23, 1994 in San Antonio in a match with Bob Backlund, a few-day transitional champion before the Diesel reign.

OVER THE NEXT FEW YEARS, Owen worked mainly as a tag-team wrestler, teaming first with Yokozuna and later with Davey Boy Smith as a championship heel team with Jim Cornette as manager, before Cornette was phased out of the picture and Bret went heel leading to the Hart Foundation's role in the Canada vs. USA feud in 1997 that turned the company's house show fortunes completely around and established Austin as a great babyface drawing card.

Owen was a major singles player, with Bret the top heel but missing time with knee surgery. He won the Intercontinental title on April 28, 1997, from Rocky Maivia, before he was simply The Rock. In an infamous incident at SummerSlam on August 3, 1997 in East Rutherford, New Jersey, he accidentally put Austin's head too low on a tombstone piledriver attempt a few minutes before the scheduled finish. Austin was temporarily paralyzed, and for a few moments was scared he'd never walk, let alone wrestle again. Hart still managed to unconvincingly pin himself as per the plans, and Austin gained the title back. With Austin on the shelf due to the injury, Hart was given the title back beating Faarooq in a tournament on October 5, 1997, leading to Montreal, where just before the real famous match that night, Austin returned to the ring for the first time since the injury to win the title from Hart in a quick brawl.

SUNDAY, MAY 23: 7:41 P.M. CENTRAL TIME. In what will now become the most famous moment of modern wrestling history, Jim Ross was setting to pitch to a pretaped Owen Hart interview under the mask as the Blue Blazer, and stunned, just before the tape ran, said, "We've got a big problem out here." The tape of Owen Hart's last interview ran anyway.

After a silly Blue Blazer interview, kind of a spoof to make Hulk Hogan look like a dated, out-of-touch character, the show went on. Jerry Lawler wasn't there. Unbeknownst to the audience watching on PPV, he ran into the ring immediately because of what happened. The big problem was that Owen Hart, in his Blue Blazer costume, was coming down from a scaffold near the ceiling of Kemper Arena in Kansas City to do a spectacular goofy ring entrance—a spoof on Sting. Somehow, he slipped out of his harness and fell, headfirst, landing on a turnbuckle, and flipping into the ring. Those at ringside watching said it was clear he had a broken neck. Many in the audience thought it was a crash test dummy, and part of the show. The cameras were on the crowd, standing, in stunned silence. They wouldn't shoot anywhere near the ring.

Ross said that something went terribly wrong. "This is not part of the entertainment portion of the show. This is as real as real can get (a line that may become the single most famous line uttered at a pro wrestling event in modern history). This is not a wrestling storyline."

As EMTs feverishly tried heart massage, those at ringside could hear the panic because he had no pulse. He was changing color rapidly. First he went white, then gray, then purple and finally blue. Jim Bradbury of the Kansas City fire department said he was killed instantly. They tried mouth to mouth. They tried to put an oxygen mask on. As they showed the crowd, never once getting a shot of the EMTs working on Hart, fans at ringside in the building could see Ross teary-eyed as his face was off camera and they rushed to show another promotional video for the Jeff Jarrett match that followed. Some

still thought this was all part of the show. Lawler, with his face white as a ghost, came back to the broadcast location. As people who know Jerry Lawler would attest, even when he's out of character, he's always "on" and somewhat in character. Not this time, as he somberly said, "It doesn't look good at all." Hart was wheeled backstage on a stretcher. Not another word was said again about it on television for another hour. Nothing was ever said to the live audience at Kemper Arena the rest of the night.

There is no question that Owen Hart wasn't at all comfortable in doing the entrance planned for him on the fateful night in Kansas City. He had done it once or twice when they did the Blazer gimmick a few months back. They tested the apparatus out twice before the show started, once with Owen himself and the second time with a large sand bag. But he

"WE JUST ASSUMED THEY WOULD STOP THE SHOW IF IT WAS AS SERIOUS AS IT WAS, WHEN THEY DIDN'T WE ALL WONDERED WHY THAT DIDN'T HAPPEN."

—ELLIE NEIDHART

had complained to his wife about it, and she strongly told him she didn't want him doing it. He told other friends, but it is unclear if he ever told anyone in management. Sting did something similar dozens of times over the past few years, but not exactly the same. The Sting descents were safer as he was very tightly hooked up. It made for some real clumsy landings setting up brawls when the ten heels he was supposed to beat up had to stand there while he had to unhook himself.

There was unprecedented news coverage in the history of pro wrestling to this story. Hart's autopsy listed the cause of death as bleeding to death internally from blunt chest trauma. Three men were on the cat walk at the Kemper Arena at the time of the accident. The WWF hired them from the International Alliance of Theatrical Stage Employees Local 31 to work with WWF officials who had put on that stunt previously. EMTs and the ambulance were at the scene, when normally they are not at WWF events, because they were asked to participate in an angle involving McMahon. Just as they finished the filming and were about to leave, Hart fell and they were called back in.

"We just assumed they would stop the show if it was as serious as it was, when they didn't we all wondered why that didn't happen." said Ellie (Jim Neidhart's wife) to the Associated Press. "I know my brother Owen, being the kind of person he was, would have wanted Vince to continue. That's the nature of wrestling, but I think it was something that should've been stopped."

CHAPTER 2
FREDDIE
BLASSIE

WHEN IT COMES TO THE ABILITY to talk people into buying tickets, some say the best there was at it was Freddie Blassie. Even by the mid-'50s, the saying among promoters was the perfect wrestler would have the moves and technique of Pat O'Connor, the look, psychology and mannerisms of Buddy Rogers, and the ability to talk of Freddie Blassie.

"Al Haft (the promoter in Columbus, Ohio, a hotbed of wrestling in the mid-'50s) told me to watch O'Connor, Rogers, and Blassie and take a piece of each one of them and put it into your own style," said Dick Beyer who, as The Destroyer, was one of Blassie's all-time leg-endary rivals. Blassie's ability to rile up a crowd and get people coming back for more became legendary in the South during the '50s, when he would wrestle in the same cities every week, against largely the same opponents, and had to keep inventing new ways to keep the crowds coming. His ways were both effective, and often dangerous, and fans came after him regularly. He was stabbed on more than one occasion.

He exploded in Los Angeles in the early '60s, when Dick Lane hosted wrestling every Wednesday night from 8 to 9:30 p.m. from the Olympic Auditorium on KTLA television. Many of

OPPOSITE: The classic maniacal pose of Freddie Blassie. (Dr. Mike Lano)

the biggest names in Hollywood at the time, from Elvis Presley to Muhammad Ali, were watching him. At his peak, not only were the big shows every other Friday night at the Olympic Auditorium drawing sellouts, but often the television tapings, which consisted of nothing but squash matches and one off-TV main event involving Blassie without all that much hype (the major hype was saved for the Friday shows) were selling out the same week.

"Elvis was a big Blassie fan when he was living out here as a recluse in the early '60s," said Johnny Legend (Martin Margulies), who first met Blassie when he, Glenn Bray, Terry Brodt and Jeff Walton, while in junior high school, would "accidentally" bump into him when they found out he spent every afternoon at the beach near the Santa Monica pier. "Elvis would watch Blassie wrestle every Wednesday night on TV from the Olympic, and then bring girls in to wrestle him."

Legend taped Blassie's interviews from 1961 through 1964 on a reel-to-reel recorder, which are likely the only copies of them still in existence, as the wrestling promoters saved nothing from that era. He released them under the title "Geekmania" at one point. He also produced the 1975 song "Pencil-Neck Geek," which was No. 1 for a while on the nationally syndicated Dr. Demento radio show, and the 56-minute movie *My*

Breakfast with Blassie with the late Andy Kaufman.

Kaufman was another longtime Blassie fan, who would call him up at all hours and harass him. By that point in his life, Blassie knew little other than wrestling and maybe porn.

"To him, the big celebrities were Sinatra, Engelbert Humperdink and John Holmes," Legend said. "He'd call me and say the guy (Kaufman) says he's a TV star, but he sounds like a nut. I would tell him, 'He is a TV star, and he is a nut.'"

Kaufman at first tried to use his connection, however unwilling, with Blassie, as an entree to do a wrestling angle in Madison Square Garden. But Vince McMahon Sr. would have none of it, and as it turned out, Bill Apter put Kaufman in touch with Jerry Lawler. Legend came up with the *Breakfast with Blassie* idea as a spoof of the award-winning *My Dinner with Andre* movie. It was shot in 1982 for about $1,000, when Kaufman was still a TV star. By the time it was ready for release, no video company would touch it because of Kaufman's fall from grace and the idea in Hollywood that anyone with any self-respect would want to stay away from wrestling. The most interest came from Michael Nesmith (of The Monkees fame), but it actually played at some sold-out theaters and one of its premieres was attended by Robin Williams. It was perhaps the last public appearance of Kaufman, who was dying of cancer by that point. Blassie's name was even mentioned in the famed REM song "Man on the Moon" about Kaufman.

To this day, there's debate whether Gorgeous George or Blassie inspired Muhammad Ali's shtick. According to Ali in his book by Thomas Hauser, "A couple of days before I fought Sabedong (a June 1961 fight in Las Vegas), I did a radio program with Gorgeous George. First, they asked me about my fight. And I can't say I was humble, but I wasn't too loud. Then they asked Gorgeous George about a wrestling match he was having in the same arena, and he was shouting, 'I'll kill him; I'll tear his arm off. If this bum beats me, I'll crawl across the ring and cut off my hair, but it's not gonna happen because I'm the greatest wrestler in the world.' And all the time, I was saying to myself; 'Man, I want to see the fight. It don't matter if he wins or loses; I want to be there to see what happens. And the whole place was sold out when Gorgeous George wrestled. There were thousands of people, including me. And that's when I decided, I'd never been shy about talking, but if I talked even more, there was no telling how much money people would pay to see me."

You would think the city and time frame would settle the argument over which one it was. Ironically, this settles nothing. The interview that Ali remembered sounded more like a Blassie interview than a George interview, but George had the gift of gab himself. There was a big wrestling show on June 23, 1961, in Las Vegas that sold out. The main event? Blassie vs. George in what was perhaps George's last hurrah. In 1976, when Blassie and Ali toured together to promote the Antonio Inoki match, Ali claimed he had been mistaken for all those years crediting George, and he realized it was Blassie that he'd been imitating. Still, years later, he went back to crediting it to George, which used to infuriate Blassie.

Mike Tenay believes that, along with Blassie's personal drawing power, he should be given even more credit because of his ability to get everyone around him over, both tag-team partners and opponents. Tenay noted you could list many of the names Blassie did his biggest business with, like Buddy Austin, Don Carson, The Destroyer, Pedro Morales, Mr. Moto, Black Gordman, Ernie Ladd, Los Medicos, John Tolos and Mil Mascaras, and none were huge main event stars in wrestling before coming to Los Angeles. He also drew big crowds with people who were big stars, like Bobo Brazil, Bearcat Wright, Edouard Carpentier, Dick the Bruiser, Cowboy Bob Ellis, Lou Thesz and many others. But many people who became wrestling legends owe much of their first great success to the rub from working with him, because it also established his opponents' reputations for being able to draw money, in some cases even when it may not have been deserved.

Tolos was probably his best known rival because of their match at the Los Angeles Coliseum and the famed Monsel powder angle. The build to his greatest career success started almost by accident. He had left Vancouver in 1970. He was 40 years old and not sure where his life was headed. He was driving down to Southern California, kind of hoping to get hooked up with the wrestling promotion.

"I just got in my car and went South," he recalled. "I stopped in Bakersfield. I looked in the newspaper and saw they had matches at Strongbow Stadium. I saw Blassie, Charlie Moto (Mr. Moto, who was booking at that time with Jules Strongbow and Blassie), Strongbow, Bobo and (Buddy) Austin. They said the territory wasn't great, but it wasn't too bad. They all thought I was driving in to work for Al Lovelock, who was running opposition. Blassie (who knew Tolos because they had a main-event feud in the area in 1953 when Blassie was a brunette and both were actually neighbors at the time they were feuding) said, 'Do you want to work?' and I said, 'Yeah.' He said, 'You're booked in the Olympic on Friday.'"

Blassie and Tolos feuded over the Americas' title in late 1970. The Americas' title had replaced the WWA title as the main belt in Southern California when the promotion rejoined the NWA in 1968. The two sold out several shows at the Olympic, including a cage match and a stretcher match. One time Tolos even brought a snake into the ring, which was the first time it was ever done in wrestling.

It was a huge, thick python. Blassie was scared to death. Tolos was so naive he didn't realize he should have been as well.

"The movie stars at ringside ran away," he said. "It scared the shit out of Blassie. I grabbed the snake, he had those fangs. I didn't know any better. Blassie was

"I'M GLAD HE HAD A GOOD LIFE. HE LIVED 85 YEARS. YOU DON'T SEE A LOT OF FOOTBALL PLAYERS AND WRESTLERS LASTING THAT LONG. THE HUMAN BODY ISN'T MADE TO TAKE THAT KIND OF POUNDING YEAR AFTER YEAR."

—JOHN TOLOS

saying, 'Jesus Christ, John, that snake might get scared and wrap around your body.' The guy who owned the snake was at ringside and brought a gun just in case that happened."

"I'm glad he had a good life," Tolos said. "He lived 85 years. You don't see a lot of football players and wrestlers lasting that long. The human body isn't made to take that kind of pounding year after year."

Tolos, in looking back on that angle, said he had many regrets. The biggest is that they actually only did the two matches when the feud was at its hottest. The Blassie-Tolos feud is remembered as similar to that of Bobo Brazil and The Sheik. But Brazil and Sheik probably wrestled each other hundreds, if not thousands of

times, spanning decades. His other regret is that there are no tapes of any of their matches, angles and interviews. Well, almost none. Legend remembers that in December of 1980, when Blassie was 62 years old Legend filmed the last Blassie cage match (this was two weeks after his final singles match with Tolos). It was Tolos and Victor Rivera against Blassie and El Medico. Blassie's offense for years was mainly biting, gouging and choking, so even at that age, he was able to at least do what was remembered as a Blassie match, albeit in slow motion.

While Tolos was sorry to see Blassie go to New York in 1971, and even sorrier when he left for good as a full-timer two years later, for Pedro Morales, who at the time was one of the five biggest stars in the world as WWWF champion, was happy to hear that his longtime friend was coming in.

Morales was a 20-year-old high-flying prelim wrestler in the Northeast from Culebra, Puerto Rico when Blassie came in for matches with Bruno Sammartino in 1964, which were some of the biggest matches of the era.

"He came every three weeks for TV tapings," Morales recalled. "Freddie told me, 'You're better than Carpentier, and I want to take you to California.' I told him I was going to Amarillo for Dory Funk (Sr.) And he said, 'F*** Dory Funk and f*** Texas. I can make you real money.' It was my first real break in the business."

Morales ended up a star in California for five years, and was considered one of the hottest new wrestlers in the business. He held the WWA title twice, held the WWA tag team titles four times and NWA tag titles twice during that period. The photos from the Olympic Auditorium with the belts, which, like the Kiel in St. Louis and Madison Square Garden were mythical in Japan because of the coverage in the newspapers and magazines, made him a star overseas.

"He was always special to me because I owed my career to him," Morales said. "I was excited to see him again because he was a good man, and I knew we'd draw money everywhere, and that was the name of the game. We sold out Madison Square Garden, Boston, Philadelphia. We sold out almost everywhere."

One would have thought all that television exposure as the top babyface in California in the New York market would have created a split crowd atmosphere against Morales, but Blassie's interviews were so strong, nothing could have been farther from the truth.

"I loved the guy," he said. "I could never say anything bad about Freddie Blassie. He was a lot of fun and everyone loved him. All the Spanish guys loved Freddie because Freddie would always tease us in a way where he made us feel like we belonged. All the Spanish boys knew Freddie liked them. The Mexican guys in Los Angeles loved him."

Blassie always felt when he was at ringside, his job was to antagonize the fans, even when he was pushing 70. Morales remembered when he returned to the WWF in the early '80s as Intercontinental champion and he wrestled one of Blassie's guys, fans were about to hop the rail on him.

"I still remember him yelling at the fans, saying, 'You pencil neck geeks,' and when they threatened him, he'd say, 'I'll kick you in the crotch!'"

Billy Graham came to Los Angeles with very little experience other than a stint in the Calgary territory when he arrived in 1970. Blassie was booking by then with Moto, and they built up a gimmick where Graham claimed to be the arm-wrestling champion of the world and would defend it every Saturday night. He started beating people like Walton and the photographers in almost comedy sketches, and then moved up to actually shooting with real arm wrestlers every Saturday night on television.

ABOVE: Blassie's offense usually consisted of ripping and tearing at his opponent.
(Dr. Mike Lano)

"He was a babyface by then, and in Los Angeles, he was like Bruno Sammartino on the East Coast," said Graham, 60. "Here I was with legitimate 22-inch arms at the time and was beating shooters. Freddy came out in the studio and the place went berserk. He was past 50 and had no muscularity at all, yet everyone believed he was going to beat me. Of course he put my arm down and the crowd went berserk. They believed 100 percent he could beat me. (Black) Gordman and Goliath hit the ring and got the hammer they use to ring the bell, and hit Freddie over the head with it, and he juiced. After having to face those shooters, the payoff was I got him (Blassie) later that night in Northridge before 500 or 1,000 people in the Blassie cage. Gordman got him at the Olympic. It's probably that I was so green and was hurting people, so he only worked with me that one time. Of course he beat me to a pulp in the cage. It was amazing, because his signature moves that they went wild for were biting and a low blow."

Graham also remembered that Blassie's mouth was, as they say, like a sailor, which Blassie was in World War II. "He was as vulgar as anyone I'd ever met," he said. "Every other word out of his mouth was f*** this and f*** that. I remembered years later in New York, you could see in the hallways that Vince (Jr.) loved the guy."

Blassie was also responsible for starting the career of Ernie Ladd. At the time, during the spring of 1963, Don Manoukian, an NFL star, was working the circuit in the off season as a heel and was a Blassie rival. Manoukian and Destroyer were feuding with Blassie and various partners, when Blassie recruited Ladd, the biggest man in pro football at the time, at 6-9, 315 pounds, who was a star with the San Diego Chargers. The two teamed together for a few months before Blassie turned on Ladd and they worked singles matches. Their feud got even bigger after the football season ended and Ladd came back to wrestling in 1964.

Dick Beyer was a babyface wrestler doing a gimmick that he was the old-school, college-jock type, which was legit, as he was a football and wrestling star at Syracuse University. Beyer had known of Blassie from when he broke in, first met him in 1955, and became friends with him in 1958 while both were in Tennessee hanging out at strip clubs after working.

Blassie, as WWA champion, was flown into Honolulu for a title defense against Beyer, the top babyface in the territory at the time on January 24, 1962. Because of Beyer's football ties, they managed to get an interview at halftime of a big televised football game, and Blassie made the most of it, diving over a table and attacking Beyer, which Beyer didn't even realize was coming. This led to a sell-out for their match, after which time Blassie came back to Los Angeles and told Jules Strongbow that they needed to bring this Beyer guy in, because he was the best babyface worker in the country. He went back to Hawaii on April 11, 1962, and by this time Beyer had turned heel. He told Strongbow that Beyer was just about the best heel in the country as well.

But as big as Blassie was in California, it was nothing compared with Japan, where Blassie was a household name in that country among the older generation. Blassie arrived in Japan on April 20, 1962, for both the World League and a title match with Rikidozan three days later in Tokyo. While Thesz was to be the biggest star, there was plenty of hype around the debut of "The Vampire" from California, because of all the photos of him biting opponents under the "RI9-5171" sign (the phone number to order tickets) that hung at the Olympic Auditorium. There was plenty of press there as Blassie got off the plane from Los Angeles at Haneda Airport, and when he saw it, he began filing his teeth.

OVER THE NEXT FEW DAYS, he did the best job of interviews that country had ever seen, and even though they didn't know English, his delivery was so powerful and the Vampire gimmick was so strong that he became the hottest heel ever in that country. People were so amazed that most of the shows on the World League tour sold out within days of his arrival. Rikidozan won his most famous match in Japan to keep the title with Arnold Skaaland as referee. It was four days later in Kobe when on a live TV shoot, six elderly men suffered heart attacks watching the brutality of close-ups of Blassie biting. Blassie became a household name. Even though it was the coun-

try's most popular show at the time, wrestling nearly got banned from television. The only thing that kept it on was just how popular it was at the time. Japanese children were told in school by their teachers not to watch wrestling when Blassie was on the air, which naturally made them want to watch, and made him larger than life.

While Blassie surpassed Lou Thesz on this tour as the top foreign star, he lost to Rikidozan and Thesz, while beating Antonio Inoki, Kintaro Oki, Michiaki Yoshimura, Buddy Austin, Larry Hennig, Kokichi Endo and Toyonobori. He came back for the 1965 World League, where he was the leading point-getter, even beating Giant Baba before losing in the finals to Toyonobori.

Los Angeles wasn't the biggest money territory in wrestling, although it was huge in the early '60s. Aside from the Olympic Auditorium, the weekend jaunts to Las Vegas, and the San Diego Sports Arena, they ran in mostly small buildings. But for Blassie, it was the perfect area. There were weekly cities, none more than a two-hour drive from Santa Monica, where Blassie lived. He'd spend all day at the beach working on his tan, often while leafing through his pocket porn books, and then wrestle every night as the deeply bronzed, blond-haired, larger-than-life figure with his hair always perfect. In fact, even in the hospital while on his deathbed, Blassie would smile when people would note he still never had a hair out of place. By the early '70s, he shied away from his famed spot on the beach, because his popularity had gotten so that he couldn't be in public without attracting more of a crowd than he usually wanted, so he preferred to do his tanning at the Flaming Hotel pool. He was home almost every night at a decent hour, at least by wrestler standards.

Blassie had his problems in Hawaii, because on more than one occasion Samoan gangs were out to get him, and he barely escaped with his life after he would run down Samoans in his television interviews promoting his matches against people like Sammy Steamboat and Neff Maiava.

On August 23, 1963, Blassie dropped the title to Bearcat Wright. While technically this wasn't the first time a black wrestler had held a world heavyweight title, it was the first time for what would have been considered a major world title. It was the right time for it, as business exploded with black fans supporting their hero who had, in their minds, captured the biggest prize in wrestling. Being out there as a top face went to Wright's head in the worst way possible. He had made it clear he thought he was "it." Even though business was great, the promotion was afraid they had created a monster. Rather than go with the flow, they kept trying to talk Wright into losing, fearing they couldn't trust him, and he kept refusing. It got so bad that Wright, scheduled to lose to Carpentier, double-crossed him in the ring and retained the title. Wright was about 6-6 and 270 pounds and had a real

boxing background, as opposed to the worked one that Blassie had claimed, and that was said so often that most wrestlers of that time believed it.

In his book, Blassie said that he was out of action and hospitalized with broken ribs when promoter Aileen Eaton, her husband Cal, and her son, Mike LeBelle came to see him about the problem. Others remember it slightly differently, that a week before the scheduled match, Blassie went to the hospital with appendicitis. Whether they begged Blassie to do the match far too quickly because he was the only guy Wright would agree to drop the belt to, or, according to other versions, Blassie was told they could postpone it, but he insisted on doing it for business. It depends on who is telling the story. Blassie's version is they asked him to come back way too soon. It was agreed they would protect Blassie by doing a short match, a three-fall match in just 13:00, and Blassie would go over. Like with Carpentier, Wright agreed to the finish. But once he was out there in front of a sold-out crowd going crazy for him, Wright started refusing to cooperate in the ring, and beat Blassie. Blassie claimed he was sucker-punched and knocked silly. Blassie was more irate because he was taken advantage of when he was in no condition to even defend himself. But the promotion got the last laugh three nights later. A rematch was scheduled, but when Wright came to the ring, Blassie wasn't there. It was Gene LeBelle. Even though Wright was much larger than "Judo Gene," and a former boxer, he had enough sense to read the situation, do an about face, head to the back, grab his bag, and leave town with the belt. On television two nights later it was announced that Wright had forfeited the title in a match in Indio, California, against Carpentier.

While wrestling was doing huge business and Blassie appeared on a lot of local television, the matches themselves got no mainstream coverage aside from the one paragraph lead and agate results of the matches in the sports sections. But this story about the double-cross in the ring and Wright leaving the territory without losing the title broke as a mainstream news story. The exposé was said to have killed the territory for a long time. However, Blassie's regaining the title on January 31, 1964, from Carpentier at the Olympic drew a sellout. His feud a few months later with Dick the Bruiser drew huge business and several sellouts. But Blassie's paycheck was declining, and he thought they were taking him for granted, figuring he loved his life so much that he would never leave.

So he gave notice and went to the Northeast for the Sammartino feud. He lost the title to Bruiser on April 22, 1964, and continued to work the territory, as well as taking some dates in Atlanta and Indianapolis. On May 27, 1964, they scheduled a death match between him and Bruiser, ending with the gimmick of Blassie dislocating his knee, ironic since it

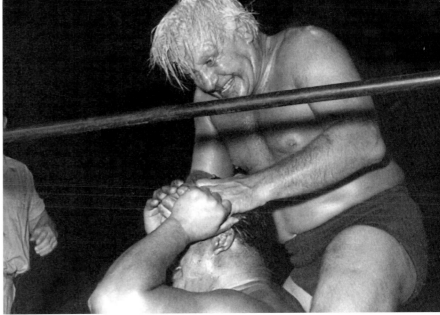

ABOVE: Blassie works on another opponent. (Dr. Mike Lano)

was knee problems that ended up plaguing him later in life, and he was unable to continue. He finally lost a "loser leaves town" match to Bruiser on June 12, 1964, in San Diego. He flew in for the match from Washington, D.C., where he had done television for McMahon Sr. the night before, which was the match with Morales that led to him recommending that Morales come to California. On June 26, 1964, billed as Pacific Coast Champion, he wrestled Sammartino outdoors at Roosevelt Stadium in Jersey City, New Jersey, before 12,000 fans, with Blassie winning via count out to set up his two sellouts for rematches in Madison Square Garden. While Blassie had lost the WWA title, almost all the communication in wrestling in those days came from the wrestling magazines, which were three months out of date.

Blassie was still WWA champion in the latest magazines, and fans assumed that the Pacific Coast title was that belt. It was never said to be a battle of two of the three major world champions of the time (the AWA title surpassed the WWA title for prominence sometime later), but it was somewhat implied and led to big business throughout the Northeast.

After finishing the run with Sammartino in October, rather than work his way down the cards, he returned to Southern California where he was going to stay on top and lived the lifestyle he wanted to live. Blassie's career as a manager started in late 1973 when he showed up on WWWF television as the manager of Volkoff. It was quite the shock, since Blassie was still one of the biggest stars in the world, and was a far bigger star than Volkoff. From there he spent more than a decade bringing in challengers for Sammartino, Bob Backlund and Hulk Hogan, including managing Iron Sheik when he had his brief title run between Backlund and Hogan. While he didn't have the beach in Southern California, the managing job in the WWWF was considered a plum job, and when it was warm, he would spend all day in his backyard in Hartsdale, New York, working on his tan.

Managers did much of the talking for their proteges, building up that this next great find would take the title, even though they would always fail. New heels would be brought in and alternate between Blassie, Lou Albano and the Grand Wizard (Ernie Roth). There was no hard and fast rule about who got whom, other than Albano almost always got the tag teams, and Blassie usually got the foreigners. The managers didn't even go on the road full time. They might interfere in matches at the television tapings, but it was rare for them to take bumps. After 1974, Blassie, unlike Albano, wasn't even put into the ring on occasions, and his wrestling was confined to his trips back to California when Tolos would talk him into coming back.

His managerial career took him to Japan on a few occasions, as he managed Adrian Adonis first, and later Hulk Hogan. Some guys, like Dick Murdoch and Jesse Ventura, didn't like the system, since they had the ability to get over on their own. Blassie would let the guys, like Ventura, who could talk, handle most of the interviews, but the two never got along, because when Blassie would give Ventura advice, or pass along instructions he'd gotten from the office, Ventura would never listen. Hogan wasn't one of them, as Blassie handled almost all his interviews in the Hogan heel run in 1979-80, including his matches with Andre the Giant.

He was Hogan's teacher on how to handle himself in Japan, as Blassie knew the ropes and taught Hogan to act like such a big star that he would never have to pay for anything in Japan, and long before his status in the U.S. reached that level, Hogan was regarded in the category with Stan Hansen, Terry Funk, Bruiser Brody and Andre as the top foreign drawing cards in the country. There is little doubt being paired with Blassie gave both Adonis and Hogan a major rub to the general public in Japan, who didn't know either of them at first, but by this point all had heard the stories, exaggerated by the years, of the night Blassie bit Rikidozan.

ABOVE: The colorful Freddie Blassie enters the ring. (Dr. Mike Lano)

CHAPTER 3
DAVEY BOY
SMITH

THE DEATH OF DAVEY BOY SMITH was a lot of different things to different people.

Within the world of wrestling, it was something people have become numb to because of the frequency of such stories. When the word reached many of his former WCW coworkers, it was, sadly, almost a humdrum reaction, with many talking about it as being something almost expected from seeing him during his darkest days. To many of his friends and even those in his former family, it was by no means a welcome relief. But in reflection, they looked on the bright side, that their friend's five years of pure hell in battling drug addictions was over.

Davey Boy Smith (that was his legal name at birth—his mother mistakenly put his sex on his birth certificate in the spot where his middle name was supposed to be) was born on November 27, 1962, in Golborne, England. By the time Smith was 11, his first cousin, Tom Billington, was a teenage wrestling sensation on television in England as the Dynamite Kid. At about that same time, Smith started getting interested in wrestling. In 1975, his father took him to Ted Betley, an old-time shooter who had trained his cousin Tom. After three years of training, Smith made his pro wrestling debut in Birmingham, England on May 15, 1978,

OPPOSITE: Davey Boy Smith toward the end of his career in his WWF days.
(Dr. Mike Lano)

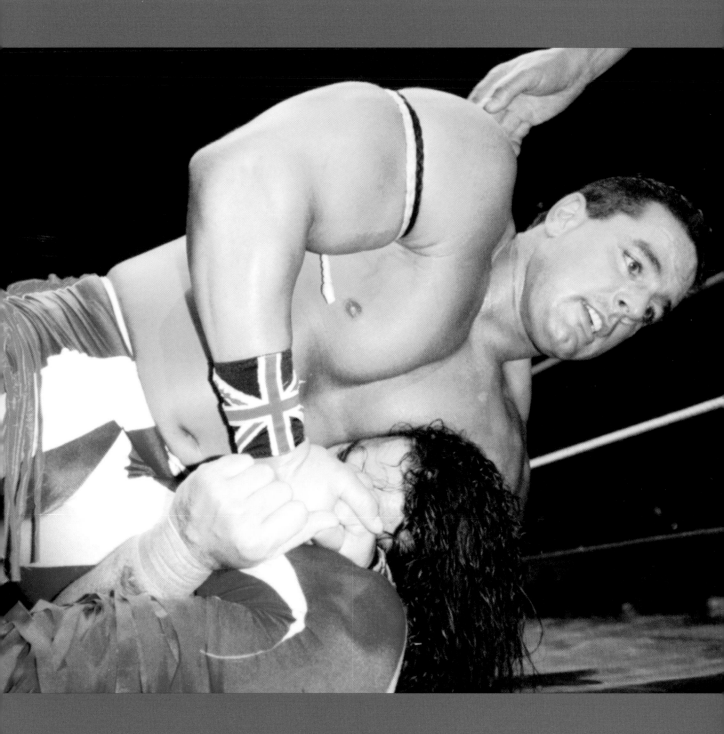

against Bernie Wright. His cousin had already become a superstar in England by this point, and left for Calgary and Stampede Wrestling.

Using the name "Young David," Smith filled the void in England of his famous cousin, being the teenage sensation on television who would carry matches while teaming with Big Daddy (Shirley Crabtree), the brother of promoter Max Crabtree. Big Daddy's awfulness inside the ring was only matched by his name recognition within the culture as its most famous wrestling star, perhaps ever.

Although Smith and Billington were cousins nearly the same age with the same passion for wrestling, their families were not close and they didn't grow up together. Billington did not know him well, but had heard from family members about his success, and convinced Stu Hart to give him a try shortly after his 18th birthday, and Smith came to Canada in April of 1981.

The Dynamite Kid was fast becoming a legend in the Western Canada wrestling scene, and had just wrestled his first match against Tiger Mask in Japan, starting a series that would break many barriers about what was humanly possible to do inside the ring and how small guys could get over in what had been a big man's world, when his cousin arrived. Dynamite was a heel, and Smith was brought in as a babyface. Their kinship was never acknowledged to anyone except those on the inside until three years later. Yet the two wrestlers who were battling each other in the ring, were living togeth-

er but they didn't get along that well, and Smith soon moved in with his future brother-in-law, Bret Hart. Smith started dating Bret's sister Diana, and in 1984, when he was 21 and she was 20, they got married in a big wedding in Calgary.

To the public, it was the fairly tale wedding of the young, good-looking wrestling star who had become an international superstar and the local beauty queen from the famous wrestling family. But it was hardly that, even at first, as just before the wedding, Davey had gotten a ring rat pregnant, and Diana nearly called the whole thing off.

"I almost rescued him after he was living with Dynamite, who was pretty hard on him in a bully kind of way," said Bret. "At the time he was a naive, innocent kid. He had a great sense of humor."

By this time, Smith had become one of the top pro wrestlers in the world. He showed up in Calgary weighing 175 pounds, but was very strong for his size and had incredible agility. While there was no question it was his cousin carrying him through their initial tremendous matches, he was also able to hold his own and keep the pace.

Billington, a naturally small guy, was already heavy into the steroids. Smith wanted to get as big as the other wrestlers. For all the steroids the two were taking from the early days, those in Stampede also acknowledge that they combined that with training as hard in the gym all day, and wrestling as hard as everyone every night.

"WE PUT HIM IN RIGHT AWAY WITH DYNAMITE. THEY HAD AWESOME MATCHES. THE FANS IMMEDIATELY LOVED DAVEY BECAUSE TOM MADE HIM LOOK FANTASTIC."

—FAMILY HISTORIAN ROSS HART

"We put him in right away with Dynamite," remembered family historian Ross Hart. "They had awesome matches. The fans immediately loved Davey because Tom made him look fantastic. But Davey could keep up with him. We had a classic British rivalry. His work was superior to everyone (in the promotion) except Dynamite in those days."

Bret recalled an incident in 1981, when he, Davey and Lou Thesz were driving and six guys in a car started making threats. He and Davey got out of the car (Thesz was stuck in the back seat and even at 65, was struggling to get out to participate) and started fighting, with Davey slamming a guy hard on the pavement.

His first title came as sort of a double-cross, not on him, or his cousin, but on the promotion. When Nelson Royal had refused to drop the NWA world junior heavyweight title to Dynamite, Bruce Hart, who was handling the booking, decided to create a title, called the World mid-heavyweight title, for Dynamite to defend. He brought in Dick Steinborn as champion to lose it, and Dynamite held it for the next three years. Since Dynamite was getting many foreign tours, that only made it appear to be more of a world title, and within the promotion, it was treated as such, with them constantly talking about stories of Dynamite going all over the world defending it when he was gone.

On July 9, 1982, Dynamite was in his last Calgary match before a New Japan tour. Bruce told Dynamite to beat his cousin, which Dynamite didn't want to do, because he was going to be out of the territory for six weeks and didn't think it made sense. Bruce told him that Davey wasn't ready for the world title. Dynamite

ABOVE: Davey Boy Smith, Louie Spicolli and Brian Pillman together. All three fell into drug problems and died at a young age. (Dr. Mike Lano)

didn't let on that he was planning a double-cross, told Davey to give him a german suplex, and stayed in that position, leaving the ref no choice but to count to three.

Dynamite hadn't even clued Davey in on his plan. But between his mid-heavyweight title, and holding the tag titles with Bruce, Smith was one of the company's biggest stars. Since he emulated Dynamite with the same look, ring style, and moves, the next stop was to follow his cousin to Japan.

In Dynamite's eyes, his cousin earned his stripes sometime earlier in Regina, Saskatchewan. At the time, Smith had

never been bladed, and he asked his cousin to do it to him in the match. Dynamite tried to claim that Smith moved, but others think Dynamite sliced him far too deeply as a form of initiation. Smith suffered a horrible gash, needing 22 stitches to close the cut. Those close to the situation say that it was the only way Dynamite knew.

"Tom wanted to make sure nobody thought he was getting an easy ride," said Ross. "It was similar to what Steve Wright did to Tom. In Tom's eyes, he passed the initiation."

Due to the steroids, Smith had already technically outgrown the mid-heavyweight division, but because of his style, they didn't acknowledge that, allowing him to keep wrestling with the smaller guys like Dynamite and The Cobra.

His career in North America nearly ended for the first time that year when he was arrested for assaulting a police officer. Stu had to use all his connections at the Calgary police department to make the charges go away, and keep Smith from being deported.

In the summer of 1983, Tiger Mask (Satoru Sayama) announced his retirement from wrestling, while holding both the NWA (although in the U.S. they had created a new belt) and WWF junior heavyweight titles. It was at this point Smith got his first offer to go to Japan as a single; Billington, feeling he wasn't ready, tried to talk him out of going. But Smith had never made real money in wrestling and was getting the opportunity.

Cobra was scheduled to win the vacant NWA jr. title against an unknown masked man on November 3, 1983, at Tokyo Sumo Hall. When Smith came to the ring under the mask, Japanese fans began chanting for Dynamite, thinking it was him under the mask. After doing some British spots that caused the crowd to go wild, he ripped the mask off and was an instant hit.

Unfortunately, the match wasn't, and as good as Smith got over, Cobra didn't. Cobra got the belt, but Smith became a sensation. The originally planned Cobra vs. Dynamite rivalry over the junior belts became a three-man program. The vacant

WWF junior heavyweight title, considered the more prestigious of the two belts because it was the one with more history in Japan, was put up in a five-week tournament in early 1984. It was a fantastic success, paving the way for what later became annual junior heavyweight tournaments with the promotion. Besides Cobra, Dynamite and Davey, Black Tiger, Bret Hart and Babe Face were also brought in from Mexico along with New Japan's Kuniaki Kobayashi, Nobuhiko Takada (in the first spotlight matches of his career) and Isamu Teranishi. Smith was protected so strongly that he won the round robin. On nights that he and Dynamite didn't have tournament matches, they worked as a tag team. Their new, faster-paced style built on outrageous moves, wowed, in particular, the younger fans, and they were all over the magazines and became television sensations at a time when New Japan was drawing huge ratings weekly on prime-time network television.

They set up a three-way, one-night program on February 7, 1984, at Sumo Hall where Kid beat Smith via count out and Cobra by pin, inventing the super gut wrench as a finisher. But it was this tour that put Smith on the map as one of the top ten in-ring performers in the business. But it came with a price. Besides the steroids to keep up the size, the punishment from all those high-risk moves started his lower-back problems.

Smith worked the next several months between New Japan and

Stampede, where he became the top singles star, beating Badnews Allen on June 18, 1984, in Vancouver before 7,000 fans, the biggest crowd in that city since the heyday of Gene Kiniski. He and Dynamite also held the International tag titles, their first belts together, beating Allen and Cuban Assassin (Angel Acevedo) on March 31, 1984, in Calgary. At the age of 21, his career seemed set. A top babyface in Stampede, and making real money in his career with New Japan. But by the end of the year, everything was different.

Shortly after Kid and Smith got back from Japan, Stu Hart sold Stampede Wrestling to Vince McMahon. Or more correctly, gave up his television contracts in Western Canada, knowing any fight to keep his territory would be a losing one. Stu only asked Vince to take care of Dynamite, Davey, Bret and Jim Neidhart, which he agreed to, and eventually did.

But not at first. Even loaded on steroids, Kid and Smith were much smaller than most of the monsters WWF was employing at the time. And nobody could work their style, except for maybe Bret, and he was a prelim guy at the time that nobody thought much of, because he didn't have a physique. They lasted all of a few weeks in the WWF before quitting, since they had the guaranteed deal in Japan that at the time nobody even knew about.

The All Japan/New Japan war had peaked over the previous few years. Even though All Japan has many huge attractions like The Funks, Bruiser Brody, Stan Hansen, Mil Mascaras and Tiger Jeet Singh as regulars and access to most of the top NWA and AWA talent like Ric Flair, Harley Race, and Nick Bockwinkel, New Japan had so much more depth and dimension, and was blowing them away. But the younger wrestlers who were getting over, wanted to move to the top. Giant Baba, in his biggest move ever, signed about a dozen wrestlers from New Japan, including its most charismatic younger wrestler, Riki Choshu, and all Choshu's regular teammates in New Japan's top feud ever. In a different deal, Baba offered Dynamite and Davey Boy a $20,000 signing bonus each and $6,200 per week, far beyond the money that junior heavyweights had ever earned in pro wrestling. The two went to Japan in November of 1984 for the New Japan tag-team tournament. Two days before the tour was scheduled to start, on November 14, 1984, at the Tokyo Capital Hotel, Giant Baba shocked the wrestling world again at a press conference announcing that Kid and Smith would instead be starting in one week in his tournament.

They debuted on November 22, 1984, with a sensational double count out against The Funks at Korakuen Hall. The Funks were already legends for 15 years in Japan as the most successful foreign tag team ever, and it was Terry's first match back after a retirement that had lasted 17 months. Just going to a draw in Terry's first match back established them at a higher level than they were with New Japan, where they were mainly considered junior heavyweight stars. Every night but one of the tour sold out. They still had to put over teams like Brody and Hansen, Jumbo Tsuruta and Genichiro Tenryu, and Harley Race and Nick Bockwinkel. Perhaps their best match on the tour was against two wrestlers, the newest Tiger Mask (Mitsuharu Misawa) getting his first push, and an unknown rookie named Toshiaki Kawada who nobody had given much thought to at the time as far as having any potential before their match, in Osaka.

The plan was to work full time in Japan in 1985, but that didn't happen, either. Reports from their Japanese tour spread to the U.S. While the AWA wasn't interested, believing them to be too small, nor was Jim Crockett Promotions, the WWF was, as was Mid South Wrestling. Joel Watts, who had become a big fan of them through watching Japanese videotapes, constantly tried to get his father to bring them in to feud with the Rock & Roll Express, huge attractions at the time. The Rock & Roll's feud with the Midnight Express had been going on for more than a year and it was time for something new. Booker Bill Dundee said there was no money in the team, and instead brought in Lynn Denton and Tony Anthony as the Dirty White Boys to face the Express. That wasn't working at all, so Bill Watts gave Joel the go-ahead. When the move was about to be made, they were informed that days earlier, the two had signed with the WWF and were given the name the British Bulldogs.

The idea was they were supposed to come to the ring barking like dogs in the cartoon world that was WWF at the time. Dynamite had the mentality from being a Japanese star, that wrestling wasn't a circus, and refused to go that far with the gimmick. So they were given dogs to come to the ring with, including Mathilda, who was even kidnapped by the Islanders in an angle.

THE WWF WAS TAKING OFF, and All Japan was on fire, and they were going back and forth making more than they'd ever imagined in both places and wowing fans all over the world with their ability. Because of the Japanese commitments, which they wouldn't give up, WWF couldn't give them the sustained push, because they were always leaving. In the summer of 1985, when the Bulldogs faced Hansen and Terry Gordy, and Smith, considered a small guy, press-slammed the 300-pound Gordy, there was talk of allowing them to be competitive with the big boys. The 1985 tag-team tournament was the biggest logjam in tournament history, with the teams (Hansen and Ted DiBiase, Baba and Dory Funk, Tsuruta and Tenryu, the Bulldogs, Race and Jesse Barr, Bockwinkel and Curt Hennig and Rusher Kimura and Ashura Hara) trading wins and losses and nobody dominating. Even though they were not pushed anywhere as main eventers, the big debate in 1985 among casual fans was involving who the best tag team in wrestling was, the Road Warriors, who never lost and were always on top, and the Bulldogs, who were in the middle but were in a league above just about everyone in the business once the bell rang.

McMahon cut a deal with Baba to get exclusivity, and the push was on to build them up for the WWF tag-team title at the second Wrestlemania. Because of their lack of interview ability, they were given Lou Albano, a legendary talker in the twilight of his career, as their mouthpiece. While a cage match with Hulk Hogan vs. King Kong Bundy, a Battle Royal involving several NFL football stars and a boxing match with Roddy Piper vs. Mr. T took center stage in the build-up, there was little doubt the best match on the second Wrestlemania on April 7, 1986, in Chicago at the Horizon was the Bulldogs winning the tag-team titles from The Dream Team, Greg Valentine and Brutus Beefcake. Dynamite took a ridiculous bump at the finish, falling backward from the middle rope to the floor after a collision with Valentine, allowing Smith to pin him in 13:03.

The injuries from working such an insane schedule in 1985, combined with the drug use, and money the likes of which few in wrestling had ever seen before, started to take its toll. Dynamite's body gave out first. He collapsed in the ring during a title defense against Don Muraco and Bob Orton on December 13, 1986, in Hamilton, and it was at first thought his career was over with two ruptured discs and temporary paralysis. In hindsight, it probably should have been. Not that he wasn't warned, as three different back specialists also advised him to give up wrestling. With the WWF running two or three shows per night, the tag titles were very important. The promotion hid the injury, never acknowledging it on television, and billed Bulldogs in title defenses for the next month that weren't going to take place. It got ridiculous after six weeks of no-shows, but they continued to play previously taped matches of the Bulldogs to make it appear he was still working every week. When those tapes ran out, Vince asked Dynamite to come to the January 26, 1987 taping in Tampa to drop the belts in the ring. The only problem was Dynamite couldn't walk yet.

McMahon wanted them to lose to Iron Sheik and Nikolai Volkoff, but Kid didn't like Sheik, and while he liked Volkoff, he thought he wasn't any good in the ring. Bret Hart, who with Neidhart was giving the Bulldogs their classic matches during that time period, asked Dynamite for the favor, and Dynamite agreed to drop the titles, but only to them. In a famous story, Dynamite Kid literally came out of a wheelchair after six weeks off steroids, being carried to the ring by Smith. Dynamite was attacked before the match started, Davey was double-teamed quickly and the title changed hands.

Davey's chemical dependencies, which gained substantial attention when they became public in 1999, actually dated back to this period.

"He had excruciating pain in his lower back from the '80s," said Ross Hart. "He was in agony and constantly seeing back specialists and getting adjustments. He was living with pain for a long time and couldn't get off the painkillers."

The WWF lifestyle was in some ways more difficult then. While the physical

"HE HAD EXCRUCIATING PAIN IN HIS LOWER BACK FROM THE '80S. HE WAS IN AGONY AND CONSTANTLY SEEING BACK SPECIALISTS AND GETTING ADJUSTMENTS. HE WAS LIVING WITH PAIN FOR A LONG TIME AND COULDN'T GET OFF THE PAINKILLERS."

—ROSS HART

trauma is greater today because of the greater expectations inside the ring, every other aspect of the business was harder, in particular, the schedule. While today's wrestlers may work 180 matches in a year, usually the weekly tours involve four shows in the same geographical area. In those days the wrestlers like the Bulldogs were on the road 300 days a year, working two or three matches at TV tapings and weekend double-shots, and constantly going back and forth all over the country, changing time zones, destroying regular sleep patterns, flying far more often and still having to train because the emphasis on the physique was equal if not greater to what it is today. Although the matches weren't as hard and the injury rate was nothing compared with today, the stress of being on the road was far greater.

Practical jokes were rampant, and the Bulldogs were the kings. Everybody did them in Calgary, probably to relieve the stress of the horribly long road trips and even worse weather. Smith was Dynamite's follower, and Dynamite had a major sadistic streak. Many of the ribs, like the ones he did with Owen Hart in the '90s, were harmless fun. Others, like putting M-80s in people's shoes or putting halcyon or heavy laxatives in people's drinks, were more destructive.

Dynamite was never the same in the ring when he came back full time just before Wrestlemania III in 1987. Smith had to carry the team; a crippled Dynamite couldn't bump much and was mainly a punch/kick guy, throwing in an occasional snap suplex or diving head-butt. The peak of the British Bulldogs was already over.

Their swansong with the promotion came the next year. Jacques and Raymond Rougeau asked Curt Hennig to watch their gear while they wrestled, largely to make sure the Bulldogs didn't destroy it, as they were known to do. So Hennig, instead, grabbed scissors and cut their clothes to ribbons. When the Rougeaus came back, they were furious. Hennig hid in the bathroom, then came out and used that as an excuse for not seeing what happened. The Bulldogs became the suspects, because that was their m.o. Jacques complained to Vince. When Dynamite found out, he slapped Jacques hard from behind. Jacques, who was by no means a tough guy, lost his temper and went to tackle Dynamite, but Dynamite, who had far more real training, ended up on top and punched him twice in the face. Raymond tried to break it up, but Dynamite knocked him out. Jacques went home to his family with his face a mess and his honor destroyed. He spent two weeks letting it build, including talking to his uncle Johnny, who was a tough guy, and eventually decided he needed to get revenge. In Fort Wayne, Indiana, he came to the building with a roll of quarters and sucker punched Dynamite, knocking out four of his teeth and ripping his mouth to shreds. There was blood everywhere, and even Jacques admitted that Dynamite, who was incredibly tough, stayed on his feet before it was broken up. When McMahon didn't fire Jacques, Dynamite told Davey they were quitting.

Dynamite, who had always called the shots for the team, called up Motoko Baba and asked her if they could return, and a deal was cut immediately. Stampede Wrestling was dying, and it was hoped a return of the Bulldogs would save the company. Stu gave Dynamite the book to work between Japan tours. Their final night in the WWF was November 24, 1988, in Cleveland at the Survivor Series, and there were rumors going around that since it was their last night in, that they were going to gain revenge on Jacques, although not in the ring. The rumors were so loud, that in a tag-team elimination match, the WWF office changed the booking plans for the match. Jacques and Raymond were eliminated 5:22 into the match. They immediately left the building. The Bulldogs, who should have been eliminated first, were kept in until the 36:02 mark of the match, giving the Rougeaus plenty of time to get on a flight to Montreal before any problems took place.

THEIR RETURN TO CALGARY drew initially, but ultimately it was a disaster. They shot an angle to turn Dynamite heel and split up the Bulldogs. Ed Whalen, a huge fan of the team, hated the angle so much that he refused to allow it to air on television. With their Japan commitments, the proposed feud, starting off as a tag feud with Davey and Chris Benoit vs. Dynamite and Johnny Smith, and building to a singles feud, was stop and start and never gained the expected momentum. Giant Baba hated that angle, and was embarrassed by reports when it was brought to his attention and he denied it had happened, since they were feuding in Canada but still working as a team in Japan. But the Japanese fans knew. Frustration mounted as the business in Calgary fell apart.

The feud stalled again as on July 4, 1989, a car driven by Ross, carrying Smith, Benoit, Tatsumi Kitahara (All Japan's Koki Kitahara) and Karl Moffat got into a serious accident near Jasper, Alberta.

"There was snow and ice on the road and we were late for the show," said Ross. "It was an icy road. The car hydroplaned. We hit head-on with a station wagon and trailer."

Ross, wearing a seat belt, had only minor injuries. Davey, sitting in the front seat, wasn't wearing a seat belt; his head smashed the windshield, and he needed 100 stitches. Moffat ended up the worst of anyone, as a spare tire crushed his ankle. He filed a lawsuit against the Hart family and Stampede Wrestling, claiming he was crippled from the accident. He probably would have collected, except an insurance company investigator secretly taped footage of him doing things like riding a motorbike and moving furniture and getting along just fine.

With Stu's savings depleting and Helen's health taking a turn for the worse from the stress, checks started bouncing, and Stu heeded his wife's wishes and closed the territory for good in December 1989.

In Japan, the Bulldogs, in their final hurrah, had some classic matches against teams like Dan Kroffat and Doug Furnas, Tiger Mask and Kawada, Joe and Dean Malenko (which won the Tokyo Sports award for tag-team match of the year in 1990), The Fantastics and Kenta Kobashi and Tsuyoshi Kikuchi. In the 1989 World Tag League, they placed fourth behind only Hansen and Tenryu, Tsuruta and Yoshiaki Yatsu and Baba and Rusher Kimura, and ahead of legends Tiger Jeet Singh and Abdullah the Butcher. No "small guy" team had ever done so well in a tournament.

When All Japan and WWF worked together on April 13, 1990, for the "U.S. and Japan Wrestling Summit" at the Tokyo Dome, McMahon saw the Bulldogs and went to Dynamite, the leader, and asked him if he wanted to come back. In front of all the wrestlers, Dynamite responded with words to the effect of, "when hell freezes over," and kind of embarrassed McMahon in front of the other wrestlers. He went to Davey and asked him the same question, and Davey responded he was ready to return. Dynamite was furious, and the two never saw each other, nor ever spoke again. Dynamite stayed in Japan teaming with Johnny Smith for the next 20 months until his physical condition got so bad that he announced his retirement at the end of 1991. He did wrestle a little in England and once more in Japan (where he was a shell of his former self) over the next few years.

"I quit with him from the WWF and went back to Japan with him, but I had a big house at that time and I wasn't making enough money, basically, to make my payments," said Smith about his breakup with Dynamite in an interview with Heath Santo conducted just a few hours before his death.

"My lifestyle was a high lifestyle because I was working for the WWF. He (Dynamite) took offense to that, but he never said anything to my face. To my face he said, 'If you go back to WWF, you won't make it as a single,' blah, blah blah, and I said, 'But I'm going back to Japan with Johnny Smith.' . . . He said, 'Good look to you,' and I said, 'Thanks,' and that's the last time I ever saw him."

When Dynamite was retired and living in England and Davey was wrestling in England, Dynamite made threats that family members took very seriously, that he was going to go after Smith and give him a beating for walking out on him in Japan and talking behind his back. The closest thing he did was go to a show and destroy his merchandise table before being taken out of the building by security, kicking and screaming about what he was going to do to Davey.

Smith's second WWF tenure, as a single, coincided with the company becoming a big hit on Sky in the U.K., with Smith catching on as the new national wrestling hero. The business was so strong that SummerSlam in 1992 was moved to Wembley Stadium. In those days, title changes were planned out months in advance, and sometimes longer. When Bret Hart won the IC title back from Roddy Piper at Wrestlemania that year, the plan was for him to drop it to Shawn Michaels at SummerSlam in D.C. When the show was moved to Wembley Stadium, the decision was changed to go to Smith. The plan was no doubt for Michaels to get it from Smith, although Smith wasn't informed he was basically a transitional champion just to get the big closing pop on the show.

Smith's biggest career match on August 29, 1992, at Wembley Stadium in London drew a record-setting 78,927 paid, which is actually the largest verifiable paid attendance ever for a pro-wrestling event. The merchandise figure of $1,456,203, much of it being Bulldog merchandise, is still the all-time record for any WWF live event. With the storyline of Diana and the family being torn apart by the feud of brother vs. husband, Smith pinned Hart in 25:13 of what is generally considered the best match of Smith's career and the one Bret Hart has also talked about being his single favorite match. What is largely forgotten about the match is that Smith had no business being in the ring, as he was hospitalized shortly before the match due to a staph infection in his knee.

Smith went from the top of the wrestling world to unemployed in just a few months. He dropped the title to Michaels, and was then fired by McMahon. The WWF had very stringent steroid testing by this point, stemming from bad publicity in the wake of the George Zahorian trial the previous year and a federal investigation into McMahon and Titan Sports.

Although the WWF claimed to be able to test for not only steroids, but also Growth Hormone, which Olympic athletes were using to beat testing, that wasn't the case. A doctor told Smith point blank there was no way they could catch Growth Hormone no matter what they publicly claimed. McMahon found out about a doctor in England who was sending stuff to Jim Hellwig, and that Smith was the connection. Even though they were the two biggest babyfaces in the promotion at the time, McMahon fired both of them in October of 1992.

Smith went back to All Japan, but both he and that company had changed greatly in the few years since he left. The new blood on top, Misawa, Kawada and Kobashi, had elevated the in-ring style. It was faster, harder and more technical than any heavyweight ring style in history. Even though Smith flourished in the faster, harder, technical style in his youth, he had become accustomed to the much less physical WWF style. His body was breaking down, and in the 1993 Champion Carnival tournament, he only placed eighth.

He had already debuted in WCW before that time, and was pushed next to Sting as the company's No. 2 babyface. While in WCW, he headlined his first three PPV shows ever. On May 23, 1993 at Slamboree, he defeated Vader via DQ in a WCW title match, which was an excellent match until the cheap Harley Race interfered after the powerslam by Smith. On July 18, 1993, at Beach Blast in Biloxi, Mississippi, he teamed with Sting over Vader and Sid Vicious in a ***3/4 match ending when Vader missed a moonsault, and Smith pinned him.

ABOVE: An early shot of the British Bulldogs, Tom Billington and Davey Boy Smith. (Bob Leonard)

Finally, on September 19, 1993, at the War Games in Houston, he headlined what was easily the worst War Games in history teaming with Sting and Dustin Rhodes and Shock Master (Fred Ottman, who made his debut falling through the wall in one of the great live bloopers in wrestling history) over Vicious and Harlem Heat and Vader. All three shows did 0.5 buy rates, and paid attendances respectively of 3,722, 4,000 and 4,500, although that was no better or worse than all WCW shows in those days were doing. By the end of the year, Smith was moved to a mid-card feud with Steven Regal before starting a program with U.S. champ Rick Rude.

Smith was fired over a contract dispute when he no-showed four house shows in protest, and WCW felt it needed to set an example—an example they'd have been well served to remember years later when similar behavior that went unpunished was a factor in destroying their business. Smith, who came in on a $1,000-per-night deal when Bill Watts was in charge, claimed Watts told him he'd earn more for shows in Europe, since he was being counted on to be the big draw there. When Watts was gone, there was no written record of such an agreement, and WCW would only pay him $1,000 per European date. He started missing shows unless he got more from his European dates. After being let go in the middle of a program with Rick Rude over the U.S. title, they announced a match on the flagship TBS Saturday night television show and played his entrance music even though he had already been fired. When he didn't come out, it was said he was backstage, and chicken to come out and face Rude.

He went on tour in England for the next several months, resurfacing in the crowd at SummerSlam on August 29, 1994. The main event was Bret vs. Owen in a cage match, and they were doing the family feud angle once again. All of the family sat ringside for the match in Chicago, including an incredibly jacked-up Smith. It was a major item at the time, because WWF was still doing the strict steroid testing, and Smith, a poster child, showed up looking like he did. McMahon immediately signed him and pushed him.

On January 22, 1995, at the Sun Dome in Tampa for the annual Royal Rumble, in one of the most memorable Rumbles in history, Michaels and Smith started together. When the dust settled, they were the last two. They did the finish where Michaels did the tight-rope act, brushing one leg, but not the other on the floor, apparently losing, only to re-enter, it was ruled he wasn't eliminated, and tossing a celebrating Smith over the top to get the Wrestlemania title shot.

He was then put in a tag team with Lex Luger, called the Allied Powers, and they were being groomed for the tag titles when Luger walked out without warning. Smith turned heel after Luger left, and went with manager Jim Cornette. His first ever WWF PPV main event came on October 22, 1995, in a terrible match on an awful show before 10,339 fans paying $93,422 and a poor 0.4 buy rate from the Winnipeg Arena against WWF champ Kevin Nash, then wrestling as Diesel. Nine days earlier, Smith, Sean Waltman and Michaels were partying in a bar in Syracuse, New York on the night of the infamous brawl where Michaels suffered a pretty bad pounding from a group of marines, the number of which has varied greatly depending upon the report from four to ten (the official police report listed the number as ten, although even WWF wrestlers thought that may have been those involved attempting to save face. Michaels ended up not pressing charges, apparently so as not to further the publicity that a WWF superstar had been beaten up by marines.

Smith, who was in the backseat in a two-door car, and because it was a small car, took some time getting out before he largely cleaned house, but not before Michaels took a pretty savage beating. Smith actually worked the next night, but had scratches on his face and a reddish black right eye from broken blood vessels in the fight.

After Hart won the title from Nash, he defended the title against Smith on December 17, 1995, on a PPV from Hershey, Pennsylvania, before 7,289 fans paying $100,000 and the company's all-time lowest ever buy rate of an 0.3. It was promoted as a rematch of their classic match three years earlier, except this time Diana was firmly behind Smith and vehemently against Bret. Hart won with la magistral cradle in 21:09 of what was another of the greatest WWF matches in history up to that point. The match was worked total babyface style, and strongly teased a Smith turn, as he hugged his consoling wife in mid-ring after losing.

SMITH MADE HEADLINES throughout Canada in February 1996 based on an incident that took place on July 25, 1993, at the Back Alley nightclub in Calgary. Kody Light, 20, asked Diana to dance,

and may have made a rude remark to her involving sexual practices. Diana got Davey to get Light to back off. Davey went to shake his hand, and Davey testified that Light said to him, "You got a nice f***in wife." When Smith tried to let go, Light squeezed and tried to outmuscle him, as strange as that sounds. There are several versions of what happened next. There were about a dozen witnesses. Three testified that Smith attacked Light, and either picked him up and threw him into a wall, using a powerbomb-like maneuver, and maybe punched him. Light suffered serious permanent injuries. However, none of the witnesses against Smith gave stories close to what the others did. All the other witnesses testified that Smith grabbed Light in a guillotine choke after Light started the fight, and brought him over to the bouncers to get rid of him. Versions of this story varied as well, as either Smith let go of Light for the bouncers, but Light had passed out and hit his head on the floor. Another version is that Light escaped from the bouncers, went to attack Smith, but was still woozy from the guillotine and slipped on the wet floor, hitting the back of his head. A bouncer testified Light had been warned earlier in the evening about harassing female patrons.

What made headlines was in testimony, Smith admitted on the stand that pro wrestling was fake, saying, "Every single thing in wrestling is a fake." Prosecutor Gary Belecki then called Smith's profession a fraud perpetrated on the public, which Smith replied saying, "If you want to put it that way." Six years ago that was considered front-page news, not that anyone didn't know it, but that a huge star would be forced to say so under oath. Smith said a power bomb would be impossible without the cooperation of the opponent (which isn't actually true, as power bombs have been done in MMA competition). Karl Moffat, who had a grudge against the Hart family stemming from the auto accident lawsuit, was a surprise prosecution witnesses who said one could physically do a power bomb in a combative situation without cooperation from the person taking the move. Another witness against him was local police officer Sydney Sutherland, who was a witness to the 1983 incident that nearly got Smith deported, saying Smith had the strength to do what was alleged. Sutherland said he saw him in 1983 grab an officer by the gun belt and collar, lift him up and throw him almost six feet across a lane of a city street.

JUDGE JACK WAITE ACQUITTED SMITH, saying he sympathized with Light because of his injuries, but was convinced Smith hadn't caused them, and also believing everything Smith had done physically was in self-defense. The key witness was Dr. John Butt, the former chief medical examiner for Alberta, who testified Light's injuries were likely caused by him falling. Light's injuries included a skull fracture at the back of his head just above where the neck muscles were attached, which caused deafness in his left ear, slurring speech and

impairment in motor functions, intellect and memory. Butt said, "I find it difficult to see how somebody is going to land that low on their head (after being flipped), but I can't deny the possibility."

Instead of turning Davey babyface, the decision was made to turn Yokozuna face, to feud with Vader, who had just been signed. Yokozuna had been teaming with Owen, and Owen and Bulldog were put together as partners and relatives who were always trying to one-up each other.

But before that came yet more controversy. Michaels had beaten Hart for the WWF title, and Hart took a leave of absence from the company while his contract expired to try his hand at acting, and even considered retirement. They constructed an angle where Diana Smith accused Michaels of hitting on her to get Davey jealous, and set up a WWF title program, including an angle where Davey attacked Michaels and tried to drown him. The angle was supposed to end with it turning out that Diana had been the one hitting on Michaels. Stu, Davey, and Bret were all vehement about the angle being in poor taste, which was actually the first major disagreement between Bret and Vince over content that probably played a small part in their eventual bigger problems.

In what was probably the single greatest disaster of a PPV in WWF history, the Beware of Dog show took place on May 26, 1996, in Florence, South Carolina. A combination of a poor advance and horrible weather limited the crowd to 4,796 paying $63,435 and an 0.45 buy rate, although many refunds from that buy rate had to be offered. An electrical storm caused power to go off. At one point during the show, there was a blank screen of 25 minutes, with clips of Vince McMahon and Jerry Lawler imploring viewers to stay tuned because the Michaels-Smith main event would take place. Power was restored with just 25 minutes of TV time left. Michaels, a brilliant performer but very immature under pressure, lost his cool because the power outage had ruined the show and neither he or Smith even wanted to go out, wanting to save the match for the next Tuesday when part of the show was going to be re-done. Michaels, the babyface, also got mad at a heckling fan and by yelling back at her, the ringside fans started booing Michaels, which caused him to pout during the match. The match wasn't terrible, but fell far short of expectations and the lofty standard of work that Michaels's main event bouts were known for. At 17:21, the average match ended with a double-pin draw to build for a rematch.

The rematch on June 23, 1996, at King of the Ring was the opposite. Milwaukee sold out three weeks in advance for the show at a time when wrestling shows rarely did such a thing, with 8,762 paying $142,568 and doing an 0.6 buy rate. He and Michaels did a ****1/4 match over 26:25 with Curt Hennig as ref with a weak-looking superkick. Hennig refused to count to three, so Earl Hebner did, for the finish.

He and Owen defeated The Smoking Gunns for the tag titles on September 22, 1996, on a PPV from Philadelphia. They even defended them in a totally forgettable match on December 15, 1996, at a PPV from West Palm Beach over the new Razor Ramon and new Diesel. They feuded with the likes of Mankind and Vader, The Road Warriors, and Doug Furnas and Phil Lafon, the latter in a disappointing program as injuries had crippled Lafon by that time.

Their most memorable, and as it turned out, most important match as champions, wasn't a title defense. It was February 26, 1997, in Berlin, Germany. While a heel in North America, Smith was the company's most popular wrestler in Europe stemming from his early '90s success. A tournament was created for a European title, largely as a reason to allow Smith to headline those tours. In the beginnings of the political maneuverings that would set the stage for the explosion months later, the soon-to-be DX faction wanted HHH to beat Bret Hart in the tournament, and in turn lose to Owen. Bret got that changed to where he beat HHH, and he himself put Owen over. Smith pinned Owen in 23:00 in a ****1/2 classic, considered by many to be the best match up to that point in the history of Raw, when it aired one week later. The two heels wrestled a totally babyface Japanese-style match, and the live crowd went crazy for all the near-falls. The ratings told a different story. The production values for the Germany taping were a throwback to '70s wrestling. The live audience rejected a classic match with poor production values. *Nitro* did a 3.41 rating to *Raw's* 1.91 for the night. Head to head, the *Nitro* main event with Luger and Giant vs. The Steiners drew a 3.7 to Owen vs. Davey's 1.9. It was the day that number came out that Vince McMahon agreed with those who had convinced him the current direction was a failure, and the direction of going for the sleaze was the only way to fight. Attitude was born on March 4, 1997.

Smith and Owen reunited with Bret, shortly after he turned heel in the Wrestlemania match with Steve Austin, which was even more monumental for turning Austin face. Austin's feud with Team Canada was the beginning of the turnaround of what had been a weak company to what eventually became the strongest company in history.

While losing the ratings, many will remember 1997 as a banner year creatively, largely based on the week-by-week antics of that top feud. With shows being taped in Canada, where so-called Team Canada (consisting of two Americans, two Canadians and a British wrestler) became almost national heroes, even though they worked as heels on television. At the U.S. tapings, the crowd reaction became just as vehement, only in the opposite direction. The peak was July 6, 1997, at the Saddledome in Calgary for one of the greatest shows in WWF history, the Canadian Stampede PPV which drew 10,974 paying $229,598, setting what was at the time the all-time Calgary gate record.

Team Canada, consisting of Bret and Owen Hart, Brian Pillman, Davey Boy Smith and Jim Neidhart won over Goldust and Road Warriors and Austin and Ken Shamrock in 24:31. The thunderous ovation of the Hart family, several generations worth, celebrating in mid-ring, was probably the biggest pop in a North American wrestling ring in more than ten years. It's eerie to think it was only five years ago. What was probably the second high point of Smith's career, turned out just like the first one, a prelude to leaving the WWF.

The Shawn Michaels European title win continued the heat between the Michaels clique and the Hart family, both in storyline and in reality. McMahon must have loved it, because it made for fascinating weekly television that had more than an edge of reality because many of the hard feelings and statements made were not made up. While the numbers were nowhere close to the levels they would eventually become, ratings and live attendance were improving with the three-pronged feud of Team Canada, Austin's group, and Michaels's group.

But Smith's tenure in the WWF was already questionable. With the situation with Bret tenuous once he turned down the request to get his money deferred, there were thoughts about Smith's future as well. He had signed a four-year contract, which some in the company were regretting, largely because WCW was after him as his WWF deal was about to expire in 1997. Smith had friends in the company like Hogan, who knew of his European

ABOVE: Davey Boy Smith at an autograph session with Terry Funk and Woman (now Nancy Benoit, wife of Chris Benoit). (Dr. Mike Lano)

popularity and WCW was talking about expanding there.

Ironically, this was the peak of the Team Canada feud, and Bret convinced Smith to sign for less money in WWF. Smith was 34, but there were no secrets in the business of his painkiller and steroid problems. The problems were nowhere near the level they would become. He had been wrestling for 19 years, and his knees in particular were showing the effect, not only of all that wrestling, but of years of doing so weighing 245 to 270 pounds on a frame built for maybe 195. Smith's legit knee problems were the backdrop for the

angle for him to lose his European title to Michaels on the first ever U.K.-only PPV called "One Night Only," a decision changed from the first plan, and something he wasn't told until the day of the show. He missed time after the match with a bad knee, which friends felt was at least partially due to his frustration at losing the match and the reaction of his dying sister. He claimed to have reinjured his knee in the Bret Hart-Vince McMahon dressing room altercation in Montreal, although his story has changed many times, from pulling Bret off Vince or pulling Shane McMahon off Bret.

Those who were in the dressing room don't remember either taking place, but Smith claimed a knee injury in the fracas and went home, also out of loyalty to Bret. Hart got WCW to offer Smith a deal, but McMahon demanded $100,000 from him to get out of his contract, which he paid. His new WCW deal would have made him more than that $100,000 anyway, although he never came close to collecting the money on his contract because he was fired a little over a year into the deal. When he came to WCW in 1998, he was a different wrestler, in poor shape physically, a virtual zombie at times, and totally unpushable.

The last four and a half years were a total nightmare. His mother and sister died. His career was in ruins. His drug problems were way out of control. His marriage was falling apart. He had one overdose after another. He was injured badly in a motorcycle accident. He had two stints in rehab. His back was shot, with crushed C-9 and C-10 discs and four more fractured discs. He was still seeing Dr. Joel Hackett even when told by WWF officials to steer clear of him. Hackett, who prescribed large quantities of drugs to many pro wrestlers including three who died with drugs as a factor, was under investigation by the authorities. WWF officials knew he was hot, banned him from dressing rooms in 1997 after the death of Pillman, but a few wrestlers continued to see him. He was portrayed horribly in two autobiographies, one by Dynamite and the other by Diana. He was

totally ineffective in stints with both WWF and WCW. He alienated some family members by siding with Vince McMahon, who had just hired him, in the lawsuit filed by Martha Hart for the death of Owen. It was actually Owen who got Smith back in, and the two were scheduled to become tag-team partners again.

Smith was near death once again with another staph infection months earlier and was fired by WCW while in the hospital. He blamed Bret, noting he stayed in WWF out of loyalty to Bret, and left for the same reason. However, Smith's condition was such that in hindsight, WCW had no choice, and there was nothing Bret could do after convincing him to go to rehab and him falling back off the wagon. But his near-death experience soon thereafter made him a sympathetic and tragic figure, and Owen convinced WWF management to give him another shot if he could recover.

Long before he was ready to start with WWF, Owen died in Kansas City. The deal had been consummated and people knew of it, but it came across terribly to many when they made the big announcement of his signing as the family feud heated up. Bret was not against his going back to WWF, recognizing there were only two companies and he'd just been fired by one. He was furious that after the accident and while the police in Kansas City were still investigating potential manslaughter charges and with a lawsuit being filed, that several family members led by Davey, Diana and Ellie (Jim

"I'D LIKE TO FOCUS ON THE GOOD MEMORIES.

HE HAD A LOT OF GOOD QUALITIES."

—ROSS HART

Neidhart's wife, as Neidhart was hired as a trainer by the WWF in the wake of Owen's death) came out publicly on McMahon's side against their sister-in-law.

Davey and Diana taped an interview for *Raw*, designed to bury Bret, who Vince by this point had seemingly hated with a passion due to the post-Montreal furor. The contents were unknown, but apparently they were so bad that even after plugging the interview on *Raw* that next week Davey would give his true thoughts on Montreal and on Bret, the decision was then made to not let the interview run. Smith was having problems with downers and morphine, but as always, he was in total denial when the subject came up.

Diana, sick of it, tried to shock him into seeing himself, and gobbled up dozens of pills like he would take. She, being half his size, didn't have the tolerance, and ended up OD'ing to shock Davey into action. Davey went to rehab twice, but he injured his back coming out of it while training and relapsed on pain pills. His back was already a mess from taking the bump on the trap door while in WCW. While in rehab the second time, he got word his wife was seeing James Trimble, a rookie wrestler working for Bruce's Stampede Wrestling under the name Dick Butkus Jr. Andrea, Bruce's wife, who always had animosity toward Diana and visa versa, left Bruce for Davey, creating yet another family wedge.

Eventually Davey and Diana divorced, and she filed restraining orders against him and he was charged with at various times, threatening the lives of several family members. The stories got worse and worse. They were surreal by 1999, and well past that over the next year. To those close to him, and for that matter, to many in wrestling, very much like Brian Pillman, his death was not a surprise.

"I'd like to focus on the good memories," said Ross. "He had a lot of good qualities. He got caught up with pain killers and other addictions to fight his pain. He was caught in the middle of relationships. We wanted him to get his life together and make a comeback."

CHAPTER 4
CURT
HENNIG

CURT HENNIG USED TO BRAG to his friends that he had a horseshoe up his ass because he was so lucky. And friends, dumbfounded how Hennig would routinely hit jackpots on quarter slots and managed to make big money from wrestling without giving up his family and hanging out with his friends, were even more shocked when hearing that he had passed away.

For Bobby Heenan, who Curt would always say was like a second father to him, it was eerie, reminding him of the death of Heenan's favorite traveling partner, Ray Stevens.

"He called me last week and it was strange," said Heenan. "It was like Ray Stevens, who never called me, other than to say pick me up at five. Stevens called me the day before he died. He said he just wanted to talk. I'd known him for 30 years and he never called to talk. That's just how he was. Curt called last week, and I wasn't home. He left a message saying that he just wanted to see how I was doing."

Heenan, like many of the wrestlers who worked the AWA during the '60s, had known Curt since he was 10 years old as one of the three boys in the Hennig

OPPOSITE: Curt Hennig was one of the most talented wrestlers of the late '80s and early '90s. (Dr. Mike Lano)

house. Randy, the oldest, was the best amateur wrestler in the family, but had no interest in pro wrestling. Jesse, the youngest, tried pro wrestling, but it never worked out.

"Curt was a better person than 99 percent of the people on this planet," said Don Frye, who was originally trained for pro wrestling by Hennig and Brad Rheingans. "He's a lot better person than I am. He and Ric Flair were the best workers who ever lived."

Tom Zenk, the last survivor of the four wrestlers who graduated in 1976 from Robbinsdale High, first met Hennig in 1974 when both were sophomores in high school. He actually knew Hennig's wife dating back to second grade in Catholic school.

Zenk thought growing up was tough for Hennig because as an athlete he had a lot of pressure on him because of his father and older brother. Larry Hennig and Verne Gagne both had attended Robbinsdale High in a previous generation and become high school football and wrestling stars and local pro wrestling legends long before Curt entered high school.

That legacy probably explains why seven different guys from their school in Hennig's era ended up at one time or another on the WWF roster during the first big era. Larry had kept the family at home in 1973-74 when he went to the WWWF as a heel, doing a program with then-champion Pedro Morales.

In 1975, Larry recognized there were only going to be one hometown hero in the AWA, and it was the owner of the company, Gagne. He brought his family with him to Scottsdale, Arizona, and Curt spent his junior year there, as his father attempted to start a wrestling territory based out of Phoenix that didn't take. Curt lost as many matches as he won as a high school wrestler that year. He returned to Robbinsdale High as a senior, and played football as a linebacker and wrestled. He lettered in both sports his senior year, but was nothing close to a star in either sport.

Verne Gagne rushed Hennig into the ring on January 30, 1980 for a match in the Twin Cities against prelim wrestler Billy Howard. Hennig's debut and early prelim wins were more to create an angle to bring his father back for a feud with Adrian Adonis, who was in the role of the older bully picking on Larry's son, a natural angle for that market. But the AWA already had its father/son tag team.

"You could tell he had it in the ring from the beginning," remembered Heenan, who rated Hennig and Flair as the two greatest wrestlers ever to come out of Minnesota, which covers tremendous ground. "He was agile and coordinated. Barry Windham had it from the beginning, and so did Dustin Rhodes."

IN MANY WAYS, Hennig's career mirrored that of Windham's. Both were second-generation wrestlers whose fathers were not what would be called good workers by any stretch in the ring, but were noted for being 300-pound, physically tough men outside the ring. Both were tall, but naturally slender and far more agile than their fathers and really blew them away inside the ring. By the late '80s, Hennig and Windham were right up there with Flair, Ricky Steamboat and Ted DiBiase as the best workers in the game.

It appeared in the late '80s that they would, along with Shawn Michaels, Bret Hart and Rick Rude, inherit the mantle as the top performers inside the ring. But both had injuries stall their careers before they reached that top level of stardom that many expected from them. Both had their careers inside the ring seem to end on more than one occasion. Both continually came back, to where newer fans had no idea that they were ever top stars.

Ironically, they wound up being paired together in the West Texas Rednecks gimmick in WCW in 1999, with Kendall Windham and the late Bobby Duncum Jr. It was a mid-card thing that wasn't supposed to get over. Even if it was, it was supposed to make the Rednecks heels against the rapper baby-face group led by Master P. The Rednecks, with Hennig as lead singer, would perform "I Hate Rap," which was supposed to get heat, but ended up with fans singing along, "I, I, I, Hate Rap. Rap is Crap." Inadvertently, through a combination of bad booking (Hennig, always outnumbered, always managed to outsmart his opposition and come back and look strong) and a backwards premise in the first place with the idea the WCW audience base would prefer gangsta rap to country music, wound up turning him babyface and should have saved his career.

The song even got some play on country stations and was turning into a cult favorite. But, as things were in that company, it was then mysteriously buried and dropped. And it was the last hurrah for both wrestlers.

"You made me laugh and gave me some of the greatest times of my career, even though it was a tough time in my life," wrote Windham in a guest book for Hennig's funeral, which had hundreds of entries from wrestlers, people in the business, and fans from all over the world. "I will always remember that. You always said that one day we would be joining up in Heaven with Rick (Rood) and Bobby (Duncum Jr.) And raise so much Hell in Heaven, they'd have to change the name."

Hennig was sent away from the AWA in 1981 to learn the trade the old-fashioned way. He started in 1981 as a prelim wrestler in the WWF. His first match in Madison Square Garden, where his father main evented eight years earlier, was on June 8, 1981, beating veteran jobber Johnny Rodz, and he followed it up with a win over washed-up former Japanese legend Shozo Kobayashi, as well as wins over Baron Scicluna and Joe Cox and a loss to Mr. Fuji.

Then, in probably the best place to learn at the time, he went to the Oregon territory for Don Owen, debuting on January 16, 1982. At the time, his family remained in Minnesota. Hennig had met Buddy Rose when both were in the WWF. Rose opened the doors for Hennig to come into Oregon. As soon as he did,

ABOVE: The Destroyer, Dick Beyer, and former ring rival Larry "The Axe" Hennig, with Larry's son Curt. (Dr. Mike Lano)

Rose made Hennig a local star by putting him over on his arrival and feuding with him.

Although Rose put him over at first, he mainly worked prelim matches. Hennig's first championship belt was when his father came out for a week to visit him. It was a natural program, with heels Rip Oliver and Matt Borne double-teaming the newcomer to the territory, and his big father, an old-school type who knew how to cut a believable promo, saved his son and won the tag titles for a few days.

He returned to the WWF in the fall of 1982, where this time he was pushed as the top babyface television jobber and would look competitive often before losing to the top heels. He returned to Portland on March 26, 1983, for his first push as a star, working main events with all the top heels in the territory. That included some classic singles matches against Dynamite Kid, who was considered by many to be the top worker in the country at the time. Hennig was frequently challenging for the Pacific Northwest heavyweight title, and finally, about a year into his stay, on May 10, 1983, defeated Sheik Ali Hassan to become champion, holding it for four months before dropping it to Dynamite.

It was about that time that Rose did his babyface turn in spectacular fashion, and the two often teamed in main events, including great six-man tags with Billy Jack Haynes on the face side against "The Clan," heels Oliver and The Assassin and Dynamite. Hennig worked the territory through early 1984, when he returned to the AWA.

During that period, he got his first Japanese booking in New Japan's MSG tag-team tournament, where his partner was former AWA regular Bobby Duncum Sr. The two worked as basically a jobber team in the tournament, won by Antonio Inoki and Hulk Hogan over Dick Murdoch and Adrian Adonis. During the tournament they also wrestled Andre the Giant and Swede Hanson, Riki Choshu and Animal Hamaguchi, Tatsumi Fujinami and Akira Maeda, Killer Khan and Tiger Toguchi, Seiji Sakaguchi and Rusher Kimura, and Otto Wanz and Wayne Bridges.

After becoming a regular in the AWA, he was sent to All Japan for the 1985 tag-team tournament to be the jobber half of the team with AWA legend Nick Bockwinkel, in the tournament won by Stan Hansen and Ted DiBiase, and featuring Jumbo Tsuruta and Genichiro Tenryu, Harley Race and Jesse Barr, Giant Baba and Dory Funk, Choshu and Yoshiaki Yatsu, Dynamite Kid and Davey Boy Smith, and Kimura and Ashura Hara.

By the time he came to All Japan for his second tour in January of 1987, he was elevated to star status, as he'd become the leading contender for then-champion Nick Bockwinkel. Probably with the idea of setting up a program for the title at some point, on January 17, 1987, in Tokuyama, Hennig was pinned when challenging Choshu for the PWF title. But by the time Hennig won the AWA title, Choshu was gone from All Japan. After winning the AWA title, his only title defense in Japan was a loss via count out to Tiger Mask (Mitsuharu Misawa) in January of 1988.

He didn't work Japan much after that, mainly working on a few major Tokyo Dome events. He worked the April 13, 1990 U.S. and Japan Wrestling Summit before 52,743 fans, where he wrestled as Hennig instead of Mr. Perfect, even though it was a WWF show, because they put him in a tag team with Rick Martel as ex-AWA world champions losing to Jumbo Tsuruta and King Haku in a match where he took a lot of unique bumps. He worked the SWS Wrestlefest on March 30, 1991, before 42,000 fans, retaining his IC title in a DQ loss to Kerry Von Erich in a match that didn't get over with the fans because of an Americanized ref-bump finish and Von Erich looking bad in the match. He also worked the January 28, 2001 Tokyo Dome show for All Japan, teaming with Windham and Mike Rotunda in losing to Johnny Smith and Jim Steele and George Hines in a midcard match before about 32,000 fans.

There was always underlying tension between Hennig and Greg Gagne during the AWA days. Hennig, who was a far bet-

"HE DIDN'T WANT TO BE MR. PERFECT.

HE WANTED TO BE A COWBOY CHARACTER."

—BOBBY HEENAN

ter worker, largely took Gagne's spot as the local second generation babyface and No. 1 title contender.

Eras changed, and the 190-pound Gagne, a big local star in the late '70s and early '80s when teaming with Jim Brunzell, could no longer overcome his lack of physique by a viewing public that viewed nearly everyone who didn't take steroids as having a subpar physique. Still, it wasn't an easy pill to swallow, and Hennig was turned heel, a role he flourished in as a performer. But to show how dead the AWA was, on the big Thanksgiving show on November 26, 1987, at the Minneapolis Auditorium headlined by Curt vs. Greg with Larry and Verne in the respective corners, drew just 1,800 fans. Verne, who was 61 by that point, KO'd Curt with a foreign object to win the title for Greg (as announced in the building that night, but reversed on television the next week). The only thing at the time keeping the company going was that ESPN was paying them for the TV show.

The two most unknown factors about Mr. Perfect were that he was not a superstar athlete before pro wrestling, and

he never liked the gimmick he played so well.

"He didn't want to be Mr. Perfect," noted Heenan, who managed him. "He wanted to be a cowboy character. He loved that. His WCW (West Texas Rednecks) gimmick was his favorite character because he loved country music and singing country songs. His dad always wore cowboy boots and loved country music, too. Made no sense to me, since they were both from Minnesota. You'd think they'd like Viking music or something."

But it's doubtful anyone could have played the character as well. The WWF was filled with outlandish gimmicks during that era. Deep down, everyone knew that Kamala wasn't really from Uganda and that Honky Tonk Man didn't really believe he was Elvis. But a lot of people did believe Ted DiBiase was rich, and that Curt Hennig was one of the world's most gifted athletes. Shawn Stasiak, a decade later, flopped when given the same role in WCW ("The Perfect One") by Vince Russo. Hennig's role was to put him over and theoretically pass the Perfect gimmick torch to him. Hennig begrudgingly did so in the ring, but it only underscored it was the guy playing the role who made it work, not the gimmick he played.

His style at the time was to make the babyfaces shine by taking big bumps. Often compared with Flair, Hennig was bigger and came across more athletic and took more outlandish bumps but didn't have Flair's charisma. While many of Flair's big moves were spots that you could see coming, Hennig's knack in his big spots was that fans didn't see where the spot was going. Two of his trademarks were where he begged off backwards, and not seeing where he was, would crotch himself on the ringpost, and then he'd hurdle the ropes into the ring and trip and fall on his face. He was also known for what later became a Lucha spot, where his opponent would sweep his leg as he held onto the ropes and he'd take an exaggerated bump on his neck.

"We called it the Hennig," said Frye, who noted that he and Johnston tried to work it into their repertoire when they feuded in Japan in 1998.

Among the wrestlers, he was the ringleader. As the best worker in the locker room during that era, he ran the show after hours, as the life of the party, and terrorized wrestlers with his ribbing. He'd shave the eyebrows of younger wrestlers if they had passed out from too much partying. He'd put Ex-lax in people's drinks so he and the rest of the crew could get a laugh. He'd cut up people's clothes and sneak around and watch people explode and blame others for it. When guys were in the ring, he'd chain their bags to poles in the arena. Joe Scarpa (Chief Jay Strongbow), one of the agents at the time, nicknamed him Dennis the Menace. A few years back, while training some of the Japanese, he told one of the kids that it was an American tradition to shave their heads at the end of camp. So he shaved one of the newcomers heads while everyone else laughed. He pinned the hair on the wall like it was another trophy.

In WCW, he once put a dead fish in Mark Madden's suit hours before a *Nitro* broadcast, and when Madden put the suit on, he discovered the fish, but the suit reeked for the rest of the night.

Heenan noted that some of his favorite moments ever in the business were when he and Hennig worked together during one of Hennig's injury sabbaticals on the set of *Prime Time Wrestling*, the show that later morphed into *Raw* on Monday nights on the USA Network, where the two, along with Vince McMahon, would do cutaway segments. The two remained friends, seeing each other most Christmases at Wade Boggs's Christmas party. Heenan even agreed to accompany Hennig to the ring, sort of coming out of retirement after 11 years to be a manager, although they called it a sports agent for the XWF TV tapings where Hennig was pushed as the heel the top programs were being built around.

"Between Curt and Brad, I learned so much in such a short period of time," Frye said. "The one thing I always wanted to do was wrestle against him. I'd have been afraid, because as a rib, he might make me look like a complete idiot."

Nick Bockwinkel, who capped off his memorable career at the age of 52 by dropping the AWA title to Hennig in 1987, had known Hennig since he was a teenager.

"He was second generation, like me," said Bockwinkel, whose father, Warren, was a contemporary of Lou Thesz and Fred Blassie breaking into wrestling in St. Louis in the '30s. "Larry was a lot like my father. He drank a little, like most of the boys, but he set a good example and Curt had a good upbringing. His mother (Irene Hennig), was very no nonsense."

His first clear memory of Curt came when a lot of the wrestlers got together to do some boating on a lake. Bockwinkel had a new speedboat, and his tag-team partner, Ray Stevens asked to take it for a spin. Bockwinkel told him no way. A little while later, Curt, then 14, and brother Randy, 16, asked if they could take a ride on the boat with their two dates from high school. Bockwinkel gave them the keys, which infuriated Stevens. He told Stevens that he knew he'd push the boat to the max while the Hennigs, because they were brought up right, would take care of it.

"When they were done, they put the boat in the dock, tied it up by themselves, and their dates were wiping the boat down," he said. "I looked at Ray and showed him, and said that's why I let them take out the boat."

Bockwinkel fondly remembers the match the two had that firmly put Curt Hennig on the map as one of the best wrestlers in the world.

"I was 52 years old and was at the Showboat in Las Vegas taping a New Year's Eve special for ESPN," he said. "The match was going fine until he hit the ringpost and needed ten stitches. He was bleeding a lot worse than he wanted to and didn't know if he could go the 60 minutes. He panicked a little when he saw how much blood he was losing. I just told him not to worry and keep going. We went the distance because he was a trooper and understood what the business was."

A few months later, just before Bockwinkel planned to retire from the ring and take a job as an agent with the WWF, he dropped the AWA title to Hennig, who was involved in his own manipulations with negotiations with Vince McMahon to pressure Verne Gagne to get the title.

"At the time, a champion needed to be a guy who looked the part, with an athletic body, and either be able to wrestle or at least make the people believe he's able to wrestle, have charisma, and be able to talk," Bockwinkel said. "Plus, he had heritage. I think Verne could see that he was the man. There was no doubt in my mind he should have been."

He was in the main event on the January 27, 1990 *Saturday Night's Main Event* (taped January 3, 1990 in Chattanooga) that drew an 11.1 rating,

OPPOSITE: Barry Windham with Curt Hennig in their WCW days as a team called The West Texas Rednecks. (Dr. Mike Lano)

among the highest ratings in the history of television in the 11:30 p.m. to 1 a.m. Saturday night slot. He teamed with manager The Genius, losing to Hulk Hogan and Ultimate Warrior in a match that was the epitome of a one-man show in the ring. Hogan and Warrior as a tag team just before their Wrestlemania match drew the fifth largest TV audience ever to watch a wrestling match in the U.S. that night, but it was Hennig who, once the bell rang, saved what, on paper, looked like a catastrophe. He headlined the next *SNME* airing on April 28, 1990 from Austin, Texas, losing to Hogan in 7:58 of a Hogan formula squash, but well above the usual levels for such a match, due to Perfect being a better worker than almost all of Hogan's foes.

Mr. Perfect first won the IC title on April 23, 1990, in a tournament final over Tito Santana, but was not publicly recognized as champion until the match aired on May 19. It was a unique tournament in that the finals were taped before some of the first-round matches were taped. He was scheduled to lose the title to Brutus Beefcake at SummerSlam on August 27, 1990 in Philadelphia, but Beefcake suffered severe injuries in a parasailing accident on July 4, 1990, and Kerry Von Erich was brought in for the spot. While Hennig was the master of making people look good, Von Erich, who had lost half of his foot years earlier in a motorcycle wreck and whose drug problems had gotten out of control, was unable to be carried by this point. The bout only lasted 5:13 and was a bad match. After poor house-show

matches around the country, it was quickly recognized the decision was a mistake, and the belt was put back on Perfect. The switch took place on November 19, 1990, in Rochester, New York at a TV taping when Ted DiBiase hit Von Erich with the title belt, setting up a Perfect vs. Roddy Piper program.

Hennig's prime years ended right about the time he appeared on the verge of being considered the best wrestler in the country. After suffering the back injury in late June of 1991, he still had to wrestle on television because he was IC champion. In those days, belts meant money, and even though the plan was to get the belt to Bret Hart, there were more than two months before that match was going to happen. In those days, the WWF was more flagrant about false advertising at house shows. Since Hennig and the belt meant a lot, he was billed for months' worth of house shows and title defenses that he wasn't at. To keep fans from realizing he was gone, or not seeing the belt, he was brought in for TV tapings on July 29 and 30 of that year. He was in so much pain on the first night in Worcester, Massachusetts, that he couldn't even rotate his body to do the perfect plex and had to win a squash via a bad-looking count out, unheard of in that period. He taped a second 30-second squash match the next night that was scheduled to air after SummerSlam, so he went out to the ring without the belt, foreshadowing the ending of what would probably be considered his most famous match of his career.

AFTER THE LOSS TO HART in Madison Square Garden, it appeared Hennig's career as an active wrestler was over. He was making his regular wrestling salary through disability insurance payments from Lloyd's of London, while remaining in a featured TV role, having taken over for Heenan as the manager of Flair.

A year later, Ultimate Warrior and Davey Boy Smith were fired just before the 1992 Survivor Series, allegedly for using Growth Hormone to beat the company steroid tests, when they were two of the four top babyfaces. Left in a lurch, McMahon agreed to buy out the remainder of Hennig's insurance settlement to get him back in the ring, since business was already on a dangerous decline and he needed a top babyface. Because of the nature of the times in wrestling, McMahon's top stars couldn't have steroids written in neon letters on them. A rushed angle, with no build-up, was set up on Prime Time Wrestling where Heenan (who did a masterful job) and Perfect got into an argument leading to Perfect turning face and agreeing to team with Randy Savage against Flair and Razor Ramon, winning via DQ in the November 25, 1992 match in Richfield, Ohio. Hennig hadn't had time to get back into his best shape and was rusty in his first match back after 15 months off, but they still had a good match. It was probably a bigger draw than the title match, but inside the ring it was overwhelmed by the classic Hart vs. Michaels co-main event.

Probably no wrestler put Vince McMahon through more hell as a pro-moter during the '80s and '90s and got so little long-term heat for doing so. Once, in 1993, on a snowy night in Connecticut when Hart was WWF champion, Hennig let what were probably his inner feelings out, saying that if he hadn't had the back injury, it would be he who was in that spot as the top guy in the company. Soon Hennig and Scott Hall were arguing with Hart. Moments later, Hennig and Hart were drinking and laughing together.

Much like his friend Rude, Mr. Perfect was far better both as a worker and personality as a heel. Once he beat Flair in their loser leaves town match, Hennig's run as a face got stale in a hurry. He was sliding down the cards, putting over the likes of Lex Luger, Diesel (Kevin Nash) and Ludvig Borga (current pro boxer Tony Halme from Finland), and hardly wrestling like Mr. Perfect. He did a heel switch by turning on Lex Luger at Wrestlemania X, costing him the WWF title in a match with Yokozuna, but then walked out on the program with his second career-ending back injury. He was again getting paid twice, collecting on disability insurance, while working as a television announcer on *Superstars of Wrestling*, the company's top syndicated show, during a period when syndicated television still meant something.

He was brought back as a character in 1996 for a run as the manager and mentor of Hunter Hearst Helmsley, to give Helmsley his superstar rub, since the heel announcer in those days was one of the highest profile personalities in the company. The wrestler now known as

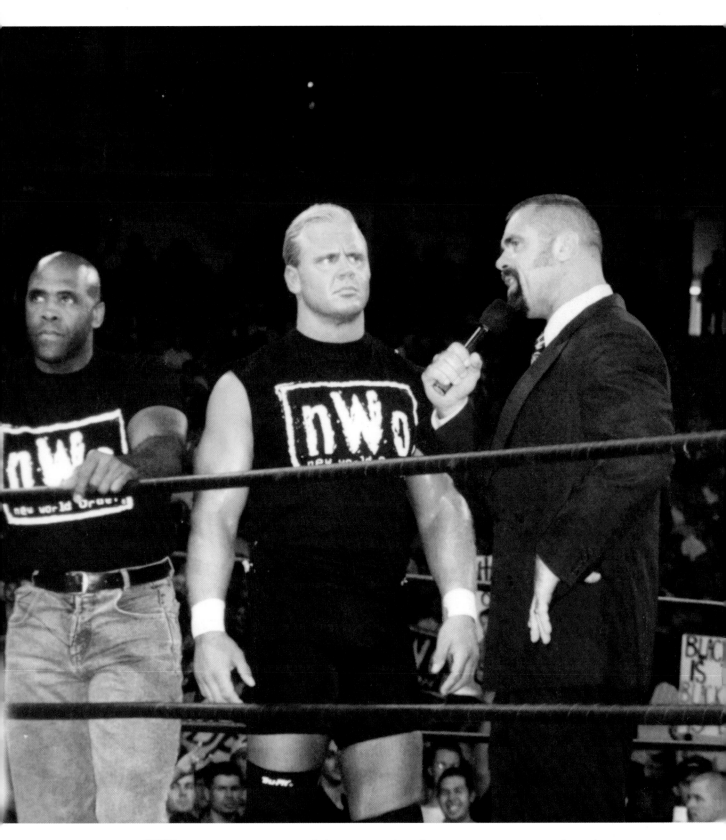

ABOVE: Curt Hennig as part of the nWo with Mike "Vincent" Jones, Rick Rude, Hennig's best friend from childhood, and Scott Hall. (Dr. Mike Lano)

HHH was playing the role of a Greenwich snob, whose gimmick was that he came to the ring with a different centerfold model every week. They set up a program where Mr. Perfect and Helmsley had a falling out, with Mr. Perfect threatening to come back and teach him a lesson. Mr. Perfect cost Helmsley television losses to the likes of The Stalker and Freddy Joe Floyd. They spent weeks building up the October 21, 1996 episode of *Raw* from Fort Wayne, Indiana, continually comparing the return of Mr. Perfect to the ring for his grudge match with the recent return of Michael Jordan to the NBA. At the time the angle started, Bret Hart was in the middle of negotiations with WCW, and there was talk of buying Hennig out of his policy once again and making him a babyface to work near the top. But from the start, the basic angle was for Mr. Perfect's return to be the swerve it turned into.

They did a screw job, as during the show, Helmsley injured Perfect's knee. IC champ Marc Mero came out to avenge Perfect, but the storyline was that it was all a swerve on Mero (who had stolen Sable from Helmsley). At the end, Perfect hit Mero with a chair, allowing Helmsley to win the title, in what, after the fact, was billed as "The Perfect Angle." This came on the night Hart returned and gave his speech about being WWF for life after having just signed a 20-year contract that day. Against heavy competition, which included the World Series and *Monday Night Football*, *Raw* did a 2.6 rating that night compared to a 3.2 for Nitro, the closest the ratings race had been in many weeks (the previous week's margin was

3.2 to 1.78, which at the time was the lowest rating in the history of the *Raw* show).

But as well as that angle played out, it was a double angle. Hennig was about to get a large cash settlement on his insurance policy of somewhere between $150,000 and $300,000. To get the settlement, he would have had to sign a statement saying he was permanently disabled and would never wrestle again. Hennig supposedly never outright told the WWF he was coming back for the match with Helmsley, but he did give everyone the impression that he might. He never said no until a few days before the taping. Because of the insurance situation, the WWF legal department sent a memo to Lloyd's to open negotiations on another settlement, going on the idea Hennig was coming back as a top babyface (this was coming at the time when they thought there was a good chance they were losing Hart to WCW).

When Lloyd's got the memo, they informed Hennig they weren't paying him the lump sum because of the belief he couldn't be permanently disabled if he was contemplating a return to the ring at that same time. Hennig was furious, feeling the company had double-crossed him, and for revenge, contacted Eric Bischoff.

AFTER NO-SHOWING several house show dates as well as voiceover sessions for two television shows, WWF sent out legal threats to WCW, claiming WCW was tampering with Hennig's contract, which didn't expire until May of 1997. McMahon was scared that Hennig would debut on the November 11, 1996 *Nitro*, although that was never the plan, as WCW was aware they couldn't debut him until his contract expired. After a meeting with McMahon, the two verbally agreed to work things out, as McMahon offered him a five-year contract with a $300,000 downside guarantee. McMahon felt whatever bad feelings there were had been settled, since he was guaranteeing Hennig more money than he would have made through his disability policy. Hennig started training to return. Bischoff then offered Hennig a three-year contract at a significantly higher figure. Hennig never told McMahon about the negotiations.

Hennig then no-showed an autograph session, the company's annual Hall of Fame dinner, the Survivor Series PPV and a voiceover session for Superstars, a unique way of letting McMahon know he had jumped to the opposition.

After sitting out and waiting for his contract to expire, Hennig debuted the next year in WCW, billed as "Minnesota's greatest athlete," a takeoff on the gimmick Gene Kiniski did in the '60s as "Canada's greatest athlete."

He came in first as a mystery tag-team partner for Diamond Dallas Page, who he never seemed to have much respect for, thinking Page was a wannabe because of their similar looks. He was then being groomed for Arn Anderson's spot in the Four Horsemen. Hennig turned on the Horsemen on September 14, 1997, in Winston-Salem, North Carolina, costing the Four Horsemen (Flair and Hennig and Chris Benoit and Steve McMichael) a

War Games match with the nWo (Kevin Nash and Konnan and Syxx and Buff Bagwell) by smashing the cage door on Flair's face (an angle designed because Flair was getting a face lift). The angle would have worked had it played out with the Horsemen getting revenge, but that never ended up happening. And for that reason, it was the beginning of the end for WCW in the Carolinas market. The next night on *Nitro* in Charlotte, McMichael, going for revenge, was pinned cleanly by Hennig for the U.S. title with a fisherman suplex. He lost the title to Page on December 28, 1997, at the famed Starrcade show in Washington, D.C. to Page, with the Hogan vs. Sting match that ended up being the peak of the company on PPV.

With the exception of the Rednecks angle, Hennig spent the remainder of his career in WCW as a "B"-level heel, usually as one of the uncool members of the nWo. His final hurrah was on November 21, 1999, at a PPV show in Toronto. They were doing an angle where Hennig, at this point a babyface feuding with Vince Russo, would be forced to retire the next time he lost a match. This led to a series of fluke wins every week by Hennig that started getting him over as a babyface. But on the PPV, Hennig lost to Bagwell, and got a huge standing ovation and loud "Perfect" chants from fans who actually believed they were seeing him for the last time. Of course, he wound up wrestling the next night on *Nitro*, and the stipula-

tion was forgotten about. He faded from WCW.

Hennig got to maneuver himself one last time as the key guy on the XWF. Hennig worked as a heel against the top faces, Bagwell (who the fans booed against him), and Vampiro, as well as working a dark match against Hogan. WWF announced the return of Mr. Perfect, supposedly as a one-shot gimmick worked through XWF, in the 2002 Royal Rumble in Atlanta. Hennig was supposed to fly out after the show and join the XWF contingent at the NATPE convention in Las Vegas as they attempted to sell their show. Instead, he stayed with WWF, signing a three-year contract. But after the thrill of the steal faded, and Hennig's performances in the ring weren't up to the new standards, he wound up relegated to syndication, and soon, disappearing even before losing his job from the incident with Lesnar on a flight coming back from England.

Hennig's career ended with a series of forgettable matches on NWA TNA. He was likely working an old-school angle once again, continually on interviews talking about being the man who took Brock Lesnar down at 35,000 feet. While it came off as a knock on the opposition, Hennig probably had the mentality of an old-time wrestler, whether correct or not, that if he said it often enough, people would want to see the match, and he'd be back in the big show. This time, Hennig's angle didn't play out.

CHAPTER 5
ANDRE
THE GIANT

KNOWN IN THE BUSINESS simply as "The Giant," Andre Rousimoff wrestled professionally for 28 years, and was an international superstar attraction. During the 1970s, Andre was the most famous wrestler in the world, the biggest international box-office attraction, and the highest-paid performer. He was also one of the most recognizable athletes on the planet. Andre headlined before one of the largest recorded paid wrestling crowd in history, his Wrestlemania III main event match against Hulk Hogan. The bout was the first million-dollar live gate in history, was the largest closed-circuit gate in history, and set a pay-per-view buy rate record.

The closed-circuit and buy rate figures appear to be safe bets to remain on the books forever.

On February 5, 1988, Andre's rematch with Hulk Hogan from Indianapolis aired on the first live prime-time network special in the United States in more than 30 years, and the viewing audience, 33 million, made it by far the most viewed pro wrestling match in U.S. history. That record also appears safe forever.

The story of Andre the Giant's life was the ultimate Faustian bargain. Born Andre Rene Rousimoff on May 19, 1946, in Grenoble, France, Andre was born with

OPPOSITE: Dory Funk Jr. battling it out with Andre the Giant. (Dr. Mike Lano)

a rare glandular disease known as acromegaly. The disease comes from the body's continual oversecretion of Growth Hormone. It caused him to grow and grow and be one of the largest and most powerful men around. He became what doctors would say would be the ultimate result of too many megadoses of Human Growth Hormone, both in positives and in side effects. Once he could no longer grow in height, his body turned against him. The continual growth in his head, hands, and feet, caused them to continually thicken and somewhat distort his already unique, oversized proportions. He started aging extremely fast.

IN HIS YOUTH, the size and power from the acromegaly made Andre one of the biggest and most powerful men in the world. The upside was that wherever he went, he was always the center of attention and loaded with friends and hangers-on. When he was in pain, the same public was still mesmerized by his transforming look. In many ways, Andre was luckier than most with the same disease, because he was able to live life to its fullest during his short period as a veritable superman among men. He saw the world, earned tons of money, was recognized everywhere, loved and admired by millions, and in his passions, eating and drinking, he was able to consume more than just about anyone he came in contact with.

Many men claim to have started Andre in wrestling, to have first discovered him in France, to have talked him into entering pro wrestling, to have brought him to the United States, etc. His beginnings are somewhat mired in mystery. Already six foot three, Andre left home at the age of 12. Because of his size, he tried rugby, soccer, and even a little boxing, before falling in with a crowd of wrestlers.

His first pro match was in France in late 1964, at the age of 18. At the time, he was about six foot seven and 245 pounds, certainly a huge man for his age, but nothing out of the ordinary. How big he wound up will forever be part of the legend of Andre the Giant.

Andre will forever be known as being seven foot four and 520 pounds. He was not seven foot four or even close to that height. The 7-4 figure, created when he first came to Montreal in late 1970, was probably because the most famous tall athlete in the world at the time, basketball superstar Lew Alcindor (who became more famous as Kareem Abdul-Jabbar), was 7-2, and promoters wanted to bill him as the tallest and largest athlete in the world. The last time he was measured in France, at the age of 24, he was 6-9 3/4.

In the mid-'60s, when Andre "The Butcher" Rousimoff started wrestling in France, there was no such thing as international news or communication. He actually wrestled for about six years before all but the most ardent wrestling fans and promoters in North America were even aware he existed. Frank Valois, who was Andre's best friend and business manager during his wrestling barnstorming heyday, said that he first met Andre in 1966 while he was wrestling as a headliner in France and brought him to England and

Germany with him the next year before bringing him to Montreal in 1971. Edouardo Carpentier was always given credit for discovering Andre as part of the first legendary "worked" story introducing him to fans in Montreal. Carpentier claimed Andre approached him in France in 1964, and Carpentier saw to it that he got started in the business.

In Japan, the story was always that Isao Yoshihara, the president of the International Wrestling Enterprises, was in Europe scouting talent for his annual Grand Prix tournament. Yoshihara had "discovered" other European attractions and gotten them their first notice in the Western World, most notable of which was Billy Robinson a few years earlier. Billed as the seven-foot-tall Monster Rousimoff, Andre debuted in Japan for the IWE on January 3, 1970, as part of a six-week tour. In early February, during the final week of the tour, Verne Gagne, who supplied the IWE with talent, arrived in Japan to defend his AWA title against the IWE's top star, Shozo Kobayashi. Gagne got his first glimpse of Monster Rousimoff, and immediately saw the dollar signs, but not where you'd think.

Verne talked with young Andre, who was at the time a physical specimen at 335 pounds, and wanted to turn him into a boxer, figuring the boxing world was at the time desperately in search of a white heavyweight title contender, and a white giant would be that much the better at the box office. Andre didn't take Verne's advice, but in Japan the story was Verne was the first American promoter to find out about Andre, and then sent him to Montreal to live, since at the time he only spoke French, and brought him in a few times as an undercard attraction for major shows.

By early 1971, American wrestling magazines started showing pictures of this "seven-foot-four, 385-pound" superman, who in Montreal was given the ring name Jean Ferre, the always-smiling giant, with little bodyfat, who could do dropkicks. Billed upon arrival as "The Eighth Wonder of the World," he was an immediate sensation in Montreal. He arrived with the famous Paul Bunyan-like storyline. Carpentier introduced him to the new world. Carpentier said he was driving around in the French Alps when a huge redwood tree had fallen in the road. Carpentier, who although only 5-7, was one of the most muscular men of his era, said he tried in vain but couldn't even budge the tree.

Suddenly out of the woods came the biggest man he had ever seen, who lifted up the redwood tree as if it were a twig, and Carpentier befriended him and brought him to Montreal to become a wrestler. The young Giant got over fast as Carpentier's big buddy, and started making big money and living life like there was no tomorrow.

Carpentier remembered when he first made it big. "Andre was really living fast," Carpentier said in an interview with the *Montreal Gazette*. "As soon as he started making money, he bought a big white cadillac and drove it all over town. He'd have a stogie (cigar) in his mouth and had women draped all over him. I used to worry about him living so fast, but I guess he felt he didn't have a long time to live, so he had to make the most of it."

Jean Ferre, the name he used in France and Montreal (named after a mythical giant lumberjack "Great Ferre"), was usually booked in handicap matches against two men, or in three-on-two matches teaming up with Carpentier, who was the most popular wrestler in Montreal. His occasional singles matches were limited to the huge heels of the time, which in the Montreal territory were either Killer Kowalski or Don Leo Jonathan. Photos of this huge newcomer who made the giant Kowalski look like a skinny midget hit all the wrestling magazines.

News of his box-office potential started leaking to the United States promoters when Ferre was booked in his first main event, billed as "The Match of the Century" in the Montreal Forum against Jonathan. The Battle of the Giants with Andre (billed as 7-4, 385) against Jonathan (billed as 6-9, 320, although he was legitimately closer to 6-5 and 285 at the time) set Canada's indoor wrestling attendance and gate mark.

Officially, the always smiling Ferre "lost his temper" for the first time in that match, and was disqualified with every wrestler on the undercard trying in vain for moments to pull his huge hands off Jonathan's throat, with one swat of the huge paw sending one big wrestler after another flying.

The idea was set in stone. He's the nicest guy in the world, but if you get him

mad, there is nobody or nothing that can physically stop him. During that time period Ferre worked some big-card matches as a special attraction on major AWA spectaculars, which was actually his first foray into the United States.

Jonathan was known at the time as the most agile big man in the game. "What I remember most about wrestling Jean (Andre) was how far it was to the canvas when I was over his head. He was so big and so tall, it was nearly impossible to get the leverage you needed to get him off the ground. We met maybe 20 times during our career. We had some awfully hard matches over the years, but I never lost respect for him. I remember Jean with much fondness. I knew him fairly well in the early years, and we came to travel together in Montreal, Texas, Europe and Japan."

Just before his first meeting with Vince McMahon Sr. and being christened Andre the Giant, Jean Ferre was given a shot at headlining a few AWA towns in singles matches against that territory's top heel, the ever colorful and controversial Superstar Billy Graham.

"I was probably the first person he ever let take him off his feet," remembered Graham about their early meetings. "At the time, nobody ever took him off his feet. It wasn't a planned spot, either. I was holding him in a bearhug and he said, 'Lift me up and take me over to the ropes.'

"I told him, 'I can't do that.' He just told me to do it. I was amazed at the time he let me do it. He was a real nice person in that if he liked you, he'd let you do

"PEOPLE WENT TO SEE HIM ORIGINALLY AS A NOVELTY, BUT AFTER SEEING HIM, THEY RECOGNIZED HE WASN'T A ONE-NIGHT STAND."

—FRANK VALOIS

things with him in the ring. I don't believe there was ever anyone in wrestling who could impress you as much by looking at him like Andre the Giant in his prime. He was a super athlete, for his size, when he was still able to move. For a man that huge, he was a little clumsy, but he was light on his feet. And he was a great worker in that he never hurt anyone. You'd never hear of anyone getting an injury against Andre. He'd throw that big punch with that big paw and never threw a potato. His hand was so big, but you'd never feel it."

The name Andre the Giant was born in 1973. The Montreal territory, which had been going great guns behind Ferre, had started to falter because fans didn't believe there was anyone who stood a chance against him. The promoters knew they had to get him out of the territory because no heel could get any serious heat, because he was so physically impressive nobody was even perceived as a threat to him. Frank Valois, a wrestler who had been a major star in France during the '60s, became Andre's caretaker, taking care of everything for him. Valois represented

Andre and set up a meeting with Vince McMahon Sr. who changed his name from Jean Ferre to Andre the Giant, debuted him in Madison Square Garden where he became an immediate sensation, and realizing the mistakes that had been made in booking him in Montreal because of overexposure, sent him on the road around the world doing one-night stands working every territory that was affiliated with the NWA, WWWF and AWA, which in those days meant just about everywhere, and not only in North America.

McMahon Sr. booked The Giant during the days when all the major promoters cooperated with one another, and Andre toured the world, staying a week or two in each territory until the wrestling war broke out in 1984, and Vince McMahon Jr. no longer allowed Andre to work for any other promotion aside from his New Japan tours.

"People went to see him originally as a novelty," said Valois, "But after seeing him, they recognized he wasn't a one-night stand."

But by the time he hit New York, and then the rest of the United States, the dropkicks and the like went out the window. "I remember being amazed at seeing a man that big do a dropkick," noted Wladek (Walter) "Killer" Kowalski, one of Andre's first major opponents in Quebec. "But when he moved to the WWWF they told him, 'We only want you to be a big, hulking monster who goes into the ring and destroys people.'"

He was generally booked in handicap matches and Battle Royales and kept away from the top heels so as not to damage the territory for the long term. In most cases, his opponent in the handicap matches would be Valois, his manager, who would call the match, and a local small preliminary wrestler who would take all the bumps. In the Battle Royales, which at the time were the biggest drawing gimmick match, he more often than not was put over. He was the most in-demand wrestler in the world.

Every promoter booking a major event wanted Andre in as the so-called French dressing. *The Guiness Book of World Records* used to list Andre as the highest paid wrestler ever with documented earnings of $400,000 in 1974. In later years, when Andre spent more time working the major Northeastern arenas, his income probably topped the $500,000 mark, and he certainly earned more than $1 million in his best years during the mid-'80s when Titan Sports went nation-al. Sam Muchnick, then president of the NWA said that Andre, Buddy Rogers, and Jim Londos were the three biggest drawing cards in wrestling history.

"He was like a big, loveable baby," Valois recalls of his days barnstorming with The Giant. "I used to treat him as a son, and he used to treat me as his father."

Somewhere along the line, the ever-smiling giant also became the undefeated giant. Wrestling legend has it that he was never pinned until the Pontiac Silverdome match with Hulk Hogan. While not entirely accurate, Andre did exceedingly few jobs during his career.

As the years went by, people no longer wanted to see Andre laugh through comedy matches with undercard wrestlers, and he'd start going into territories and face the top heels. His best drawing matches would be against men who were at least close to his size, with famous feuds with the likes of Big John Studd, Hulk Hogan (when Hogan was a heel, not only in his first WWF tour but even earlier in Alabama and Georgia as Terry Boulder and Sterling Golden), Blackjack Mulligan, Killer Khan, Bruiser Brody, Superstar Billy Graham and perhaps his biggest opponent during the 1970s, Ernie Ladd, a 6-9 1/2, 320-pound former all-pro football lineman whom he drew many big gates against in Battles of the Giants. Ironically, because Ladd had achieved so much fame in football before wrestling as his real height was known, promoters

OPPOSITE: A frequent opponent of Andre was one of the strongest men in the world, former Olympic weightlifter Ken Patera. (Dr. Mike Lano)

never tried to exaggerate his height as would have normally been the case in those days. It was funny, because Andre at the time was billed as 7-5, yet the two were roughly the same height.

In the late 1970s, Valois went back home, and Frenchy Bernard, a former referee out of Florida, became Andre's road mate and lived with him until the time of his death. Valois still received a check from the New York office until Sr. passed the torch to Jr. in 1984, at which point he was cut off and lost touch with Andre.

Within wrestling, stories of Andre are legion. While there are stories of his awesome presence and strength, the most famous stories are eating and drinking stories. There would be fighting stories as well, but Andre got into such few fights that the stories were more like a fight about to break out, Andre showed up, and the fight ended before the first punch was thrown, so Andre stories mainly revolved around drinking.

A rare fighting story came out of South Africa, where the country's most popular wrestler, Jan Wilkens (who naturally doubled as the promoter), who held that country's version of the world title for most of the '70s, apparently wanted to embarrass Andre to build his own reputation, or perhaps believed in his own self-created hype. The story has it that Andre threw one punch and Wilkens woke up three days later. Another story was out of Los Angeles, when Andre had a match against "The Monster," a guy named Tony Hernandez who dressed up in a

Frankenstein outfit with huge boots to make him look about 6-7 and doing an indestructible gimmick. Apparently Andre wanted to unmask him, not realizing the promotion had billed the man as a Frankenstein built in a laboratory rather than as a masked man, and the guy fought for all he was worth to avoid it because it would kill the gimmick, and wound up getting way on the short end of that stick.

Andre was legendary among wrestlers for his capacity to drink. Stories of him drinking 50 beers and not having a buzz are common. How exaggerated they are is another story. One of the most famous stories was of him drinking 119 bottles of beer at one sitting and passing out in a hotel lobby. Since he was so huge, nobody could move him. They simply put a piano cover over him and let him sleep it off and acted like it was covering a large piece of furniture. There are dozens of stories just like them.

Wrestlers joke about being out in bars in the mid-'70s with Andre, and some local wanted to provoke a fight with the "normal-sized" wrestlers to prove how tough he was or that they were fakes, and they'd laugh about it and signal for Andre, and the local's face would turn eight shades of albino and he'd high tail it out of the pub. McMahon Sr. built a special trailer so Andre would be comfortable as he was driven from town to town, and always kept it stocked full.

Andre was a notorious eater with stories of him going into restaurants and ordering everything on the menu. There

"WHEN IT COMES TO PULLING POWER, HE WAS ENORMOUSLY STRONG. PUSHING POWER, HE WAS NOTHING EXCEPTIONAL."

—SUPERSTAR BILLY GRAHAM

were also legendary stories about Andre's strength. Andre never lifted a weight, but he had the thickest bone structure and largest in-condition torso that anyone had ever laid eyes on. Andre was invited to the World's Strongest Man contest when CBS-TV sponsored the event, but he declined, and wrestling sent names like Billy Graham, Ken Patera, Ivan Putski and Jerry Blackwell to compete. Stories of Andre being able to pick up and move big cars in his youth are legendary. But how strong was he really?

"When it comes to pulling power, he was enormously strong," remembered Graham. "Pushing power, he was nothing exceptional. Anything having to do with a pulling motion like pulling you around the ring, he could pull anything with the greatest of ease. Pushing he wasn't that strong, like in doing something like pressing guys overhead or something that

would be like a bench press or military press motion."

As the years went by, Andre got older and heavier. For a while he was billed as 7-5, but 7-4 become much more famous and a little less of an exaggeration. The weight went to 445, 485 and passed the 500-pound mark.

At this point he was far from being solid muscle. Many have said that if Andre had taken care of himself physically, had gone to the gym, had drank less, that he could have been the most awesome specimen ever. But it never seemed to interest him, and really his fate was sealed at the time he was born, anyway. As the years went by, the ever-smiling giant smiled less and less. Perhaps it was the pain of his incredible body turning against him. Perhaps it was the pain of the realization of his own inevitability.

"I REMEMBER THE QUANTITY HE COULD DRINK. HE USED TO DRINK TO NUMB HIMSELF FROM THE REALITY THAT HE WOULDN'T LIVE LONG IN THIS WORLD."

—KILLER KOWALSKI

"I remember the quantity he could drink," remembered Kowalski in an interview with the *Montreal Gazette.* "He used to drink to numb himself from the reality that he wouldn't live long in this world."

In the 1970s, when wrestlers never received any mainstream publicity—it was almost like there was a law against it—Andre was the lone exception.

He appeared on *The Tonight Show* and compared hand size with Joey Bishop, he did *The Six-Million Dollar Man*, and had a lengthy feature article in *Sports Illustrated* about him. In 1974, many newspapers around the country aired photos of Andre talking about him getting a tryout with the NFL's Washington Redskins. Andre never took the tryout, which was mainly a publicity stunt. When he first arrived in Quebec, the Montreal Alouettes had similar ideas about trying to make him a football player, but he was slow afoot and had never played the game.

The first chink in the invincible armor came in 1981 when he woke up one day, got out of bed, and collapsed on the floor. His ankle had been badly broken. It was attributed to a match with Killer Khan, a 6-4, 280-pound Japanese star billed as the Mongolian giant, whose feud with Andre in 1981 after the legitimate injury was his main claim to fame in wrestling.

Andre was already closing in on the 500-pound mark by this point. While his mobility was limited because of the weight, he still had enough left to have numerous genuinely exciting matches with Khan. Andre's peak as a worker was probably the late '70s, when he had picked up the ring psychology, his weight hadn't gotten too far out of control although he was no longer a physical specimen, and he still had his mobility and stamina. He had good matches in the United States, at least for what he was, even doing occasional 60-minute draws against Nick Bockwinkel and Race, but he excelled as a monster heel while in Japan.

Perhaps his most entertaining matches were his cat-and-mouse encounters with the much smaller but gifted Tatsumi Fujinami, then a junior heavyweight champion, who worked a believable series of spots with Andre before finally getting caught and squashed at the end. Andre even let Fujinami, barely 200 pounds at the time, slam him.

Andre the Giant and Hulk Hogan wrestled for the first time around 1978 in Dothan, Alabama at the Houston Farm Center. Hogan was the newest big guy who could presumably be built into an attraction to give Andre a new opponent. Two years later, Andre participated in the angle that made Hogan a national star. On a WWF taping, Hogan, then a heel managed by Freddie Blassie, loaded his armpad and busted Andre's head with a lariat and left him laying. Just before the finish, Hogan lifted Andre up for a bodyslam. While Andre had been slammed before, surely no slam in the United States at least up to that point had been seen by so many people.

Andre and Hogan took their feud to all the major arenas, and not just in the old WWF territory, but across the United States and Canada and into Japan. The first Andre-Hogan match in New York was at Shea Stadium on August 9, 1980, underneath the Bruno Sammartino vs. Larry Zbyszko cage match main event, which drew 35,771 paid and a then-record $541,730.

Unfortunately, Andre's most famous matches were also among his worst. The two Hogan matches, one setting the PPV and attendance record of 78,000 at the Pontiac Silverdome for Wrestlemania III, and the other on NBC, both came when he was long past his physical prime and badly crippled from injuries. His matches with the likes of Warrior and Studd were even worse, since neither were Hogan's calibre when it came to charisma. Few of his main events from the '70s in the U.S. were ever videotaped. With the exception of the Hogan matches, perhaps the most famous match of his career was in many ways one of the strangest matches ever. And it could have been the most dangerous.

In April of 1986, Andre got into the ring with Akira Maeda. The circumstances behind what happened were never explained. Maeda was one of the leading stars for the first UWF in Japan in 1984-85, which worked matches in a so-called "shooting-style" and many of its wrestlers, particularly Maeda, decried pro wrestling for not being true sport, and Maeda in his youth often had outbursts at fans, wrestlers and reporters regarding such a thing. The first UWF went out of business at the end of 1985, and Maeda, who was first trained in New Japan, was invited back to the fold. Apparently swallowing his pride because he needed to work and it was the only way to remain in the business, Maeda agreed, and actually turned into a phenomenal worker, combing his submission-style moves with some pro spots. Maeda never did a job in the New Japan rings except to Yoshiaki Fujiwara, which was okay since Maeda acknowledged Fujiwara as a true wrestler. Maeda's statements about wrestling and American wrestlers in general often led to a lack of cooperation in those matches. Andre never sold any of Maeda's submissions and was almost mocking his shooter gimmick. It appeared Andre kept going for Maeda's eyes, which would be scary when someone of that size makes a move in that direction. Soon, all cooperation was gone, and the match had fallen apart and nearly turned into a real fight.

Andre, as immobile as he was by this time, was still more than 500 pounds. Maeda started getting into a fighting stance and throwing wicked kicks at Andre's knee time after time. Andre just stood there, acting like he didn't feel a thing; maybe he didn't. The few times Maeda got closer and went for a single-leg, Andre's lack of balance was evident as he went down easily, like a redwood tree that had just been chopped through. Maeda never jumped on him, because strategically, if Andre snatched him, the size difference could prove embarrassing to the self-proclaimed super shooter. Andre would get to his feet, Maeda would kick the knee, go for the single leg and Andre would go down. Andre, who wasn't in any kind of condition by this time in his career, after a few series, just decided to

stay down and dare Maeda to jump on him. At this point Maeda asked one of the older wrestlers if he had permission to finish Andre off, but the wrestler shook his head no.

Antonio Inoki, the promoter, finally jumped into the ring with no explanation, and they broke the match up without an ending. Andre was furious and screamed to Frenchy Bernard, his traveling companion and the referee of the match, that he wanted Maeda back in the ring. Maeda threw his best kick of all after being ordered out, only the opponent was the guard rail.

Just a few weeks earlier, Andre won the most famous Battle Royale of his career, at Wrestlemania II in Chicago, a match which included a half-dozen NFL football players including William "Refrigerator" Perry, who was coming off a season where he was the most popular player in the league. Andre got some wire service coverage again, because being around the 500-pound mark, he dwarfed the 6-3, 330-pound Fridge. Because the football players weren't workers, they did a dress rehearsal a few days earlier in secret. A few of the wrestlers and footballers were traveling back from the rehearsal when one of the football players, Ernie Holmes, a former all-pro with the Pittsburgh Steelers, was bragging about how tough he was. Everyone was getting tired of it, but nobody said anything until suddenly Andre blurted out in that guttural voice, "You talk too much, you know what I mean," and Holmes didn't say another word the rest of the trip as apparently one of the wrestlers whispered to Holmes that you don't know what tough is until you get this guy mad.

It was hardly a stroke of genius to turn Andre heel and have him feud with Hogan, which led to Wrestlemania III. Andre had been a heel for 14 years in Japan. He knew what to do and when to do it as a heel, probably better than in his more familiar U.S. role as a face. He looked the part as well. Unfortunately, by the time his biggest money run was about to start, his physical condition had already badly deteriorated.

Andre's last run as a babyface came under a hood as Giant Machine. About one year earlier in Japan, as a gimmick that was largely decried and considered unsuccessful, manager Ichimasa Wakamatsu brought in Andre as The Giant Machine and teamed him with Super Machine (Bill Eadie) and Strong Machine (Junji Hirata, who still uses that name in New Japan) as the Machine Gun Army. Titan ran an angle where Andre was unjustly suspended by Jack Tunney, and he came back as Giant Machine, teaming with Super Machine against longtime nemesis Studd and massive King Kong Bundy. Unlike most angles involving Andre, this one was not a success, and he quickly disappeared from the scene and headed to England to make *The Princess Bride*, a movie where he played a loveable giant and got rave reviews. This led to a few commercials, most notably for Honeycombs cereal.

Andre's back and spine were already giving him major problems by this time. He walked with a major stoop, and his longtime smiling face had a hard time making the smile. He became reclusive and was largely introverted except around his trusted friends, who were mainly wrestlers.

IN LATE 1986, Andre underwent major back surgery while in England. Because of his immense proportions, the operating crew had to build customized surgical equipment for the operation.

Andre went heel in January of 1987, leading to the most successful wrestling show of all time. Nearly every wrestling attendance and gate record was shattered for the "first" Hogan-Andre match (Titan went to the extent of actually denying they had ever wrestled previously, let alone had a big-money feud that spanned many territories). The Silverdome sold out two weeks in advance and it's no exaggeration to believe that if the building had been large enough, they could have put 125,000 people in the Silverdome that day. By this time, his physical condition was all but gone. Andre, who wore a backbrace underneath his long wrestling tights into the ring, was almost completely immobile. Legend has it that he had total numbness from his knees down when he was in the ring. He was largely kept out of the ring until the rematch on NBC, where he won the WWF title from Hogan with the famous twin Hebner referee finish, and he immediately made the famed faux pas of selling "the world tag-team title" to Ted DiBiase. He went back on the road working programs as a heel against Studd, Jake Roberts (where he faked a heart attack from fright the snake) and Ultimate Warrior (where he did the bulk of the total number of jobs of his entire career) and in his last run as a heel, held the tag-team title with King Haku, winning and losing the titles to Demolition. He did very little walking by this point, except when in front of a crowd. Backstage he spent all his time sitting. He was often wheeled to and from his hotel to the car that would take him to the arenas.

He returned as a babyface and did his final U.S. angle being attacked from behind by Earthquake, since he was legitimately going to undergo knee surgery and this would be the wrestling cover reason. However, Andre never returned for his expected series with Earthquake. The closest he got was an appearance at Summer Slam where he came out as a cripple and the Legion of Doom kept Earthquake and Typhoon from attacking him so set up their tag program.

In 1990, Seiji Sakaguchi and Giant Baba had a meeting. Sakaguchi asked Baba to bring Andre back to Japan. He'd always be able to draw money, but New Japan worked a very serious style and he had no place. All Japan always booked one pure comedy match per show, largely to give Baba a place on the tour, and the idea of Baba and Andre as a tag team would be a nice touch. Andre toured for All Japan three times per year from September 1990 until his final tour at the end of 1992. It was not a pretty sight. Each tour he grew progressively worse. However, out of loyalty, Baba continued to book him.

Anyone who ever saw Andre the Giant will never forget him. He had that unique look and that unique presence. Probably many reading this can vividly remember the first time they saw him live. It's a moment you don't forget. Anyone who ever shook that gigantic hand will never forget it. Even the largest men in the world felt small in the grasp of the monster hand. Those memories only made the sight of him toward the end of his career that much sadder.

But it can't be denied that Andre made his mark in his profession in a way that only a handful will ever be able to.

OPPOSITE: Hulk Hogan and Andre the Giant, together in 1982, as a tag team in the AWA. (Dr. Mike Lano)

CHAPTER 6

THE SHEIK

IN A 45-YEAR PRO WRESTLING CAREER, The Sheik experienced the highest of highs and lowest of lows that pro wrestling could offer. At his peak, he was the top heel in the business, one of the biggest drawing cards of all time, and one of his era's most successful promoters and wealthiest wrestlers. But to show how quickly things change, it was only a few years later that his luck would run out.

During the good years, he'd book himself into Los Angeles so he could shop on Rodeo Drive in Los Angeles, lavishly wine and dine his friends, and scare his fellow NWA promoters when they would see how much money he'd put on the tables in Las Vegas during their annual conventions ("I work hard for my money and I deserve to play hard," he'd respond to their pleas from experience that business wasn't always going to be that good).

He also had a reputation for helping out wrestlers down on their luck with loans that he'd never expect to be paid back. Harley Race noted that early in his career, when he had a bad auto accident that kept him out of action for months, Sheik would send him a check every week until he could get back in the ring, so he could take care of his bills. Many other wrestlers from the era related similar stories about Sheik.

OPPOSITE: The Sheik carving up the forehead of longtime partner and rival, Abdullah the Butcher. (Dr. Mike Lano)

But just as suddenly, he was the one down on his luck, desperately trying to find the lost secret to rebuild the empire he both created and saw collapse through the same methodology.

He wrestled virtually every major name of his era, both every top babyface and every top heel. No matter how great a heel they were, they became instant babyface in their grudge matches against The Sheik.

The Sheik kept pushing the same formula that built his company, namely, himself in short bloodbaths, building up a level of crowd heat that became legendary, against the biggest names in the industry. Even as an outsider, Sheik would get more intense heat quicker than the people in the territory who had the benefit of appearing on television and doing weekly promos to incite the crowd, with his act of heavy violence. Fans in his home territory eventually got tired of the same thing, and got burned too many times, but Sheik forged on with the method that made him so much money and that he knew best.

Even after he could no longer run at Cobo Hall, a 10,000-seat auditorium he once packed every other week and some would say he put on the map in that city, he tried the same act at a tiny auditorium in nearby Taylor, Michigan, or the IMA Hall in Flint, Michigan. He was hoping that he, in his mid-50s, and Bobo Brazil, pushing 60, would heat things up for that run of business that would never come again, and return things to how they once were.

By this point, instead of promoters calling him to pop gates against the local babyface when business was getting slow, he was down to working mainly for promoters as desperate as he was, who had burned their own territories, who were clinging on to a similar belief, remembering the days when The Sheik would come in and pop their territory.

"He was one of the most respected characters in wrestling," remembered Detroit native Jim Meyers, who grew up as a fan of his and later copied some of his maniac act and timing to become George "The Animal" Steele. "It's too bad so many people remember him as what he was later in his career and didn't see him when he was younger. Like many of us, he wrestled too long. He and Bobo Brazil, when I was younger, I'd watch them wrestle and I was in awe."

HE IS BELIEVED TO HAVE CAPTURED his first championship while wrestling out of Chicago in late 1953, when he and the original Gypsy Joe won the Midwest tag-team titles. At the time, for all real purposes, there was no wrestling in Japan. Who would have believed that nearly 40 years later, Sheik would be an active wrestler, working with two artificial hips, and holding a version of the world title in that country?

Even though he had held the Texas title, beating Johnny Valentine, one year earlier, legend has it that the singles match that made his reputation was on November 18, 1955, in Chicago, when he faced Lou Thesz for the NWA heavyweight title.

According to his son, Ed Farhat Jr., who wrestled as Captain Ed George in

Detroit in the late '70s, Thesz, known for roughing up guys who couldn't wrestle, told Sheik he was going to beat him, and then break both his legs. The more likely story is that Thesz told Sheik that on this night, whether he liked it or not, the two were going to have a wrestling match.

Sheik responded, "I don't think so," and when the bell sounded, he rolled out of the ring, and ran out of the building. This was in the middle of a snowstorm, and Sheik crawled underneath a bus and wouldn't get out. It became such a scene, with police and firefighters trying to talk him out of the bottom of the bus, getting major publicity.

Thesz got a kick out of all the publicity the incident got and how it was a unique way to be put over, and the two became friends. Years later, in 1969, when Sheik was ruling Detroit and Toronto and Thesz was planning on getting out of the game, Thesz put him over on three occasions in main events.

Thesz once wrote about it on the Wrestling Classics message board, simply saying, "Once in Chicago, when I didn't buckle to his antics, and wanted him to wrestle, he just walked out of the ring and didn't come back. He was a great guy, but not a wrestler."

In the area of television production, Sheik was well ahead of his time. While most companies in that era would either tape wrestling in a studio or a small arena (or in Texas, weekly from the local arena), Sheik owned his own production truck and would tape arena main events from all over his territory. He built a TV studio into his home in Lansing, and the wrestlers would come and do their interviews.

While Sheik was notorious for not doing jobs, it was apparently more belief in a star pecking order than outright not doing so, as he would put over people who were considered stars on his level in his mind.

During his 1968-69 feud with WWWF champion Bruno Sammartino, he put Sammartino over in both Boston and Philadelphia in cage matches, although they never did the climactic battle in Madison Square Garden. During Sammartino's second run as champion, after Sheik had been banned from New York, they did a match in Pittsburgh, which had separate television from the rest of the WWWF circuit, ending with Sheik losing to a bear-hug submission, no doubt his only submission loss of that era. He and Dick the Bruiser headlined in Bruiser's main cities, Chicago and Indianapolis. In Chicago, it built to a chain match, where Bruiser wrapped Sheik's leg to the bottom rope with the chain and Sheik hung outside the ring to get counted out. In Indianapolis, their cage match drew one of the city's biggest crowds of the era, and ended without a finish when the Masked Stranger (Jerry Hill aka Guy Mitchell) attacked Bruiser to start the next area feud.

Meyers's most vivid memory of Sheik was actually something that took place outside the ring. Meyers, long before he was a character babyface pining after Elizabeth, was a high school teacher and football coach in Michigan, and wrestled most summers for Vince McMahon Sr. in the Northeast. Once, after arriving late for a show in Lansing after football practice, he bumped into a huge kid. The kid, who wrestled heavyweight at Michigan State, saw Meyers as he was coming in and said that he knew The Sheik was Ed Farhat from Lansing, and that wrestling was fake and he was real, and he was going to beat him up as he came to the ring. Meyers said he alerted Sheik (even Meyers never dared call him Ed), and told him there was a crazy kid who was going to stretch him as he came to the ring.

Sheik came out back and came right up to the kid, who was a lot bigger than he was, breaking character and softly speaking English, and said, "You're right, my name is Ed Farhat," all the while doing his crazy eye gimmick. But he talked calmly, taking the kid off guard, and suddenly with no warning, stuck his fingers in the kid's Adam's Apple and began choking, and said, "But I will kill you." The wrestler broke free, and took off as fast as he could.

The Sheik first started appearing in Madison Square Garden in 1958, during the era where Argentina Rocca and Miguel Perez were arguably the greatest drawing tag team in the history of American wrestling. New York was a tag-team territory, so Sheik started teaming with another legendary heel of the era and frequent rival more than a decade later, "Wild Bull" Curry (Fred Koury Sr.). On October 20, 1958, the teams sold out Madison Square Garden, with a best-of-three fall match only lasting one fall before Curry didn't answer the bell for the second fall.

The two also lost the next month to the famous Mark Lewin and Don Curtis duo. Sheik and Johnny Valentine had main events against Rocca and Perez in May and June of 1959, losing the first match via DQ, before losing 2/3 falls in the rematch in 30:09 before 12,000 fans.

At one time or another, he headlined just about everywhere during the '60s and '70s, with the exception of St. Louis. The Sheik/Sam Muchnick relationship didn't get off to a good start when he no-showed a May 24, 1974 date in a prelim match with Rick Renaldo. He debuted on August 9, 1974, third from the top in the famous match with Pat O'Connor which lasted less than one minute. After that fiasco, Muchnick kept his commitment and brought Sheik in on August 24, 1974, for a quick squash win over Devoy Brunson, and publicly apologized for Sheik's actions in his program, saying he wouldn't bring him back.

In 1967, he worked much of the year during the week based out of Amarillo for a major program with Dory Funk Sr. During that year, he was the top heel draw in Lubbock, Texas, which shockingly because of the size of the market, was the top grossing city for wrestling in the state, averaging 3,500 fans per week in the 4,000-seat Fair Park Coliseum.

"He'd work here three weeks out of every month," remembered Dory Funk Jr. "He didn't talk to anybody. His timing in those days was impeccable when it came

"HE'D WINE AND DINE YOU IF YOU KNEW HIM, BUT IF HE DIDN'T, HE'D SLICE YOU IF YOU LOOKED AT HIM THE WRONG WAY."

—PROMOTER JEFF WALTON

to when to get heat, how much heat to get, and when to finish it. People hated his guts in the right way to make them keep coming back. I can't tell you another wrestler who ever matched him for getting heat. Fritz Von Erich is the only one close. Terry (Funk) was up there. But I don't think anyone got more heat for as many years."

Years later, during Sheik's drawing power heyday, Dory Jr. was the biggest star in the game as NWA champion, and they wrestled on several occasions. Those were not the classic 60-minute matches that Funk was remembered for.

"That's one guy I can't say I ever went an hour with," he said. "It was get in, get the fans hot, and get out. For the people who drew the money in Detroit, in those days, he paid well."

"He first came to Los Angeles when Bobo was hot in 1967," remembered Los Angeles promoter Jeff Walton. "The first program I ever did for Aileen Eaton (Mike LeBelle's mother, who was the promoter at the Olympic at the time) was in May of 1968 with Bobo vs. Sheik as the main

event. We'd bring him in for some of the big shows as an attraction, the same way we used Mil Mascaras. He was in and out for years."

They were very protective of who they booked Sheik with, noting that Brazil knew how to work with him, and strangely, as limited as they both were as workers, he and Blassie understood how to get the best out of each other.

"But you couldn't book him with a guy like Dick Beyer (The Destroyer), because he didn't know any holds."

While Walton recalled Sheik as being great to people who knew him, he was dangerous to those who didn't.

"He'd wine and dine you if you knew him, but if he didn't, he'd slice you if you looked at him the wrong way."

Sheik won the Americas title from Brazil on February 21, 1969, at the Olympic, and then started a famous feud with Fred Blassie, who was replacing Brazil as the area's top babyface. With Sheik on top, it became a period of screwjob finishes on top. Sheik was counted out in a match on March 21, 1969, and the title was held up. A rematch, since the title was vacant, on April 11, 1969, in a cage match was won by Blassie via DQ. Sheik pinned Blassie to retain the title two weeks later, before a gimmicked finish against Mascaras saw him lose it again. He returned the next summer for his hottest program ever with Blassie, culminating with the debut of the Blassie cage and Blassie cage rules. He was brought in as an attraction on August 27, 1971, for what is to this day the largest crowd ever to attend pro wrestling in Los Angeles, when 25,817 fans paid to see the famous Blassie-Tolos match, with Sheik vs. Brazil being a main undercard attraction.

The actual Toronto unbeaten main-event streak was 109 matches, ending with the DQ loss to Tiger Jeet Singh. It was his 149th main event in that city when he suffered his first pinfall loss, well after the glory days were over. More impressive was his streak of matches that drew more than 10,000 in that city, which included a rotating group of babyfaces like Thesz, Dewey Robertson, Ernie Ladd, Lord Athol Layton, Whipper Billy Watson, Gene Kiniski, Fred Curry, Bull Curry, Haystacks Calhoun, Brazil, Mighty Igor, Tex McKenzie, Tiger Jeet Singh, Funk Jr., Angelo Mosca, The Assassin (Jerry "Guy Mitchell" Hill), John Quinn, Luis Martinez, Pampero Firpo, Magnificent Zulu, Valentine, Tony Marino, Chief Jay Strongbow, Eric the Red, Johnny Powers, Bearcat Wright, Domenic DeNucci, Billy "Red" Lyons, Andre the Giant, Edouard Carpentier and Jack Brisco.

While many of Sheik's matches in that streak period lasted more than ten minutes, many, with big names and huge crowds, also lasted less than five. The lone 60-minute draw during that period, no doubt with significant time shaved off, was May 13, 1973, against Brazil, the month after the first time he went 20 minutes with Strongbow. After three monster houses with Andre, all drawing more than 15,500, ending with Sheik winning a death match on February 17, 1974, which was also the seventh straight main event lasting less than five minutes, business started to fall. The streak of short main events continued with opponents like Chief Jay Strongbow, Crusader, back with Andre and Carpentier, and even a September 8, 1974 NWA title match with Brisco that went to a double count out in less than five minutes. Only Tiger Jeet Singh went longer during that period, and even a Sheik and Butcher vs. Andre and Lord Layton tag match went four minutes. The first recorded crowd of less than 10,000 was January 5, 1975, when Sheik was scheduled to headline against Killer Kowalski, and ended up no-showing (a few months earlier he'd no-showed a main event with Johnny Powers), and it was never the same after that.

The Sheik also had a great history in Montreal, where he still holds the record crowd, legitimately selling out Jarry Park with 26,000 fans for a 1972 match with Johnny Rougeau. He was an attraction brought in for big shows.

Montreal was a wrestling hotbed, and when longtime top heel Mad Dog Vachon

OPPOSITE: The Sheik was still main-eventing shows past the age of 60. (Dr. Mike Lano)

was injured in an auto accident, Sheik was brought in to plug the vacant hole. He won a tournament to become the vacant IWA world heavyweight champion on October 23, 1967 in Montreal over Gino Brito, to springboard into a program with the area's top babyface, Edouard Carpentier. In 1971, that city became a war zone between the established office headed by Bob "Legs" Langevin, Jacques Rougeau Sr. and brother Johnny, and the rival Grand Prix Wrestling headed by Paul Vachon. Vachon was able to lure area legends like his brother Mad Dog, Carpentier, Killer Kowalski, Don Leo Jonathan and the LeDuc Brothers. Most notably, Grand Prix Wrestling was where Verne Gagne sent Andre Roussimoff, after he had been discovered in Japan, since Roussimoff knew French and could be brought in as an attraction for AWA big shows after Gagne gave up on the idea of making him a heavyweight boxer. He took the name Jean Ferre, a take off of his name in France, Geant Ferre, the name of a mythical cultural giant lumberjack. Grand Prix was clearly winning the war behind Ferre's matches with the likes of Kowalski and Jonathan, the latter drawing one of the biggest crowds anywhere of the era. The Rougeaus countered by bringing in Sheik and Valentine for big matches with Jacques and Johnny with their world belt at stake. By this point, both sides were doing huge business, but it burned out the area. Sheik continued to draw until an incident took place where he caused a riot in 1973 and was banned by the athletic commission. Business went down unbelievably fast for both sides, and after a merger because both

were losing so much, the entire scene had disintegrated a few years later.

His violent character was a massive contradiction to his generosity, but that was a massive contradiction to his reputation among so many in wrestling once business got bad. He was married to the former Joyce Fleser. The marriage lasted 53 years, and she served as his slave girl in the '50s and early '60s and always traveled with him except during the period he was falling apart and his business and life were spiraling out of control. When he would work an outside territory, he tried to make a rule of never staying at the same hotel as the wrestlers. When he was working his own area, he'd drive back to Lansing almost every night to get maybe an hour of time with his two kids, before making the long drive back.

But even his family members knew him as Sheik. David Farhat, his nephew and a member of the Michigan House of Representatives, knew him as "Uncle Sheik," who was almost never out of character, even at family outings. David said Sheik used to have a picnic for their huge family (Sheik's parents had 11 children, most of whom also had a lot of children), and he would be in character and would scare the kids. He'd go swimming, wearing his wrestling trunks with the camel on them, or when going out with the family, would wear the expensive suits he was known for outside the ring, and would always drive a purple Ford Continental Mark III with white interior. Politics ended up running in the Farhat family, as Sheik's brother Edmund was a lobbyist, and niece

Debbie Farhat was a member of the state House of Representatives.

The Sheik was a long-forgotten part of a different era of wrestling when he ended up performing before the largest crowds of his career in the '90s with FMW.

By that point, he was playing off the fact Japanese fans had longer memories when it came to wrestling stars, and that he was a huge star in the '70s, when wrestling was a prime time hit. Sheik never even wrestled in Japan until September 6, 1972. While he was tailor-made for that country, because in those days, characters and American stars were a big hit, the promoters were fearful of his violent act as television executives in the '60s had vivid memories of the problems with older people having heart attacks the night Fred Blassie did his biting act with the Great Togo in 1962. Besides, the JWA already had its guy doing much of the gimmick in Abdullah.

BUT THINGS CHANGED, as a wrestling promotional split broke out that year. Antonio Inoki was fired by the dominant Japan Pro Wrestling Association, which was running into financial problems even though business was great, due to its leaders piling up huge gambling debts. Shohei Baba, who at the time was an even bigger star than Inoki, quit to start All Japan Pro Wrestling.

After Baba and Inoki left, the company went with Seiji Sakaguchi as its top star. Sakaguchi had wrestled in Michigan and Texas a few years earlier as "The Big Saka," including some main events against Sheik, and they were looking at ways to give him credibility as a bigger star than

Baba and Inoki, who were both ahead of him and never lost to him before leaving.

The idea to compete with Baba's opening press conference was to bring in The Sheik, who was the biggest name foreigner wrestler of the era who up to that point had never worked in Japan. The Sakaguchi-Sheik match for the United National title at the old Denen Coliseum in Tokyo was a huge hit, drawing a sellout 13,000 fans for the dying company. Japanese fans had seen photos of Sheik in magazines and newspapers, seemingly forever, from his main events against all the big names in Detroit, Toronto, Madison Square Garden and the Olympic Auditorium, all of which carried a great mystique in that era. Sheik came out of the dressing room and caused a riot, attacking fans, who ran away in fear after he popped anyone within reach.

When he got to the ring, he was presented with flowers, as was the tradition before main events. He began eating the flowers and praying to Allah. He attacked Sakaguchi with a foreign object and put him in the camel clutch to win the first fall in just 3:16. Sakaguchi came back to win the second fall after an atomic drop in 1:21. During the third fall, a bloody Sakaguchi was pinned after numerous blows with a pencil in just 56 seconds. Sheik was made, even though he actually dropped the belt the next day in Osaka in two straight falls (first fall via DQ) going less than eight minutes total.

After the company folded, Sheik made a deal with Baba and debuted on April 24, 1973, for two nights, challenging for Baba's PWF title with a DQ and a pinfall finish respectively in bouts in Osaka and Tokyo.

He got a better offer and jumped the next year to New Japan. However, after a singles match with Inoki in Okinawa in November 1974, Sheik canceled a series of Japanese bookings due to problems with his home territory, which resulted in the company filing suit against him.

With Baba mad at him for jumping, it left Sheik out of Japan until his most famous tour, in December of 1977. Without question, the tour that made him a legend in Japan was the first of what came to be the annual World Open Tag-Team Tournament in December 1977, as it was called, where he teamed with Abdullah.

The two went to the championship match where they faced The Funks, in what turned out to be one of the most famous matches in Japanese wrestling history. For the Japanese television audience, the bloody war was like real life, Wild Middle Easterners against Texas Cowboys. Sheik and Butcher used a pencil and stabbed Terry Funk numerous times in his arm, which was bleeding. Terry was taken away for medical attention, leaving Dory by himself for several minutes. Even two on one, Dory survived. Terry returned, with his bad arm in a sling, using his good arm to punch Sheik and Abdullah. The perfect finish would have been The Funks winning via pinfall, but the actual finish was a cheap disqualification when Sheik and Abdullah attacked the referee.

But that match established Sheik and Abdullah as a legendary heel team. Even more, it established The Funks as the most popular foreign wrestlers in Japan, and almost honorary Japanese for the spirit they showed. And it also established the December tag-team tournament, which has now lasted 27 years as the oldest unbreakable tradition in wrestling.

Sheik was a regular for All Japan just as his star had dimmed in the U.S., working from 1977-1981, continuing the feud with Baba and the Funks, and eventually after the inevitable split, with Butcher, before Baba stopped using him after the 1981 tag team tournament.

By this point, Detroit was dead, his promotion had closed up shop, and while a superstar in Japan, in the U.S. he was wrestling in small high school gyms before few fans for Angelo Poffo's outlaw ICW promotion.

He made 15 more tours of Japan from 1991-95 with Sabu, and even wrestled once for ECW as Sabu's partner during that era. His last match with Brazil was in 1990, nearly 40 years after they first hooked up. His final high-profile match in the U.S. was February 5, 1994, at "The Night the line was Crossed," at the ECW Arena.

Sabu was already a headliner. Paul Heyman was against using Sheik, believing the role of the older veterans in a growing company was to put over the young talent, something Sheik wasn't willing to do, and at his age, 67, wouldn't be able to do effectively. Tod Gordon was a big fan of The Sheik, and remembered how Sheik did tear down the house three years earlier for Joel Goodhart's promotion in Philadelphia by drawing Goodhart's biggest crowd and gate ever, and a bigger crowd than ECW had ever drawn up to that point in its history (1,800 paying $32,000), while slicing everyone in sight in a match with Butcher.

Gordon insisted on bringing him in anyway. He teamed with Pat Tanaka to beat Kevin Sullivan and The Tazmaniac (Tazz) when he pinned Tazmaniac after throwing a fireball in what was the No. 2 match on the show, and the match did get over strong live. It is believed his final match ever in the U.S. was a few months later in Lincoln Park, Michigan. He was scheduled against Butcher, but as happened more than 100 times during his career, Butcher's mother passed away that day, and Sheik ended up wrestling promoter Malcolm Monroe.

Even after his career was over, Sheik served as Sabu's mentor, which, because the industry had changed greatly, was probably not the best thing for Sabu's career. He instilled in him the belief of never trusting anyone, and the idea of not doing jobs as much as possible. It hurt

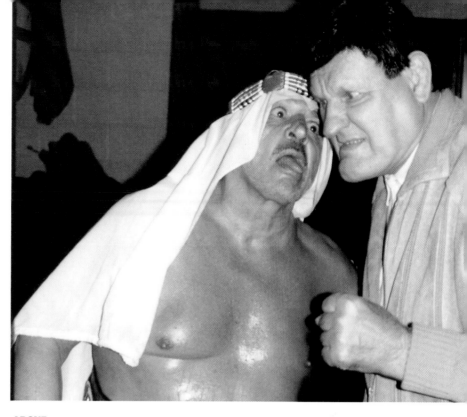

ABOVE: Two of wrestling's all-time villains, The Sheik and Walter "Killer" Kowalski. (Dr. Mike Lano)

Sabu's career, because not doing jobs when asked largely ended his career in the U.S. mainstream. Sabu clung to the idea that one day, like his uncle, he would run a territory in Michigan and wear the U.S. title belt as its top star, but those days are long gone. Even to this day, his son, Ed Jr., talks about getting television, reopening a territory, and bringing back the famous U.S. title belt.

Shortly after his final appearance in the ring in Japan in 1998, his accumulation of ring injuries and various health problems left him bedridden and crippled over the last two years of his life.

But he does leave wrestling with a legacy, because in his time, there was never a heel more hated by more fans, who drew more people, in more places.

CHAPTER 7

STU HART

STU HART'S LIFE WAS WRESTLING, and it made him a real-life mythical legend of Canada's Wild West. While he was neither an international drawing card on his own, nor one of the top-level promoters when it came to drawing gigantic houses, he probably influenced the history of the business, both in and out of the ring, more than all but a few men in history.

Stu received Canada's highest honor, the Order of Canada, in 2001, the only wrestler in history to receive such a high award, although he never could figure out what he did to deserve it. Like him being one of wrestling's most beloved legendary figures, it was largely due to him being a

uniquely likeable personality, even as some of his exploits made him deadly scary. He was a member of the first class of the Wrestling Observer Hall of Fame, mainly because if there was never a Stu Hart, this industry would be so entirely different today, that there is no way to realistically measure his influence.

There would have been no Fritz Von Erich, Wilbur Snyder, Joe Blanchard or Gene Kiniski as pro wrestlers, all of whom he started as Canadian football stars, and all of whom became major promoters and among the game's biggest stars. There would have been no Superstar Billy Graham, who in hindsight was one of the

OPPOSITE: Stu Hart, the patriarch of North America's most famous family of wrestlers, the Harts from Calgary. (Dr. Mike Lano)

most important figures in modern wrestling since he spawned Hulk Hogan, Jesse Ventura, and a hoard of other guys who thought being a big bodybuilder and pro wrestler was the coolest thing. Billy Robinson may never have come to North America. Dynamite Kid almost surely never would have come to North America. So without Hart, there would have been no British Bulldogs opening up a new style of wrestling in the WWF. The WWF would most likely have never taken off like it did from the start in England without Davey Boy Smith. Bret and Owen Hart would have never been born. Sylvester Ritter may have been a wrestler, but there he would have never been discovered by Jake Roberts and become the Junkyard Dog. Chris Benoit would almost surely be in another profession, as it was watching Dynamite Kid as a child in Edmonton that got him into wrestling, and it was the Hart family that trained him. Brian Pillman would have never been a wrestler, although he and Davey Boy Smith probably would also be alive.

Stewart Edward Hart was born May 3, 1915, in Saskatoon. Stu was a teenager when he saw what would change his life, a match involving Jack Taylor in Calgary. Taylor was something of the Canadian version of Frank Gotch, as the country's first national wrestling hero in the '20s. Hart had already started amateur wrestling, and trained with the old-time shooters in brutal training sessions that influenced his life. He was literally tortured with submission holds until he learned to defend himself and became

proficient himself. In his own mind, his own personal knack for torturing people, including sometimes his own family, was because he believed it built self-respect. To outsiders hearing about it in the movie, *Wrestling with Shadows*, it came across as scary child abuse to Bret and Owen, who he'd take to the brink of injury, and then let go. Bret talked about going to school with eyes that were bloodshot because his father put him in holds and squeezed until the blood vessels in the eye burst. Owen talked about being deathly afraid of his father.

In Stu's mind, he was preparing them for amateur wrestling. But while both were good amateur wrestlers, neither liked it and really did it only to please their father. Stu's dream of winning an Olympic gold medal, ruined by World War II, he pushed on his sons, but neither son wanted to pursue it at that level.

"When he was around us, he was always generous and compassionate," said Ross Hart. "But in the gym, it was a different world. It was his way of teaching guys. He felt there was no soft or easy way to learn wrestling."

Throughout his long life, he went through experiences that few people living in modern U.S. or Canada could ever relate to. He grew up destitute. When he was a teenager, his father lost his farm and was later arrested for refusing to leave the property. His mother took Stu and his two sisters to Edmonton, where they lived in a canvas tent, battling the frozen Canadian winter. They lived on money made milking cows, and Stu ended up in the YMCA

"HE DETESTED SMOKING OR DRUGS OF ANY KIND. HE WANTED THE SAME FROM US."

—ROSS HART

as a 14-year-old and learning wrestling. He got into pro wrestling in 1946 in New York, when he couldn't wait for the 1948 Olympics. Before long, he was married. From 1950 to 1965, he and wife Helen had 12 children and operated a wrestling company that became legendary. For the most part, it was not legendary because people made big money from working there, but because of the experiences they gained.

To those wrestlers who became students of the game, Stu's stories became the lost link to a history that didn't exist, and he was the most imitated man in wrestling with his unique accent and his trademark, "Ah, ah," before starting a sentence. He loved telling the stories. Even though many of the family members were on television regularly, Stu, unlike just about every wrestling promoter in the world, always kept his home phone number listed, and would talk at length to fans that called the house.

Stu started training at amateur wrestling in 1929, and was also a good football player, who dreamed of getting a college scholarship to Notre Dame as a football player or wrestling in the Olympics. By 1938, while still an ama-

teur, he came across the pros and began training in submission style. He was a Western Canadian champion in 1938 and qualified for the British Empire games, but neither he nor the city of Edmonton, had the money to send him to Australia. From 1937-39, he also played center and place kicker for the Edmonton Eskimos of the Canadian Football League. His mother, Elizabeth, died in 1939 of complications from diabetes, largely because the family had no money and she didn't want to be a burden, so refused to let anyone know how badly she was suffering. It hit Stu so hard that he buried it in his mind, and he almost never spoke about it, because of the heartbreak of the knowledge that it was preventable.

He was assistant wrestling coach at the University of Alberta, earning $75 a year, and trained on primitive equipment and even more primitive eating regiment, supplementing his meat and raw egg diet with things such as wheat germ oil and cod liver oil, believed to be the optimum way to build muscle and power in those days. He got into clean living and lived that way for the rest of his life.

"He detested smoking or drugs of any kind," said Ross. "He wanted the same from us. He would never let us eat junk food, chew gum or eat candy. He ended up mellowing on that later."

In 1939, Stu placed second in the Canadian national wrestling championships at 191 pounds in Montreal.

After his mother's death, he went to a small city called Yellowknife, where he heard he could make money working in the mines. As it turned out, there was little money to be made, and he had to brave that winter living in a canvas tent, but unlike years earlier, he at least had a sleeping bag and stove to his name. An old sports contact brought him back to Edmonton and sent him to Vancouver, where he won the national championship at 191 pounds, qualifying him for the Olympics. However, after winning the trials, before he could even prepare for the games, the decision was made, due to World War II, to cancel the Olympics. Even worse at the time, there was uncertainty about there being Olympics in 1944 either. He was in the navy, kept training, waiting for the 1944 Olympics, but his heart was broken when they were also canceled.

He was discharged in 1946, and he hitchhiked to New York to find Toots Mondt, a name he knew from Jack Taylor. When Mondt saw the muscular specimen and found that he had trained with Taylor and heard he was a Canadian amateur champion, he hired him. While not a top-level superstar, he was pushed well, and in his first few years as a pro, had three world title matches with Frank Sexton and one with Thesz. Stu wrestled regularly through about 1960, facing just about every big name from that era. Even though he was often the most popular wrestler in the area because he was a regular and the fans locally all knew the stories of how tough he was, he never pushed himself hard in the limelight, always looking to develop younger wrestlers. He was probably the biggest territorial star in wrestling history never to win a singles championship. He stopped wrestling full time when the athletic commission in Calgary ruled that a promoter could not also be a wrestler. The timing was right because he had a big family, and while Helen handled the bookkeeping, Stu made the meals for the kids and took them to school, so Stu stopped going to most of the road shows.

Stu was an early advocate of weight training, something most athletes of his era were told to avoid. He was a muscular, good-looking, stud athlete when he hit New York in 1946. In the '50s, he became a promoter and feared shooter, known for being his own policeman when somebody wanted to be a wrestler. He would show them, through his real wrestling ability, that it wasn't a business for dreamers, but only for big, legitimately tough athletes. Most left screaming, never to be heard from again. By the '60s, while still recognized as a dangerous man, his kids were constantly teased—they were the weird family in the Addams Family house surrounded by beat-up Cadillacs. In wrestling, the Harts were the butts of jokes in the '70s and early '80s, but not so much in a mean-spirited way as a unique way.

By the mid-'90s they became almost like a wrestling royal family, particularly to Canadians in the Western half of the country. There was the beauty-queen daughter married to Davey Boy Smith and a whole family of local wrestlers and women married to wrestlers. Stu was the gruff old-shooter father, and two sons dominated worldwide while other sons taught wrestling in the city. The Harts were possibly the most well-known people worldwide to come from Calgary in the '90s, a far cry from the taunts all the children had faced growing up about their father being a fake. In wrestling circles, the city of Calgary suddenly had special meaning. It was the city where real technical wrestlers came from. Even to this day, the city Calgary evokes a special meaning among wrestling fans and wrestlers worldwide.

Hart, who trained with them all, usually mentioned George Gordienko, Rube Wright, and Luther Goodall as the toughest of them all. When he'd get nostalgic about his youth, he'd mention Jack Taylor as the toughest wrestler who ever lived. Goodall was said to be the one man he couldn't handle, who could escape from his best holds and put them right back on him. There was a funny story, the veracity of which is as unknown as are all wrestling stories from that era, of Goodall reversing Stu and getting him in a submission, as Stu screamed that he heard the phone ring and had to take a call. The story, as the years went on, grew in legend to where Goodall, who had learned submission wrestling from Stu the hard way,

told Stu that the caller was just going to have to wait.

While Stu was legendary for making football players, big weightlifters, or tough guys around Calgary scream for their lives while his children listened to the scary sounds, he never used his skills in the ring. There are no famous incidents of Stu shooting on an unwilling competitor in the ring.

One situation came in the late '50s and involved the person who went on to make Stu a lot of money, Archie "The Stomper" Gouldie. He was in his early 20s, from Carbon, Alberta, and showed up at the matches as a big, powerful fan. He hit the ring and went after the Mills Brothers, who were Stu's top heels. Stu talked him out of it by inviting him to his home to show him what he could do. Stu used every vicious tactic in the world on Gouldie to teach him not to disrespect wrestling, figuring that he'd never see him again. Gouldie stormed out of the house after the humiliation.

ABOUT SIX MONTHS LATER, Gouldie came back and said, "Sir, I want you to teach me to wrestle." He became so believable as a heel within a few years that the Hart children used to have nightmares years later when he would wrestle Stu in grudge matches, and people in the Alberta area talk of him the way fans in Detroit talk about The Sheik.

"Anyone who he ever stretched, he did it because he thought he was trying to teach them, and to appreciate wrestling," said Bret. "He was a mark for shooting. He loved it. He'd do it at any time. It you woke my dad up at 4 a.m. and told him two Chippendale dancers are downstairs wanting to be pro wrestlers, he couldn't get his pants on fast enough."

He also had an affinity for strongmen and bodybuilders. Stu helped train strongmen types like Tom Magee, Terry Albritton (No. 1 in the world in the shot put when he came with college teammate Jim Neidhart to Calgary in 1979), Ted Arcidi (the first man ever to bench press 700 pounds) and Bill Kazmaier (perhaps the strongest man who ever walked the Earth), none of whom had success in wrestling. One who wasn't quite at that level was Wayne Coleman, a bodybuilding champion as a teenager who was among the strongest men in the world when he met Stu, about a year before he became Superstar Graham, as the younger brother of Dr. Jerry Graham. Bret once said his father considered Graham the biggest fish he ever reeled in.

He trained Graham, and in his first angle, Stu had set up a battle between CFL football stars during the off season, Bob Lueck, who was actually the person who made the connection to get Graham in, and Angelo Mosca. Stu told Graham to run in and attack Lueck right when the match started.

"I hadn't been smartened up at all," said Graham. I didn't know what was a work and what wasn't, so I told Stu, 'I can't go. The bell has already rung.' Can you imagine saying that? Stu grabbed me by the neck and took me backstage and said, 'You do what I tell you to do, because I'm your boss.'"

Stu joked that when Graham, who he always called "Billy Graham, Superstar," hit it big, one day, out of nowhere, he got this big package in the mail. It was a television set, sent by Graham, as a thank you for starting him out. Stu noted that the back of the set had "Holiday Inn" on it.

By the late '90s, a new group of third-generation guys like T.J. Wilson (a current New Japan wrestler who was practically raised in the family and lives in the family's carriage house), and Stu's grandchildren Matt and Ted Annis (Teddy Hart) and Harry Smith as teenagers were doing high-spot tag-team matches and training with the other family members to follow their fathers and uncles.

Stu and Helen were married on New Year's Eve of 1947 (as Helen often said, "We were married in a blizzard, and have been snowed in ever since"). He talked the New York socialite into moving to Great Falls, Montana, as he continued his wrestling career. That territory included most of Western Canada. It wasn't long before Hart started helping promoters Larry Tillman and Jerry Meeker with booking, and started running shows on his own in Edmonton, his former hometown, which had no live wrestling. He used the name Klondike Wrestling, a name he used in Edmonton as late as the '80s. His business in Edmonton was so strong that in 1951 he bought the wrestling rights to Calgary from Tillman for $50,000. The company, called Foothills Athletic Club, was first known to the public as Big Time Wrestling, and

ABOVE: Stu Hart during his wrestling days. (Dr. Mike Lano)

later Wildcat Wrestling, before changing to Stampede Wrestling in 1967. Business was good in the early years, as he flew in the big names that appeared on local television from Chicago, Los Angeles and Canadian stars out of Toronto. At one point his territory included Alberta, British Columbia, the Northwest Territories, and parts of Washington and Montana.

Stu's favorite rib was what became known as "Mable parties." They would do it to the new guys. They'd tell them about this woman who lived in a farmhouse just outside of town who loved to take care of the wrestlers, but she was married and her husband was out of town. They usually found a good-looking woman to play the role. They would take the wrestler to see her, and just as something was about to happen, the husband would come in, furious, with a gun, and kick in the door. The gun would have blanks and one of the wrestlers in on the gag would jump in and try to calm him down. The guy would shoot the wrestler, who would go down, preferably readied with ketchup. Stu would tell the guy to run as fast as he could.

Sometimes he'd have the "husband" chase the newcomer sprinting down the vacant highway for miles. While there were many victims, the most famous was the Great Antonio, as he freaked out seeing the guy get shot, the ketchup blood, and people laughed for decades at idea of this 450-pound man with unkempt hair and a scraggly beard running for his life for a mile down an empty road.

In the '50s, the family was rich, both from wrestling and investing the profits in real estate, another booming business. It was so successful that many of the biggest names in the business worked the territory regularly, and he'd fly in talent regularly from Frank Tunney's larger Toronto office and the wrestlers often flew from city to city, much different than the legendary bus trips from hell the territory became known for. But just as suddenly it ended.

It would almost seem amazing by today's standards what happened. Heel Mike DiBiase (the adopted stepfather of Ted), cut a promo to announcer Ernie Roth, saying, "If brains were dynamite, the people of Calgary wouldn't be able to blow their nose." For television and the community in 1963, that was way over the line, and Ch. 7 immediately canceled wrestling.

Without television, Hart's business collapsed. By this point, they had a house filled with children, and struggled to keep food on the table, clothes on the children, and fund a losing business. Bret, who was barely old enough to comprehend the sudden change, remembered the kids having to wear hand-me-down clothes and being made fun of at school for their tattered clothes. To keep afloat, they had to sell much of the land they'd acquired during the boom period, and take out second and third mortgages on their home. It fell so badly in one year without television, Stu nearly went bankrupt. He had invested money into the Vancouver office with Rod Fenton, and they got their television in Stu's cities.

Stu flew the Vancouver talent into his cities (thus not having to keep a crew of his own on the road and run a territory), using their TV to promote his Calgary and Edmonton shows. The Calgary and Edmonton fans didn't go for the Vancouver talent, didn't care about the angles shot in a television studio when they were used to arena footage and a higher class of workers, and the new wrestlers didn't get over. The whole thing ended up being a huge financial failure, and they were about to close up shop completely. In both 1964 and 1965, the territory closed down for months at a time while they attempted to regroup, sending the wrestlers scattered around North America trying to find work. He had to borrow money to re-open. In January 1966, things started turning around, and the territory became strong when former announcer Ed Whalen was able to get them back on television, this time called Wild Cat Wrestling.

THE EARLY '70s were a boom period, with frequent appearances of NWA champion Dory Funk. The first sign of the boom came by accident in 1969. Dory Funk was brought in for two weeks, and the idea was that one week he'd face Archie "The Stomper" Gouldie, and the next week he'd face Billy Robinson. The week before he came, Robinson and Stomper were supposed to have a disputed finish in a match for Stomper's North American title, to lead to each getting a title shot during Funk's visit. However, Stomper was furious at what he believed was Robinson's lack of cooperation and

shooting on him during the match (Robinson had a reputation for being a bully). Stomper walked out and quit, forcing them to go with Robinson for two straight weeks, and giving Robinson an unplanned North American title reign. Because Stomper was such a feared heel at the time, the idea that he would walk out and quit, even though it wasn't the planned ending, ended up making the fans think Robinson had to be tougher than anyone they had seen previously.

In the first match with Funk, the two had a 60-minute draw, the match was at a pace and skill level that nobody in the area had ever seen. Even to this day, Dory rated that original series with Robinson as the physically toughest matches of his career. The rematch the next week sold out the 7,500-seat Corral. It gave Robinson local credibility as being the best real wrestler in the world, and he became a great draw, particularly in his feud with Abdullah the Butcher.

Robinson, who many wrestlers considered the best wrestler in the world at the time, had been a hit in Japan, but was unknown in North America when Stu brought him in. Americans who had toured England knew of Robinson, who had already won the IWA world title in a tournament in Japan a year earlier. Robinson, schooled at the famed hooker school in Wigan, England, had the rep of being unbeatable in a shoot, incredible in a work, and unable to sell tickets. Ironically, Hart brought him in, and his wrestling skill was at a different level from anyone the fans had seen, and he became

ABOVE: Stu Hart and his constant companion in life, wife Helen Hart. (Dr. Mike Lano)

a top draw, leading Verne Gagne to hire him, and he became one of the biggest stars of the '70s.

"It was always a tough crowd to please," said Bret about Calgary wrestling. "We had the miners, the lumberjacks, who wanted to see a very real style. When you walked out of the arena after the show, everyone was buzzing about the show. There was real tension in the matches. When the work was bad, it didn't draw. It didn't really draw because of the talking, although we had good talkers. It was all about the work and the credibility. Next to Japan, it seemed the most real. Amarillo and Portland were like that. I'd go to Florida and see Dusty Rhodes, and think that our fans would never buy this."

In fact, when Rhodes won the NWA title in 1981, Stu switched to bringing AWA champion Nick Bockwinkel in for the big shows.

By the late '70s, like in much of North America, business started to struggle. With Stampede, the fall of business came in 1975, when Hart brought in Mark Lewin, King Curtis Iaukea and Big Bad John. All three had come from Australia where they had done well with bloodbath matches. Whalen hated this style of wrestling, complained about it on the air, and finally, in the middle of a TV shoot, gave a speech about how bad wrestling had become and walked off. The new announcers who took his place were clueless, and that, combined with the belief that all the blood, foreign objects and stretcher jobs had turned out the territory, and things got bad in a hurry.

With Helen's health failing from the pressure of the business, Stu had a deal worked out to sell in 1977. She was insistent, but he was reluctant. As it turned out, the deal fell through, and he decided to keep things going. Things started getting better, which led to a successful period where Stampede Wrestling changed wrestling in North America.

Bruce Hart was wrestling in England in 1978 when he came across Tom Billington, the Dynamite Kid. Then 19 years old, the 165-pounder was the best worker he had ever seen. His father, enamored with big guys, was skeptical. Dynamite could do things in the ring that nobody in wrestling at the time had ever seen in North America, and his Canadian exposure opened the door to Japan for him. The company created a mid-heavyweight division, largely based on Dynamite as the top star, and then their own world championship when NWA jr. champ Nelson Royal refused to put Dynamite over for the title as agreed upon in a business deal Stu had set up with Leroy McGuirk. The belt allowed people like Bret (then a junior heavyweight), Bruce (who was always really a junior heavyweight) and later Davey Boy Smith and many others to be put in the spotlight. Bruce noted that while his father was at first not happy seeing how small Dynamite was when he was flown in, he was open-minded enough that when Dynamite surprised everyone and got over, he quickly embraced pushing smaller wrestlers to work with him on top, and Whalen praised the fast paced and more

athletic action. Most who followed Stampede Wrestling from start to finish consider Dynamite to rank right up at the top of the company's biggest draws ever, and most who saw him at that time would claim he was the best worker in the history of the territory.

Stampede Wrestling became a melting pot of styles, combining the European style, the Japanese style, the Southern U.S. style (using top heels like Honky Tonk Wayne Ferris and David Shults), and the old-fashioned Canadian style. This allowed the Stampede wrestlers the unique ability to wrestle anywhere in the world and be somewhat familiar with the style. Both Owen and Chris Benoit were able to wrestle in every style and be considered top hands. Many of Japan's biggest names from years later came in during this period.

The peak seemed to be when Badnews Allen was brought in as top heel. But after a controversial angle involving Allen and Stomper, designed to finally turn Stomper into a babyface, things fell apart just as quickly. The match pitted Bret Hart and Davey Boy Smith and Two Rivers against Badnews and Stomper and a wrestler billed as Jeff Gouldie, a young kid who from Kansas City who was billed as Stomper's son. The idea was to injure Jeff, turning Archie babyface, for what was thought to be a dream program of bullies against Badnews, who had run through all the territory's smaller babyfaces.

Allen used a fork and a fire hydrant to take out Smith and Two Rivers. Kerry Brown then took out Bret. Allen piledrove

Jeff on the floor, and it was sold as both a broken neck and a career-ending injury, leading to Stomper doing one of the greatest interviews in the history of Canadian wrestling, turning face and vowing revenge. But what should have been a big angle turned into a disaster. A riot broke out, and a woman fan injured her ankle and was trampled on. As this was going on, Whalen, broadcasting live, said he was repulsed by what was going on, since he hated blood, and this angle had it in abundance. Between the injury of the fan, the riot, the supposed career-ending injury to the wrestler (which was a total work) and Whalen walking off, this ended up being front-page news locally.

The result was the city of Calgary banned Stampede Wrestling for six months, forcing Stu to run at a nearby Indian reservation, which killed local business. Stu brought Menacker back as announcer, but Menacker was too old to keep up with or comprehend the much faster action, plus he couldn't even remember the names of the young crew of wrestlers. TV ratings dropped and business fell way off. This was tough for Stu, since Menacker had made him so much money as a booker and an announcer in the past. Helen's health, largely from the pressure the money losses were taking on her again, was going bad. Again, there was hope, as Stampede had gotten television in Vancouver, which had been Gene Kiniski's territory, and the new style of

action was such a success that the first show and repeat business was strong.

Vince McMahon at the same time had already starting running nationally in the U.S. and parts of Canada. There was no way, even with its superior workrate and high-flying smaller wrestlers, that the modest look of Stampede Wrestling and its two-camera shoot could compete with Hulk Hogan. McMahon came to Stu, and instead of just running him out of business like he was about to do with everyone else, offered him a deal. He'd buy Stampede Wrestling for $1 million, an amazing total if you consider that a few months earlier he purchased a controlling interest in the far more valuable Georgia Championship Wrestling office for somewhere between $675,000 and $750,000, which included a national TV contract. The deal was that McMahon would pay Hart $100,000 per year for ten years, and in addition, Hart would get 10 percent of the gate from all house shows in Calgary and Edmonton. McMahon also got Stu's television network, giving him coverage in all of Western Canada. Stu, who was 69, said he was too old to fight McMahon, and recognized even if he wanted to, it was a fight he couldn't win. Stu's only stipulation to McMahon was to give jobs to his three most talented wrestlers, son Bret, son-in-law Davey, and Dynamite.

At first, the fans in Western Canada, weaned on the hard work and fast-paced action of Stampede Wrestling, rejected

OPPOSITE: Stu Hart at ringside in Calgary with longtime friend, announcer Ed Whalen. (Dr. Mike Lano)

ABOVE: Stu Hart flanked by family members at his 80th birthday party. (Dr. Mike Lano)

WWF and the early Calgary and Edmonton shows drew poorly. While Hulk Hogan was a big draw, most shows did not do well, and WWF started running in the area less and less frequently. One year later, McMahon told Stu that he wasn't going to pay him the promised $100,000 per year, and told Stu he could reopen Stampede Wrestling. Of course, McMahon by this point had his top stars, and more importantly, the familiar TV time slot for fans in the area, and was now the established major league promotion. Stu had to restart from scratch, clearly as a minor league operation catering to the die-hards, and servicing the small towns in the middle

of nowhere that WWF wouldn't go near. Stu decided against filing a lawsuit, feeling it would ruin the careers of Dynamite, Davey, Bret and son-in-law Jim Neidhart, who had been hired by this point.

It was this final semi big-time version of Stampede Wrestling, from October 1985 through December 1989, that actually gained the most worldwide recognition for the group, largely due to its biggest star, Stu's youngest son, Owen. Stampede Wrestling became known throughout Canada during that time period, as its television appeared on TSN. The group was struggling, using Bruce, Keith and 18-year-old rookie Chris Benoit, fresh out of high school in Edmonton, as the top stars. Owen was a junior at the University of Calgary, and in 1986 placed second in the CIAU nationals at 177 pounds. The college dropped its wrestling program, and Owen lost his scholarship. Bruce talked him into coming to work, since the company was lacking a top singles babyface.

Because of his high-flying moves and quickness, taken from studying tapes of Satoru Sayama, Owen quickly became the most spectacular wrestler in the world. Brian Pillman, Johnny Smith, and Hiroshi Hase also debuted at about the same time, while Jushin Liger wrestled under his real name of Keiichi Yamada, Shinya Hashimoto was Hashif Khan and Kensuke Sasaki was Benkei Sasaki. It was clear to anyone watching at the time that this was becoming the place where the superstars of the future were being developed. In particular, the tag-team feud of Owen Hart and then-brother-in-law Ben Bassarab vs. The Viet Cong Express was the introduction of the high spot after high spot style, often going 45 and 60 minutes and picked up interest all over Western Canada. This led to Owen Hart's stardom in Japan.

While the territory sometimes drew well during those years, largely when Bret or Davey would appear, or when Owen would have a big grudge match, or the peak of Karl Moffat as Jason the Terrible, Stu was generally losing tremendous money. When Owen left for his first run with WWF as the Blue Blazer, business went way down. When Dynamite and Davey quit the WWF in 1988 after Jacques Rougeau sucker-punched Dynamite, the last-ditch effort to save the territory around a Dynamite and Johnny Smith vs. Davey and Chris Benoit feud didn't work, partially because Whalen was dead set against the break up of the Bulldogs and would edit virtually everything with heat or blood off the television show. Many felt Whalen was killing the territory. Stu thought otherwise, since Whalen was a local broadcasting institution. No matter what was said elsewhere, Stu would talk of Whalen as the best wrestling announcer in the business, since his ups and downs over the previous 20 plus years often coincided with whether or not Whalen was on television selling the product to the masses.

"They had lost money before, but in that period they lost a fortune," Bret said. "Stu just didn't want to give up."

Practically fearless because of what he'd been through, he once wrestled a live Tiger, not even thinking about how stupid that could have been. He continued to train and stretch people until a week after his 77th birthday. On May 23, 1993, he tore his quad completely away from the bone and messed up his knee going into the ring for a legends presentation at the WCW Slamboree PPV show at the Omni in Atlanta. Even though he underwent surgery to reattach the muscle, he never fully recovered from it. He was basically crippled from that point on, as it changed the way he could walk. Inside, that had to be killing him, but he learned early on that life wasn't about complaining.

CHAPTER 8
GORILLA
MONSOON

BOB "GINO" MARELLA (Gorilla Monsoon) was a fixture in the pro wrestling world for four decades. Marella's career in pro wrestling, which began in 1959 after being a three-sport star in college and an Olympic hopeful in wrestling, took on many forms.

In the early '60s he was marketed as Gino Marella, a huge man with some agility. He was marketed as a friendly clean-cut babyface local college sports hero for promoters Ygnacio (Pedro) Martinez and Frank Tunney in the Buffalo, Cleveland, and Toronto areas, where Italian babyfaces were popular. Gorilla Monsoon, one of the most famous heels of the '60s, was created by Vince McMahon Sr. in 1963 and with his immense size and one of the all-time great ring names, became one of the biggest names in the business.

As with most big men in the profession, because the stress on the joints of a big man is much greater than a normal-sized wrestler, his in-ring prime wasn't long. One of the few educated men in the pro wrestling industry in those days, he rose to a position of power, eventually being co-owner simultaneously of two of the most successful offices in the world, Capitol Sports out of Washington, D.C. (World Wide Wrestling Federation) where

OPPOSITE: Blackjack Mulligan works over the 400-pound Gorilla Monsoon. (Dr. Mike Lano)

he largely ran the television tapings for years, and Capital Wrestling (no relationship) out of San Juan, Puerto Rico (World Wrestling Council). In the early '70s, he also worked as the manager and frequent tag-team partner of WWWF champion Pedro Morales.

In the '80s, after retiring from the ring in 1979 and being just about the only name wrestler in history never to come back from retirement, he gained national fame as the announcer on World Wrestling Federation television and PPV shows, as the unflappable straight man for Jesse Ventura and Bobby Heenan. In his last years, he had an on-air role as the figurehead WWF president, and once a week came to the Titan studios to voice-over matches for international WWF telecasts.

Born Robert James Marella on June 4, 1937, he grew up in Rochester, New York and was a huge man by the standards of his time. While this would sound strange today, in the '50s, there was virtually no such thing as a 250-pound high school student. With his size, he was an All-City football star at Thomas Jefferson High School, on both the offensive and defensive line, and a local shot and discus champion as well as area heavyweight wrestling champion.

He went to Ithaca College, a Division III school in upstate New York, playing both offensive and defensive line in football, and setting school records in both the shot and discus that stood well into the '60s. He earned degrees in both physical education and physiotherapy and was on the Dean's list. With his size and

power, wrestling was his best sport, and as a senior in 1959, he went all the way to the Division I finals in Ames, Iowa, placing second in the heavyweight division losing to Oklahoma State's Ted Ellis. He represented the U.S. as a national team member in several international meets in Greco-roman wrestling, but was beaten out by another future pro wrestler, Dale Lewis, for a slot on the 1960 Olympic team. Bad knees, which already slowed his mobility, kept him from being drafted by the NFL. His 18-second pin in college is still a school record for the fastest win, and led to what was his gimmick during much of his career of quick wins (and when he got older, quick countout losses to build up heels for title shots). In 1973, he was inducted into the Ithaca College Sports Hall of Fame.

He receiving his teaching credential, but with his size, which made him almost a freak in the world at that time, he figured there was a lot more money in pro wrestling. He started as a teacher in Rochester, New York, after graduating college, but only lasted a few months before being offered more money to wrestle. Martinez debuted him as a local sports hero babyface in late 1959 at the old Rochester War Memorial Auditorium, drawing a crowd of 6,000 fans, about four times the usual attendance in the building, pinning Pancho Lopez in a matter of seconds. His background as a legit athlete and his huge size kept him high on cards in his days as the babyface Gino Marella, wrestling mostly in cities like Rochester, Buffalo, and Cleveland for Martinez and in Ontario for Frank Tunney. But he was not cut out to play the face role. He was too big and powerful to sell believably to the wrestlers of that era, so he was limited to doing short matches that had no drama, and going into cities week after week doing one-minute squashes gets old.

Marella went on his first tour of Japan in the spring of 1963 in one of the early World League (precursor to today's Champion Carnival) tournaments promoted by Rikidozan as the youngest foreigner on a tour that included a crew of superstars at the time of Killer Kowalski, Pat O'Connor, Haystacks Calhoun, Cowboy Bob Ellis, Sandor Szabo and the Masked Killer X (Frankie Townsend). He was nicknamed "The White Elephant" and "The Human Typhoon" The tour was highlighted by Shohei Baba's return from the U.S. and the two had a famous singles match which Baba won, but was notable for Monsoon using a giant swing on Baba. Kowalski was impressed with Marella's potential and introduced him to his friend Bobby Davis, the top heel manager for Vince McMahon Sr.

GORILLA MONSOON, with the monsoon being a take off from his Japanese typhoon nickname, was introduced to the world in the late summer 1963 by McMahon. Davis, manager of Buddy Rogers at the time, brought him in to be one of the first in a long line of huge monster heels who would challenge Bruno Sammartino, who had just won the WWWF championship from Rogers. At the time he was the second largest true wrestling star of the era, with only Haystacks Calhoun being larg-

er. With Rogers largely on the shelf due to heart problems, Monsoon was introduced with a storyline about Davis travelling to Manchuria to investigate the legend of this Neanderthal-like man-beast who could crunch anyone at will. He arrived, finding this supposed 6-7, 400-pound man wading nude in a stream not knowing a word of English. Somehow, through an interpreter, he convinced the man to come with him to the United States and introduced him as the man who destroyed the legendary Antonino Rocca in less than three minutes.

All sorts of colorful made-up stories hyped his arrival, with him going on television and squashing one hapless foe after another in seconds. While Sammartino had faced Gino Marella previously, although not in the WWWF territory, their first meeting was actually a rush job. Sammartino was scheduled to have a long-awaited title rematch against Rogers, who he had won the title from on May 17, 1963 in 48 seconds in Madison Square Garden before a sellout crowd of more than 18,000 fans. There are disputed as to whether or not Rogers suffered a heart attack. Rogers claimed that he'd suffered the heart attack shortly before the first Sammartino match and went to the ring and just got it over with in seconds. Sammartino always disputed the story, citing that commission doctors would not have allowed him in the ring if that were the case. There is little question based on the fact Rogers wrestled so few matches during that time leading to and after the match, almost all tag matches and in vir-

ABOVE: Two of the biggest men in wrestling of the '60s, Haystacks Calhoun and Gorilla Monsoon. (Dr. Mike Lano)

tually every match he was only in the ring one minute max, and that he never wrestled Sammartino in a rematch despite its huge gate potential and after late August, disappeared from wrestling for more than three years until resurfacing in another promotion, that he was in poor health at the time.

The Sammartino-Rogers rematch, scheduled for October 4, 1963, was moved from Madison Square Garden outdoors to Roosevelt Stadium in Jersey City, New Jersey because of the expectations of a record-setting crowd and gate. Wrestling, behind Sammartino's popularity and strong local television (in New York, wrestling aired in prime time from 9-11 p.m. on both Thursday and Saturday nights), was doing huge business in the area. Just a few weeks before the show, it was announced locally that due to heart problems, Rogers had been pulled from the show and a tournament was held on television to create a top contender, sponsored by *Ring Magazine*, which saw newcomer Monsoon destroy everyone in less than one minute, including top heel Buddy Austin in the finals. A bloody Sammartino lost via DQ in that first meeting before a crowd of about 18,000 fans. A rematch on October 21, 1963, which went to a double count out, drew an even bigger crowd, selling out Madison Square Garden, which at this point was something Sammartino was doing with regularity. Finally on November 18, 1963, before another sellout, Sammartino got his win, and the Monsoon feud moved to the secondary markets on the circuit like

Philadelphia, Pittsburgh and Washington, D.C. Boston at that point wasn't part of the territory. It became a WWWF city in 1965, and Sammartino vs. Monsoon was the first major match at the old Boston Gardens.

Monsoon and Kowalski became the top heel tag team in the territory, winning the old U.S. tag-team titles from Brute Bernard and Skull Murphy, before losing them to the Tolos Brothers. Monsoon later held the same belts in 1965 with partner Bill Watts. He remained a top heel until late 1965.

He went back to Japan in September 1966 as Gorilla Monsoon, the top heel on the tour, drawing sellout crowds in Sapporo and Sendai for International heavyweight title matches with Baba, losing the first via count out and the second via pinfall, and teamed with huge George "Man Mountain" Cannon as an 800-pound tag team to lose to Baba and Michiaki Yoshimura in an All-Asian tag-team title match. He toured Japan twice more, once in 1969 in the World League tournament, and in 1972 for the World League where he went to the finals in a tournament that included such foreign names as Abdullah the Butcher, Jos LeDuc, Dick Murdoch and Jose Lothario, on May 12 in Tokyo, losing to Baba with a boston crab submission in the third fall. Said to be a talented singer, while on that tour, he crooned at Shohei and Motoko Baba's wedding.

After the death of Joe "Toots" Mondt, who was McMahon's partner in Capitol Sports, manager and former wrestling great Wild Red Berry and Phil Zacko, the Philadelphia promoter, were given the option of each buying half of Mondt's 50 percent of Capitol Sports. Berry declined, and the offer went to Marella. Eventually, McMahon made some maneuverings so he maintained 50 percent, Arnold Skaaland, his most trusted ally in the company, had 10 percent and Zacko and Marella each owned 20 percent.

Monsoon, this time managed by Berry, returned in 1967, for another three-match series with Sammartino. The first meeting on February 27, which Monsoon won via count out, drew a sell-out. The second meeting, on March 27, drew another sellout going to the 11 p.m. curfew draw. Legend has this match as going 90 minutes, although they used to exaggerate the time of long matches. There is no reliable source as to how long it was, other than it definitely was less than 60 minutes. The third meeting, on May 15 which Sammartino won in a Texas death match, drew just shy of capacity, largely blamed on the fact that in the draw match, Sammartino had Monsoon down for a two count when the bell rang and the fans hated the finish. Monsoon then became a headline tag team with Toru Tanaka before making his face turn in the late 1969.

Sammartino was wrestling in a television match and was being double-teamed by two heels when, surprisingly, Monsoon made the save. Subsequently, Monsoon was wrestling and after a run-in was being double-teamed, and Sammartino saved him, saying he owed him a favor.

WHILE THE MONSOON of the '60s couldn't speak a word of English, the Monsoon of the '70s was a very literate, well-spoken interview. When Morales was champion from 1971-73, Monsoon was used as his manager, to give interviews in English, often team with him, and be attacked by heels to set up grudge opponents for the champion. His Manchurian background was totally forgotten, and he became the 400-pound New Jersey giant from Willingboro, although his physique changed noticeably, and he had slowed in the ring greatly from his prime. If he worked undercard matches against wrestlers not being groomed for a title shot, they were generally very short squash wins.

While McMahon Sr. handled the booking, Marella was his top assistant, and on occasion, his policeman (the man to physically handle any problems with the other wrestlers). The McMahon Sr. booking was usually simple. The cards were headlined by title matches, with revolving heels brought in against a face champion. The heels would get either one, two or three title shots against the champion in all the major arenas, based on how well tickets moved. McMahon would book the top two or three matches on the show, and Marella would fill out the undercards. Unlike today's week-to-week booking, in those days, Sr. and Marella generally had the main events in the big arenas tentatively booked ten months to one year out.

In 1974, Carlos Colon, Victor Jovica, and Victor Quinones started

Capital Wrestling in Puerto Rico, and in the early days behind Colon as the top draw, were on fire, including one period of 13 straight sellouts at 30,000-seat Bayamon Stadium in the infancy of the promotion. Headliners could earn $3,000 to $5,000 working a weekend, and the climate was awesome in the winter for people living their lives in the Northeast, so even though he had slowed from his prime, Monsoon came in to reprise his role as a heel against the much smaller natives.

He came in almost every other weekend for a few years, and also worked headline matches as a heel against the likes of Andre the Giant, Bruno Sammartino (who did a rare job for Monsoon on July 22, 1978 in San Juan, losing the WWC North American heavyweight title), and even Bob Backlund.

Eventually, Jovica's brother sold his stock, and Marella owned 10 percent of the office for many years. He was the liaison for WWWF talent, booking every big star from the WWWF in those days for big-money weekends. Quinones and Monsoon became close during that period, and they had basically a father/son relationship.

Monsoon's most famous angle, however, came in June of 1976, when he was long past his prime as a headliner, and it's not even clear as to why it happened, because it built up to nothing involving him. Muhammad Ali was hyping a mixed match against Antonio Inoki, as a closed-circuit spectacular. Ali came to a WWWF taping in Allentown, Pennsylvania, to shoot an angle, which eventually appeared on TV sportscasts throughout the country and nearly every wrestling television show in the U.S. Monsoon, who virtually never wrestled on TV by this point because he had already made his name and was more valuable backstage, was wrestling his long-time friend Baron Mikel Scicluna. After a few seconds, Ali, introduced before the match, hit the ring and threw jabs at Monsoon. Perhaps because Monsoon was such a huge man, he dwarfed Ali, who at the time was considered a large, agile athlete. They used him to get the idea that wrestlers were bigger and tougher than the most famous fighter in the world. Ali circled and jabbed, and Monsoon picked him up in an airplane spin, with Ali making facial expressions that would make Steve Regal proud and gently placing him on the mat with Ali doing a great job of selling, particularly for someone who had never done pro wrestling.

Monsoon condescendingly said that while Ali may be great as a boxer, he'd be nothing in a fight with a wrestler, saying he could have grabbed any hold at will and broken any bone in Ali's body, debuting his phrase that he used on television throughout the '80s, "He doesn't know a wristlock from a wrist watch." For the public, it was felt that nobody knew Inoki and at that time, nobody believed a wrestler could beat a boxer, let alone Ali, who was the ultimate boxing legend of the generation, so they needed to do an angle showing Ali selling big for a wrestler to put the result in doubt to the public. Later Ali did other angles where he KO'd lesser known wrestlers on ABC's *Wide World of Sports* from Chicago, narrated by Howard Cosell, who made the famous call, "In all this nonsense, there is a chance that Ali could get hurt."

In the '70s and early '80s, he ran backstage at television. Before the days when referees would have earpieces to get the messages to tell the wrestlers when it was time to "go home," the job fell to Monsoon. Monsoon was visible to the referee, wrestlers and timekeeper in what later became known in wrestling as "the Gorilla position," basically wrestling's terminology for the on-deck circle, and when he took his glasses off, it was the signal to end the match.

He got his final run of singles main events challenging and putting over Superstar Billy Graham at most of the major arenas when he was WWWF champion in 1977. In 1979, he announced if he lost a match in Philadelphia, he would retire, and he lost that match and never wrestled again. He also wrote a column for a Philadelphia newspaper, and perhaps his most noteworthy column came a few years later when he wrote the obituary for Graham's death from cancer. Of course, Graham was still alive at the time. Even when Monsoon got the word Graham was alive, he never wrote a retraction. A few years later, when Graham, with a shaved bald head, returned to challenge then-champion Bob Backlund, the series drew a huge response (three straight sellouts) in Madison Square Garden, but didn't draw well in Philadelphia because the word among fans in that city was that the real

Graham had died, and that the WWF (one of the W's had been removed by this time) was trying to sell an imposter on the fans.

Marella was eventually bought out by Vince McMahon Jr. in 1982, but in return got a ten-year contract that gave him an announcing job and 1.5 times preliminary money on every WWF house show even though he never had to leave his home, which turned out to be a very lucrative deal when the WWF was running close to 1,000 shows per year. If you figure prelim wrestlers in that era were doing $2,000 per week, figure 1.5 times that, multiplied by three house shows per night, and you realize he had huge money years after selling the company when Titan flourished in its '80s heyday. He became best known nationally during this period, generally hosting *Wrestling Challenge*, the WWF's "B" show, many *NBC Saturday Nights Main Events* and PPV shows with either Ventura or Heenan as his co-host. Monsoon was not a good wrestling announcer and liked to show off some of his knowledge of body parts, which came off as arrogant to many, but played a good straight man for a comedic foil. As part of a promise Jr. had made to Sr., the partners he bought, Marella, Zacko and Skaaland had to be taken care of as long as they were alive. Since his health problems, Marella generally went into the Titan studios once a week, on Thursdays, to reminisce about the old days and announce on WWF International broadcasts. He didn't need to do it, but liked it because it gave him a need to get out of the house and be productive.

ABOVE: Gorilla Monsoon (second from left) flanked by former WWWF champion Pedro Morales (far left) and Arnold Skaaland (second from right). (Dr. Mike Lano)

CHAPTER 9
JOHNNY VALENTINE

JOHNNY VALENTINE WAS ONE of the biggest stars in an era where the top guys made good money, but not by the standards of the wrestlers and athletes today. That was just how it was for athletes of the '60s and '70s. Then a plane crash led to huge medical bills that left him destitute. Promoter Jim Crockett Jr. did keep him on the payroll for about 18 more months, and he eventually went back to Texas, where he's lived since his career ended, and tried to be a manager for supposed brother Buddy Valentine (Dale Hey, known most of his career as Buddy Roberts who gained later fame with The Freebirds), but it just didn't fit. Valentine couldn't do much from a wheelchair, and the fans who had seen him as one of the toughest and most dangerous men they'd seen since childhood, weren't comfortable seeing him that way, either.

The money he had saved from wrestling went to paying his mounting medical bills and he was left to live on Social Security disability income.

"It's a shame that somebody like John...the business ignored him," said reporter Mike Mooneyham in a *Slam! Wrestling* article, who grew up watching Valentine as the top star in the Carolinas in the '70s. "I really can't state it any other way or sugarcoat it. His own business

OPPOSITE: Johnny Valentine lays down his brand of brutality. (Dr. Mike Lano)

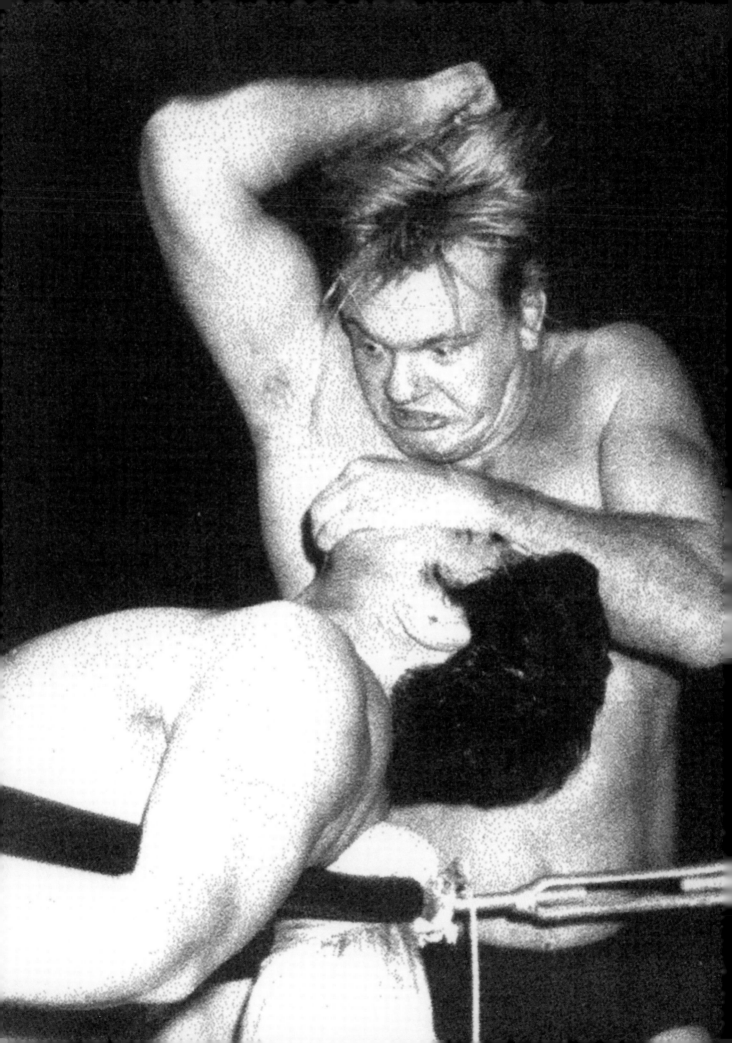

"ONCE YOU GOT PAST THE HOOKERS AND THE SERIOUS SHOOTERS, JOHNNY VALENTINE WAS PROBABLY THE ONE MAN IN PROFESSIONAL WRESTLING YOU LEAST WANTED TO MESS WITH."

—LOU THESZ

turned its back on him. It was cold and heartless. ...Especially for a guy like him...this was a guy that meant so much to the business. I would say he was one of the top five performers of my generation. In a business that has accumulated so much over the past few years, these things shouldn't happen."

Valentine was an enigma in the profession. He was one of those performers, like Ray Stevens, who was a bigger legend to the wrestlers themselves than they even were to the fans. Even Lou Thesz, who normally doesn't have kind things to say about wrestlers who weren't actually skilled at wrestling, always put Valentine over as being physically tough.

There was many a story he told in the book *Hooker* about Valentine, who grew up in Hobart, Washington, just outside of Seattle, where he was always billed. Valentine was actually training to be a boxer at first, before he ended up as a teenager in wrestling and became one of its biggest stars.

"He had almost no wrestling ability," Thesz wrote, "but he didn't need any, because he rose to the top on toughness and pure guts. Once you got past the hookers and the serious shooters, Johnny Valentine was probably the one man in professional wrestling you least wanted to mess with. The fans could sense his toughness, too, and they always turned out in droves to see him."

Thesz remembered that the wrestling office in Texas talked him into riding a brahma bull at a stock show in Houston, because they felt the publicity would be good for business, as it was billed as "the toughest man in wrestling (which was how Valentine was billed in those days) versus the toughest animal." Valentine, who had never done this sort of thing, still did it anyway, and was thrown rather quickly. But the animal then turned on him. The bull charged at him so quickly that Thesz, who was in the stands watching, remembered he thought Valentine for sure was going to wind up a goner. Valentine punched the bull right in the face as hard as he could. Thesz said you could hear the splat all over the building. The bull stopped dead in its tracks and tried to shake off the blow. This gave Valentine the momentary diversion for him to hop the fence and get out of trouble.

Thesz also recalled a situation in California where Joe Pazandak, a very good actual wrestler, had a conflict with the office over money, went public and caused some trouble. Valentine, who was known as Cowboy Rocky Valentine in California, even though he was by then already a big name as Johnny Valentine in many other places, was put in the ring with him. The match turned into a shoot, apparently, with Valentine stalling forever. When Pazandak tried some wrestling, Valentine hit him with a punch, cutting his eye. Pazandak again tried to shoot, but Valentine cut him over the other eye. Valentine literally beat the hell out of him with punches before it was stopped because Pazandak was bleeding so badly.

Valentine was remembered for always having a blank stare, like he was in a trance, both in and out of the ring. There was a famous story about one night when he was walking around the ring with the blank stare, like a man so deep into the zone you couldn't get him out of it. A fan in the front row, hot at him for bailing out on the babyface's comeback, hit him with a sucker punch hard to the jaw. Valentine not only didn't go after the fan, but just kept walking, never even blinked or registered the blow, and never broke character. To do so would be to acknowledge that the match itself going on in the ring wasn't his 100-percent focus.

"John was one of my heroes," said Dory Funk, who rated Valentine and Jack Brisco as his favorite opponents of that era. "I learned a lot from him about working. I didn't wrestle his style, but I learned so much about taking care of myself in the ring, ring presence, and what the fans wanted to see from him."

The legend of Valentine is such that nobody ever hit harder than he and Wahoo. Memories are often kind, and whether his stiff blows were any different than many Japanese wrestlers or Chris Benoit today is as much conjecture as anything. As are the pops he drew either playing face or heel; he was equally successful at either role. His m.o. was usually to come in as a heel, and when the fans respected him so much for being the toughest s.o.b. around, turn face without changing the style much except doing more early selling to build the comeback. While he was by no means anywhere close to the promo man Steve Austin was, the perception of the fans of what Valentine was probably was the closest similarity today. He was the heel who never backed down, who became a super babyface because the fans believed in him with the turn. But if he turned back, they accepted that because they knew he was never anyone to be trusted. Without the promo ability of an Austin, Valentine had to work his magic 100 percent in the ring. But even after the heart attack in 1973, once he came back a few months later, it wasn't as if he was moved down cards for being past his prime.

"The loudest crowd I ever heard was when he beat Harley Race for the Missouri State title (January 19, 1973 in St. Louis)," recalled longtime St. Louis television announcer and Sam Muchnick's assistant Larry Matysik on *Wrestling Observer Live's* Valentine special show on 4/24, who recalled the pop when he made the announcement of the title change. "I was deaf for two days after the match."

Soon after winning that title, he was booked to lose it in a match with Terry Funk. In a match at the Chase Hotel, Funk hit Valentine's knee with a chair to lead to the spinning toe hold finish. Fans in St. Louis were furious, since using chairs wasn't done in that promotion up until that point in time. Valentine was a huge face being screwed out of the title, but Muchnick hated it because he was trying to keep wrestling away from gimmicks, believing they hurt long-term business by killing credibility.

As it turned out, the two never had the rematch, which Valentine would have almost surely won since Mushnick was hot at Funk for using the chair. He had the heart attack two days before the match. Muchnick never went back to the program because he was mad at Funk for that finish.

YEARS EARLIER IN ST. LOUIS, Valentine in a television match beat up a young wrestler, pounding him so viciously that he was bleeding badly from the chest. When Dory Funk asked him if he needed to go that far, Valentine was very pragmatic. He said he had a main event coming up and had three television matches to make an impact before the show. If the show drew well because he made an impact, everyone would make more money. If the guy he wrestled got discouraged because of the beating, he didn't belong in the business in the first place.

Descriptions by wrestlers of that era, particularly the younger wrestlers who were starting their career when Valentine was one of the game's biggest stars, seem to indicate he had almost an Andy Kaufman-like eerie personality.

"I'm not sure if what he did couldn't be done today, but it won't ever be done today," Terry Funk said about Valentine's slow-building style. "He was just real to everyone. He totally got everyone to suspend their disbelief in every match to a great extreme. Even in the dressing room, you didn't know if he was working or shooting. Nobody really knew. He had a high IQ. The important thing people didn't know about him was just how smart the guy was."

Others echoed those comments. Ric Flair remembered traveling with him early in his career and Valentine would play classical music the entire trip and not even say a word, never breaking character in the car or in the dressing room. He hardly let on to the wrestlers and the fans themselves never knew that he was, among other things, a master at chess.

"He usually sat in a corner by himself with a blank stare," remembered Dory Funk, who wrestled Valentine numerous times when he was NWA world champion between 1969 and 1973. "The younger guys were afraid to talk to him. For those who would go up and talk with him, he was very much into what draws money, what the fans will buy, what works and how to draw money working a program."

Dory Funk remembered as champion, worked four times with Valentine at the Sam Houston Coliseum in Houston. By this time Valentine had done the turn and was the territory's top babyface, and top babyface challenging the world champion was an easy program at first to draw, but they worked it so well that they sold out all four shows. His favorite finish was in the third match, which went 70 minutes. Funk, as champion, had the match won when the 60-minute time limit expired. He said he didn't want to leave with a draw and asked for ten more minutes. At the end of the period, Valentine was pounding on him and had him beat. When Valentine then asked for ten more minutes because he didn't want to leave with a draw, Funk grabbed his belt and said, "I'll accept a draw," and left to incredible heat, enough to bring it back a fourth time with a 90-minute time limit, and draw another sellout. Funk noted that because the time limit was 90 minutes, to give the fans what they expected, Valentine felt they couldn't do the blow-off finish until they passed the 60-minute mark.

Valentine and McDaniel are generally given credit for rebuilding Texas in 1969 after a down period and then building the Carolinas into one of the top territories in the country after it was long just another regional territory in 1974. The Texas territory had been built for years around Fritz Von Erich as the top star. Von Erich, who shortly after winning a nasty promotional war in Dallas and Fort Worth, stopped travelling the circuit to raise his family and run his two cities, leaving the rest of the cities without a major draw. The rest of the circuit suffered greatly, as Von Erich was such a huge star and a great interview that he couldn't be replaced as the main man. It was Valentine as a heel and McDaniel as a babyface doing their stiff matches that picked the rest of the territory up to where it was one of the hottest and most lucrative markets in the country, and it stayed that way with Valentine's babyface turn, tag team with McDaniel, and heel turn again. The territory cooled down in the period after Valentine suffered his heart attack on March 15, 1973.

At the time, Valentine was one of the top five stars in the business, at his drawing power peak, and working probably the toughest schedule of anyone in wrestling except for the NWA world heavyweight champion. He was the top babyface in St. Louis, at the time considered the wrestling capital of North America. He was the world champion, as a heel, for the Buffalo/Cleveland-based National Wrestling Federation. He was still based in Texas, where he had made his heel turn and held the American heavyweight title, and was headlining Montreal as a heel, where he had just lost that area's version of the world heavyweight title to Jacques Rougeau Sr. He had one week earlier returned from a Japanese tour, where he was the leading star on tour. And he was 44 years old.

The heart attack only kept him down for a few months, and he returned, working a program in Detroit with The Sheik, which meant short matches that would allow him to rebuild his stamina, before getting back his NWF title from Rougeau.

At that point, George Scott, booking for Crockett, talked him into coming to Charlotte full time, a part of the country he had never appeared in. This was a huge risk at the time, for both men. Valentine was 45 years old by this point, and his health was questionable. He was a superstar nearly everywhere because fans had longer memories. Valentine's style worked great in St. Louis, where they had a retro promotion doing an older style without gimmicks and where serious believability was important. And it worked in Texas, because the main eventers had to be considered tough guys, as it was a hard-hitting brawlers territory.

But the Carolinas were different. It was a tag-team territory, used to fast-paced matches and high spots, such as they were in 1974. Because of the heart attack, Valentine had gotten into the best shape of his career, and for the first time, watched his diet. But his style, he wouldn't do high spots because of their lack of realism, particularly since he was put in main events quickly, totally contradicted

what had been done and what the fans had been educated to by the existing crew of main eventers and years of a more gimmick oriented product. The thought by many was that you can't go back in time, and Valentine's style was okay for St. Louis and he was a legend for decades in the places he was working, but his style wouldn't work in the Carolinas. Even worse, at first, fans were bored by Valentine's style, and crowds dwindled. But Scott's patience and confidence were virtues, as it turned out. Within a few months, business picked up to where it was good, and on occasion, very strong. Scott had been wrestling in Texas during one of the incarnations of the McDaniel program where the established tough heel finally faced a babyface tough enough to stand up to him and give him back in kind.

Soon the company, behind Valentine and McDaniel's long and brutal matches, was the hottest it had ever been. Valentine was still doing fly-ins in the big-money cities like St. Louis and Houston during this period. Valentine's strength as a believable ultra-stiff heel setting up McDaniel's just-as-stiff comebacks, with both guys having the reputation as guys who were willing to take five of the other guys' best shots to get in one of their own, and not cover up, made him an incredibly hot babyface. Even after Valentine went down in the plane crash, the territory stayed strong with McDaniel as a top face.

Terry Funk compared Valentine with Lou Thesz as the two wrestlers, when

OPPOSITE: Johnny Valentine grabs the pencil to get revenge on The Sheik. (Dr. Mike Lano)

Funk was breaking in during the '60s, who had the most presence both in the ring to the fans and out of the ring to the rest of the wrestlers. Even when they came into the dressing room, the wrestlers in the room were in awe of them.

"If you knew you had Valentine coming in, you could build a territory around him and know that he was going to make you money," said Dory Funk. "He was the best there ever was at selling a wrestling match that the people believed. He'd sell a headlock or an armlock for 15 minutes till the people bought it."

Dory Funk remembered if Valentine was a babyface when he was subtle heel champion, he could beat on him longer than anyone in the country, because fans had so much faith that Valentine would make a comeback and when he did he would kick so much ass that it would be worth the wait.

In Japan, where wrestling history is a big deal, Valentine's death was huge news. Valentine, always a headliner in that country, is generally credited as the man who made arguably the biggest wrestling star of this generation—Antonio Inoki. It was Valentine who put Inoki, at the time 23 years old, over in some famous matches in late 1966. Inoki had never beaten a foreign superstar anywhere near that calibre before those matches. Inoki made a booking deal with Sonny Myers of Kansas City, and the big coup was bringing in Valentine. Valentine was Inoki's favorite wrestler in the United States and had never been to Japan before he came as United States champion, holding the Toronto version of the title (which he actually maintained for about five years in that part of the world) at the time. Inoki beat Valentine in 31:56 via count out on October 12, 1966, at Tokyo Sumo Hall in the match generally credited with establishing Inoki as a superstar in Japan in one night.

They met twice more on that tour, a 60-minute draw for the U.S. title on October 25, 1966, before Inoki won two out of three falls in their most famous meeting, taking the title in the main event of an Osaka Baseball Stadium show on November 19, 1966. After the promotion folded, the two kept their feud going in the old IWE promotion, put together by Hiro Matsuda and Isao Yoshihara, which was able to get bigger name foreigners due to Matsuda making a booking deal with Eddie Graham. Inoki and Matsuda had won a version of the World tag-team titles in Memphis by this point in time, and went to a 60-minute draw on January 14, 1967, with Valentine and Graham before Inoki and Matsuda won a rematch four days later. On January 30, Inoki retained his U.S. title beating Valentine again.

Valentine appeared in late 1970 for JWP, with his most famous match coming on December 1, teaming with Gene Kiniski losing two of three falls to Baba and Inoki for their International tag team title. Valentine was also Baba's final opponent in 1972 as International heavyweight champion before Baba quit JWP and formed All Japan Pro Wrestling later that year.

OPPOSITE: Johnny Valentine with the Missouri State title belt. (Dr. Mike Lano)

OPPOSITE: After a plane crash ended his active career, Valentine tried his hand at TV announcing. (Dr. Mike Lano)

He never worked for either All Japan or New Japan Pro Wrestling, and after the last Baba match didn't return to Japan until long after his career was over. Inoki's wins over Valentine had so much impact at the time, that even though TPW went out of business shortly after the match, when Inoki went back the next year to the established JWA, he was so established with the win that he was put in the position directly below Giant Baba as the top star in the company, and it led to the famous Baba and Inoki tag-team era. This was one of the most successful box office periods in Japanese wrestling history, and Inoki became such a television ratings

draw in that period that he's remained a cultural icon to this day. Long after the rest of the wrestling world had forgotten him, Inoki brought Valentine back for what was likely his final public appearance at a major pro wrestling show on September 30, 1990, at a Yokohama Arena show when Inoki did his gimmick of the "Greatest 18 Club," which were mainly composed of Inoki's greatest ring rivals with the idea they had gotten together to create a championship that would represent what pro wrestling was and should be again, so to speak. While there were numerous famous wrestlers brought in for the show, including Lou

Thesz, Nick Bockwinkel, Tiger Jeet Singh, Johnny Powers, Inoki Billy Robinson, Willem Ruska, Hiro Matsuda, Stan Hansen and Andre the Giant, it was Valentine who stole the show.

"I only wrestled him once, in Houston," remembered Wayne Coleman (Billy Graham) of their match in 1975. "But when I was in Minnesota, Wahoo would tell me war stories about him and Valentine in Texas. I had all those stories in my mind when I was booked to wrestle him. The first thing I did when I met him was I said, 'Please go easy on me.' He laughed. After all those stories, I froze in fear waiting for the first shot. I didn't want those blood blisters on my chest. He was a stiff guy, but he didn't hurt me."

For whatever reason, Valentine did not have the same level of success in the Northeast that he had in most of the rest of the world, although he was a solid star and did headline Madison Square Garden on numerous occasions. He was also a frequent tag-team champion with the likes of Dr. Jerry Graham, Buddy Rogers, Cowboy Bob Ellis and later Antonio Pugliese (Tony Parisi). In the early years, he feuded with the likes of the legendary tag teams of that era when tag teams actually were dominant in the territory.

The reason he never had a Madison Square Garden program against Sammartino for the WWWF title appears more a timing issue than anything else. After Valentine turned on Pugliese, who was billed as Sammartino's cousin and often the stepping stone where heels would attack Pugliese to build to

Sammartino defending family and Italian honor, he left for Texas where he was having a strong run as the top heel in the hot territory feuding with Fritz Von Erich. He was flown back only to work a program in major cities like Pittsburgh and Baltimore for the title against Sammartino in the summer of 1966. MSG was closed that summer, and by the time it was reopened, he was working in Japan. He had been off television in the Northeast too long by the time he returned from Japan, so the heat had runs its course.

He clearly had his dark and strange side, like Kaufman. He was known as the king of ribs, but his ribs weren't always harmless pranks as the word would lend one to believe such as taking scissors and cutting up people's clothes while they were in the ring or doing strange things to arena rats while on the road. Many people in wrestling detested him. Far more were just scared of him, and others didn't like to work with him because he was too physically tough to work with because of the extremes he would go to to make matches seem real. He could be cruel and sadistic outside the ring, and because he didn't break character among most of the wrestlers, they didn't know how to take him. He thought the wrestling business wasn't for anyone but guys who were physically and mentally tough, and he tested out the newcomers. The crueler pranks often involved feces, whether on people's clothes or even while they were in the bathroom at a restaurant, would sneak it in their food.

CHAPTER 10

ROAD WARRIOR HAWK

WHEN MIKE HEGSTRAND was really living it up as Road Warrior Hawk in 1985, and a friend made a comment on how fast he was living, his response was, "I'll never live to see 40 anyway." Sometimes when you're 28, you think like that. Unfortunately for him, when he did make 40, and had already had his share of health problems, his thoughts were much different. After a heart attack in 2000, he found religion. He always had a Bible in his bag when he went on road trips. Unfortunately, he may have made the decision too late.

Hegstrand, who passed away at the age of 46, died in his sleep, probably shortly after going to bed on October 18, 2003, after spending most of the day packing to move the next day from his condo in Indian Shores, Florida, into his new house in Tampa. Perhaps steroids had nothing to do with his death, or even his health problems, but the combination of admitted heavy use, as well as heart problems, kidney problems and liver problems at a young age looks suspicious to say the least. During the '80s, when steroids were considered the big secret, from a public standpoint, Hegstrand always denied use. That's just how it was. In the '90s, when denying use would be tantamount to insulting people's intelligence, he admitted use, but also said that he didn't believe

OPPOSITE: Road Warrior Hawk in his trademark spiked outfit. (Dr. Mike Lano)

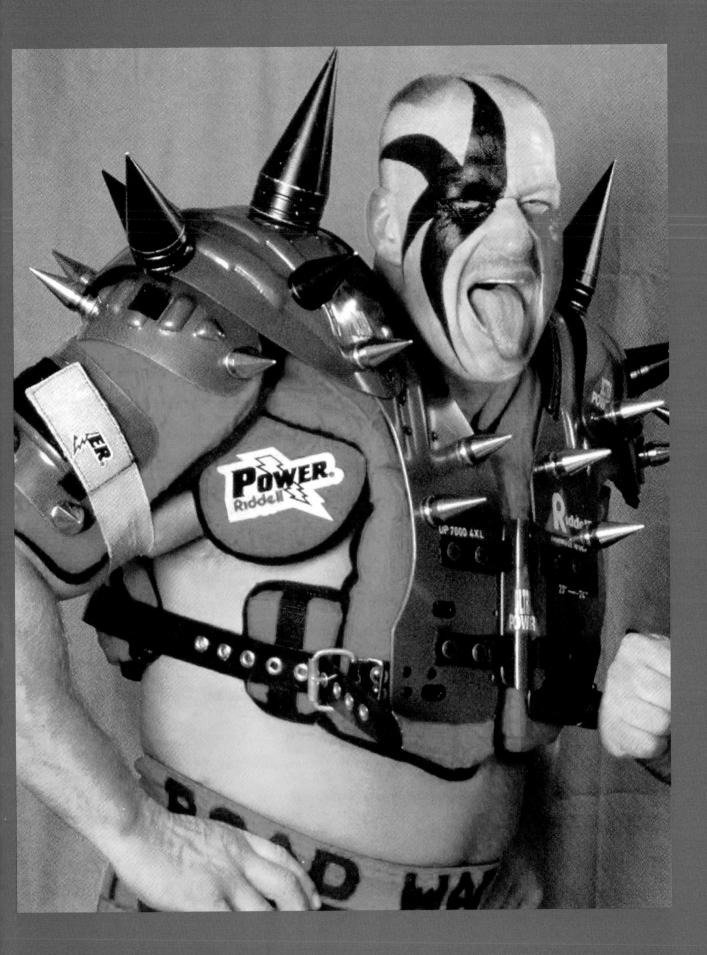

they were that dangerous and always denied any link to his health problems, even though friends as far back as 1985 remember a very different private belief.

But Hegstrand did enough other stuff that to blame steroids alone may very well be unfair, and will allow those who want to deny that it had anything to do with it enough ammunition. Certainly, Hawk was a more prolific user at his peak than most. But to believe they definitely had nothing to do with it could very well be the ultimate of all the pro wrestling deceptions.

Hawk was one of the biggest stars, most charismatic and highest paid wrestlers up to that point in history when he hit his peak during the late 1980s. The Road Warriors were so successful as a team that almost nobody argues their placing as, in their prime, the most successful tag team on a worldwide basis in the history of the industry. They had the look, the aura and a unique interview ability, with Animal screaming whatever points were supposed to be made, and yelling, "Tell 'em Hawk." Hawk would finish the promo with his twisted-sounding voice that every wrestling fan of the era tried to imitate, spewing catch phrases like, "We snack on danger, and dine on death," "That's good for us, very bad for you," and of course, "Oh, whatta rush!"

While many heavy steroid and recreational drug users will live long lives, many have their numbers called early. And now, out of the high school class of 1976 in his Minneapolis area school district, of the five men who became known pro wrestlers, Curt Hennig, Rick Rood (both of whom died from drug-related causes and had heart damage), Dean Peters (Brady Boone, who died in an auto accident while working as a ref for WCW in 1998) and Tom Zenk of Robbinsdale High, and Hegstrand of Patrick Henry High, only Zenk is alive today.

Hennig and Hegstrand go way back, all the way to a bowling alley in 1975 when the two had a fight as part of a rumble between Henry High and Robbinsdale High. Both claim they won that fight. Years later, when Hennig was in the AWA working with the Road Warriors, who were much bigger than he was at the time and selling almost nothing for him, he once joked on a television show that, "If I knew how big he was going to become, I never would have punched him."

That first meeting was very different from what would happen 25 years later. Then, after a serious heart attack, suffered after a match on August 5, 2000, in Derwent, Australia, on a tour for Superstars of Wrestling, when Hegstrand was in the hospital in far-off Australia, Hennig, who was on the tour, stayed with him in the country for ten more days until he was able to return to the States. Then when Hennig died, Hegstrand was freaked out about it, telling friends, "One day, he just didn't wake up," and appeared scared it would happen to him.

Hegstrand was a huge wrestling and Elvis fan growing up. Like all the Minneapolis-based guys who grew up in the gyms and wanted to be TV wrestlers, his hero in high school was Superstar Billy

Graham, whom he ended up being close friends with in the latter stages of his life. When Hegstrand was in his early 20s, he started training at the old Jesse Ventura Gym in Minneapolis, and approached Ventura about getting into pro wrestling.

Ventura told him flat out, "You'll never make it."

Hegstrand repeated that story many times, never losing the bitterness. But Ventura did tell Hegstrand about Eddie Sharkey.

AT THE TIME, Hegstrand was bouncing at a club called "Gramma B's," in North Minneapolis, alongside Rick Rood, Barry Darsow and Joe Laurinaitis. "It was the toughest joint in town," said Eddie Shyman, better known as Sharkey, a former area wrestler who had become disenchanted with the entire business. "One time Hawk beat up a guy in front so bad and left him on the pavement in bad shape. A few minutes later, in front of the bar, somebody got run over. An ambulance came after being called about the guy being run over, and when it got there, they picked up the guy Hawk beat up and left the guy who was run over, since he looked in worse shape."

Sharkey was a junior heavyweight prelim wrestler in the '60s. His wrestling career ended in the late '60s. Because of his size, he was not a major star, with his highest profile matches coming when World junior heavyweight champion Danny Hodge would come to the area, and Sharkey would put him over in title matches. Sharkey claimed that promoter Verne Gagne was hitting on his wife,

Dixie Jordan (the two are since divorced), who wrestled as Princess Little Cloud. Sharkey went to Gagne's Minneapolis Boxing and Wrestling Club office at the Dyckman Hotel in Minneapolis with a gun, and started firing shots everywhere. Needless to say, in a business where blackballing was common, shooting up a promoter's office was a spectacular way to end one's career.

During the '70s, Sharkey trained wrestlers in Minneapolis, which only infuriated Gagne more, since he believed only he had the right to promote wrestling or break people from the area into the business.

In 1982, pro wrestling was on fire in Minneapolis, largely due to the success of "Hulkamania," a few years before Vince McMahon claimed to have created it. The wrestlers in the AWA had a great lifestyle. Most of the stars were making $75,000 to low six figures, working 10-15 dates per month, with plenty of free time. Nick Bockwinkel turned down an opportunity for the NWA title because the lifestyle in the AWA was so good.

For big tough guys like Hegstrand, Rood, Laurinaitis and Darsow, it seemed like a fun way to make big money. Hegstrand wanted it the most of the four. They would have turned to Gagne, but he was only interested in teaching people who were worthy in his eyes, which meant either second-generation guys, or guys with real wrestling or major sports backgrounds. Sharkey told the guys he was through with wrestling and wasn't interested. Hegstrand went back to Ventura and told him Sharkey wasn't interested, and Ventura said, "Give him some money and he'll be interested."

He was right. After three months of training, Sharkey sent Hegstrand to Vancouver to work for Al Tomko as the German powerhouse Crusher Von Haig. He lasted only two weeks before he decided being away from home for no money wasn't really as much fun as he thought. He quit and returned to Minneapolis.

At about the same time Hegstrand quit, Alan "Ole Anderson" Rogowski, who was booking for Georgia Championship Wrestling, went out one night and saw the movie *The Road Warrior*. Sharkey had invited Anderson to Minneapolis to see his big students. Looking for a wrestler to play the role, Anderson picked Laurinaitis because he was the strongest looking of the four. Laurinaitis was put on Georgia Championship Wrestling, and at first, put over like a new monster on TV, but it was clear he was way too green. He was sent to Jim Crockett Promotions after about a week, and told to drop the gimmick because he needed ring time. He worked there as nondescript Joe Laurin, television jobber in motorcycle rider shorts. Within a few weeks, he also quit and came home.

Right after that, Anderson had taken over the promotion from Jim Barnett, blaming Barnett for getting the company deep in debt with his spending. Anderson cut back on big-name wrestlers and national stars, and was looking to go with cheaper headliners. In trying to work on the business end, the booking went to

hell. The company hadn't even had tag-team champions for about six months after The Wild Samoans, Afa and Sika left the territory. There was talk of a fictitious tournament for the national tag-team titles, which Anderson was grooming for Matt Borne and Arn Anderson (no relation to Ole, although the two looked alike and Anderson worked at various times as Ole's brother, cousin and nephew), managed by Paul Ellering. Ellering was a former powerlifting champion from Melrose, Minnesota, who could dead lift 745 pounds. But before he made as a wrestler, he blew out his knee badly, and his career looked to be over. He was a nice guy and was learning how to cut a decent promo, so Anderson gave him a job as a manager. Borne was arrested the week before they were going to announce them as new champions. Anderson flew back to Minnesota. Sharkey suggested Rood and Hegstrand, but when Anderson got there, he said, "You and you," pointing to Hegstrand and Laurinaitis, "You start this week." "You and you," pointing to Rood and Darsow. "You start in another week or two." Rood and Darsow did, but without nearly the same push, although both eventually made it as stars. For Hegstrand and Laurinaitis, Ole went back to the name The Road Warriors.

Hegstrand and Laurinaitis showed up at the old TBS studios on Techwood Drive on June 11, 1983, with Ellering as their manager, came out to the song "Iron Man" by Black Sabbath, and were announced as having just won the tournament for the belts. While at first, Ellering was put with them simply because Anderson liked Ellering and wanted to give him a job, Ellering had some financial acumen, and became the real-life manager of the guys as they started making big money almost immediately, and he invested it well. They bought into Zubaz early on, a company that manufactured stretch pants that became a part of late '80s culture as NFL players, wrestlers, big weightlifters and eventually the general public liked them because of how comfortable they were.

THEY WERE AN INSTANT SENSATION. Wrestling fans had never seen guys who looked as physically dangerous, and played the part, selling nothing, eating people alive, and working short, explosive bouts. Ellering called his heel stable, which also included Jake Roberts and King Kong Bundy, the "Legion of Doom," a moniker that stuck with the Road Warriors the rest of their career.

Bill Watts came up with the idea of the face paint. Anderson came up with the idea of doing the explosive squash matches and no selling, to hide how green they were. At the arena shows, he put them in top matches with his best workers, and always had the Road Warriors win in five minutes or less, even against all-time area legends like Mr. Wrestling I and II and Jack and Jerry Brisco. The idea, designed to protect fans from seeing how limited they were, worked to perfection, as fans simply thought they were so strong and powerful than even the legends of wrestling couldn't last five minutes with them. The wrestling magazines, which had major influence on the business in those days, fell in love with them, and they were on covers everywhere.

Between the spiked shoulder pads they wore to the ring, the face paint, the music, the ferocity, and Hawk's ability to flex his neck and snap dog collars, it was one of the great acts in wrestling history. When they worked with the top guys, they pioneered the no-sell spots. The top guys would give them what were finishing moves at the time, like suplexes and piledrivers, and they would pop right up. Hawk usually took the piledrivers because his traps were positively freaky, and were used as the gimmick as to why piledrivers were ineffective against him. They became the hottest act in the Georgia circuit, but that promotion was having its problems. But when they went for outside dates with other major offices around North America, they were big box office from their TBS squash matches and magazine covers.

The problems with the Road Warriors were evident quickly. Tommy Rich had been the top star on TBS a few years earlier. While he had burned out, he was still a major star. It was natural that he, with various partners, would face the Road Warriors on top. But when Rich's offense was ineffective against the new monsters, he was never thought of the same.

Nobody since Andre the Giant had made such an impact on wrestling that quickly. Their most frequent opponents were the Sawyer Brothers. To show how screwed up the booking was by this point, over the week after Thanksgiving of 1983, the Sawyer Brothers beat the Road Warriors every night of the week on a tour of Ohio and Michigan. Then, on TBS that Saturday, the Warriors came out with the belts and nothing was acknowledged. Then, the week after Christmas, they went to many of those same cities, and every night had the Sawyers win again. To make things confusing, on TBS that Saturday, the Sawyers came out with the belts, although they didn't acknowledge in which of the cities was the title change. Buzz Sawyer was fired, and without a change in the ring, the Warriors had the belts back on the January 28, 1984, television show.

The Georgia office was falling apart, and Vince McMahon Jr. purchased controlling interest in 1984. The Warriors were making good money working out dates in the various NWA groups while getting their exposure in Atlanta. It was clear Georgia was going to die, so they moved on, dropping the tag titles to Ron Garvin and Jerry Oates in Oates, home town of Columbus, Georgia on July 4, 1984. It was the last clean job they would do for years.

The AWA, on fire like never before six months earlier due to Hogan, was reeling. Hogan, Ventura, David Shults, Gene Okerlund, most of the production staff, and nearly everyone else were all leaving for greener pastures, mostly the national expansion of Vince McMahon's WWF. The Warriors were billed from Chicago, which was Gagne's top city, and they really were from Minneapolis, Gagne's home

city. They were already huge stars, so it was only natural they would be brought in to fill the void.

The deal wasn't so easy, as they showed their power. As a stipulation for coming in, they wanted Sharkey hired as a referee and trainer. Gagne agreed to it, and while business with people like the Warriors, Sgt. Slaughter, Jerry Blackwell and Bruiser Brody as headliners never reached the Hogan years, at first the territory was holding up fairly well.

Like with Hogan a few years earlier, Gagne booked them as heels, but the fans cheered them wildly. With Hogan, the crowd wouldn't boo his face opponents, but would cheer Hogan more, and Gagne did the turn almost immediately. Gagne had a harder time with the fans cheering the Warriors, and spent nearly a year searching for babyfaces who could get the fans cheers before finally giving up. The Warriors managed to turn Verne's babyfaces into impotent heels. Old-time legends like The Crusher, Baron Von Raschke and Dick the Bruiser, while long past their prime, were still seen as tough guys by fans who longed for time to stand still and remembered them as they were, and still paid to see them. As the Warriors beat The Crusher and The Baron for the belts right away, on August 25, 1984, in Las Vegas at the Showboat, and no-sold their offense, not running away from the Baron's feared claw (when Baron stuck up his hand, opponents sold it like a deadly Hogan finger point or Lawler pulling down the strap in Memphis), they became feeble old men, and their drawing power

ABOVE: The Road Warriors and Dusty Rhodes teamed together regularly in the late '80s. (Dr. Mike Lano)

that had lasted decades was no more. The same happened when they defended the title against the greatest team in AWA history, Nick Bockwinkel and Ray Stevens, treating both legends as old men Gagne's best babyface tag team, the High Flyers, consisting of Verne's 190-pound son Greg and partner Jim Brunzell, were booed as the Warriors no-sold for them, and rowdy fans laughed at the size difference. Ditto the father-and-son team of Curt and Larry Hennig, although the Warriors did sell for

Larry, who, even past 40 and with a bad neck, was respected by everyone as a 300+ pound tough guy, particularly since he knocked them around one night when they weren't selling for him and Jerry Blackwell.

The Fabulous Ones (Stan Lane and Steve Keirn), who were the hottest baby-face tag team in the country at one point, were brought in, and had a natural feud over the tag titles. Between getting booed out of the arenas and having to work with bigger, stronger guys who weren't all that cooperative and who got way too excited when the crowd went wild for them, which happened almost every night, The Fabs quit the promotion.

Reluctantly, Gagne turned the Warriors face, or more accurately, simply booked them as faces, bringing in another legendary team, The Fabulous Freebirds, as their foes. The feud did good business, although not as good as most had expected, and The Freebirds hated working in the Midwest, so it was short-lived. Probably their biggest and perhaps best AWA match was September 28, 1985, outdoors at Comiskey Park, where they beat Terry Gordy and Michael Hayes via DQ to keep their AWA tag team before 21,000 fans paying $280,000. While there were numerous big matches on the show, including Stan Hansen vs. Rick Martel for the AWA title, the house was clearly drawn by the Warriors-Freebirds and Ric Flair vs. Magnum T.A. for the NWA title.

At the same time, they were becoming instant legends in Japan. TV-Tokyo every Monday night at 8 p.m. in that era aired a show called *World Pro Wrestling*, airing an hour of tapes from all over North America, and on occasion, Mexico. The show focused itself on talent that had a name in Japan, and was built around the Road Warriors, Brody, Flair, The Von Erichs and The Freebirds. Because of the time slot on a network, the show had a huge audience and did high ratings for a few years. A lot of its weekly audience were young people who weren't necessari-ly fans of Japanese wrestling. To these new fans, the Warriors became the biggest stars on the show, because their matches, most-ly two-minute squashes and short arena matches against the bigger stars, were eas-ier to understand because it was simple power moves with fast pacing, no slow spots and no psychology. They looked the part of tough guys more than anyone else.

Understanding their popularity, Ellering negotiated a deal where he and both Hawk and Animal signed a $10,000 per-week contract with Giant Baba, which, in 1985, was as big a money con-tract as anyone was getting. Without even having wrestled there, they were making the kind of money that Brody, Stan Hansen, The Funks and Andre the Giant were making after years of making a name for themselves. Baba ran his first show after the opening of the current Sumo Hall, on March 9, 1985, with a major spectacular that sold out the 11,500-seat arena well in advance, headlined by the Road Warriors, who debuted the previous night, challenging Jumbo Tsuruta and Genichiro Tenryu for the International tag-team titles in a two-out-of-three fall match. Hawk destroyed Tsuruta to win the first fall. In the second fall they did a fluke double-pin deal where Tsuruta got his shoulder up and Hawk was pinned. He got right up and they attacked the ref for a DQ. Most hardcore fans realized the match wasn't any good, and the Warriors, when not doing squashes, weren't all that great. But they were so over at the time, the fans loved it anyway.

BABA QUICKLY FIGURED OUT how to use them. He would bring them in several times per year, but only for a few days at a time. He knew to keep their matches short and always put them over. As attractions, the Warriors drew sellout crowds almost every night in the smaller cities. Their second International tag title challenge, on June 2, 1986, at Budokan, this time against Choshu and Yoshiaki Yatsu, saw them DQ'd in 6:34. To the fans in Japan, the three top tag teams in the world were Choshu and Yatsu, Road Warriors and Tsuruta and Tenryu, who faced each other regularly in all combinations, usually with no winner.

Baba was also smart enough to never allow them to be exposed, and kept them out of his annual year-end tag-team tournaments because it would require at some point for them to do jobs. But it wasn't all smooth sailing. On an early tour, one of the Japanese prelim wrestlers tied one of them up in a wrestling hold, stopping the momentum of their one-sided explosive matches. They went to Baba afterward and told him to either send them home or they were going to go in the ring the next night and fight for real. Baba calmed them down, told his guys to work with them, and there were never any major problems.

While the AWA was their base, they were working basically every major show that any NWA promoters could put together. Probably the only place they didn't work was for World Class, because Fritz Von Erich likely recognized that at the time, Road Warriors vs. Von Erichs would be huge money, but the long-term

cost wouldn't be worth it. If the Road Warriors wouldn't sell enough for his kids, it would do more harm than good in the long run, and by that time, there was no way to get the Warriors to do a job for his kids. Plus Fritz noted at the time that while they would draw, they would also make it cool for local biker types to boo his sons, and he didn't want that happening.

Their biggest money program was probably in Crockett's territory, where the Warriors became American heroes against the hated Russians, which ironically consisted of fellow Minneapolis trainees Darsow, as Khrusher Kruschev, and Scott Simpson. Simpson, as Nikita Koloff, was billed as a bitter Russian Olympic team member who would have won a gold medal in both wrestling and weightlifting (if you're going to write fiction, you might as well go all the way), except Russia boycotted the 1984 Olympics because they were in Los Angeles. The Warriors and Russians went all over North America as strong underneath help on shows headlined by Flair, as Crockett gained strength, surpassing World Class, AWA and Mid South Wrestling as the alternative promotion for those who didn't like Vince McMahon.

In 1986, while in the AWA as faces, and with no heels left to conquer, they approached Brody. The dream feud at the time was Warriors vs. Brody and Stan Hansen (who was the AWA champion at the time). The Warriors were excited about the potential of such a feud (or a feud with Brody and protege John Nord), but Brody turned it down flat. He said that it wouldn't work. They didn't understand why. If they sold too much, their aura would be dead. But if they didn't sell for him, his aura would be dead. Brody worked with them at least once, most notably being on a major Don Owen show in Portland. Brody's partner may have been local star Rip Oliver, but whomever it was ended up doing the job.

They had dropped the AWA tag belts with a ton of interference, to Jimmy Garvin and Steve Regal on September 29, 1985, in St. Paul, largely to free them to work more dates for Crockett, as Crockett and Baba were paying better, and without a program with Brody, they had no opponents left. In 1986, with the territory hitting the skids, they left, and the AWA never recovered.

The Road Warriors vs. Russians was a strong program for much of 1985 and 1986, not just for Crockett, but all over North America for various NWA promoters. Seeing how popular it was, Rhodes, the Crockett booker, who was getting a little long in the tooth and fans were starting to turn on him, hooked himself with the Warriors. It made sense. After all, there were three Russians, even if Dusty didn't exactly look right standing next to the other two. Donning face paint, they feuded with the Russians over the NWA world six-man tag-team titles Rhodes created for his new program.

At the first annual Crockett Cup, an afternoon and evening show which saw 24 tag teams from all over the world come to New Orleans on April 19, 1986, on a show jointly promoted by Mid South Wrestling and Crockett, the Warriors were the big stars of the night. They went through Wahoo McDaniel and Mark Youngblood, the Midnight Express of Bobby Eaton and Dennis Condrey, and Ronnie Garvin and Magnum T.A. in the finals.

Because they were so hot an act, there was talk of breaking them up. Most felt Hawk had more potential as a single, and there was a thought at this time that Hawk could end up being, after Hulk Hogan, the hottest singles babyface in wrestling. But when tried out, the magic wasn't there. There was something missing when they tried both men out as singles on some big Crockett shows in 1986. During the 1986 Great America Bash tour, both got singles title matches with Flair. They did the classic Dusty finish, which was killing the company, where they would pin Flair after a ref bump and a second ref came in, to apparently win the title, and get the big pop, only to have it overturned when the first ref, usually Tommy Young, would note that before the pin, he saw the Road Warrior throw Flair over the top rope.

Flair vs. Hawk on July 1, 1986, in Philadelphia outdoors at Veterans Memorial Stadium drew a little over 10,000 fans, which was a slight disappointment, even if the $238,000 gate was an all-time record for the city. Flair's match with Animal eight days later at Riverfront Stadium in Cincinnati was a total disaster, only drawing 5,000. The idea of breaking them up was put on hold

"THEIR PERSONALITIES [WRESTLERS] WERE SO EXTREMELY MERCURIAL, OFF THE CHARTS AT TIMES, THE 'ROID RAGES WERE REALLY UNSTABLE."

—BILL WATTS

for several years after that. Flair and Hawk only had one more famous match, on January 24, 1988, at the Nassau Coliseum, where Flair saved his title by using a chair, which Hawk no-sold, for the DQ on a PPV debacle, destroyed by McMahon putting the first national Royal Rumble on free television head to head, and only drew 6,200 fans live.

Starrcade '86 was the biggest money non-WWF pro wrestling show in history up to that point, called *The Night of the Skywalkers*. It was built around the Road Warriors vs. Midnight Express in a scaffold match. The match was built up for months. But about a month before the match, while wrestling in Japan, Hawk suffered a broken ankle in a tag match when he was out of position and got his leg tangled as Choshu went to give him a back suplex. Of course, the injury was never acknowledged in the U.S., and Animal and Ellering worked arena dates for weeks that Hawk was advertised on.

However, broken ankle and all, he did go up the scaffold at the Omni in Atlanta, and took some risks of big falls, which drew the biggest live gate ($280,000) up to that point in the history of the city.

Hawk had a well-known temper and a short fuse. Bill Watts wrote that he was a huge drug abuser in those days, taking massive amounts of steroids, growth hormone, uppers and downers.

"Personality-wise, it was apparent," he said. "Their personalities were so extremely mercurial, off the charts at times, the 'roid rages were really unstable, and sometimes very difficult to deal with. Hawk once told me when he was shooting straight monkey hormones (at that time, shooting hormones from rhesus monkeys was an "in" thing among those in the physique community) that the first thing each morning when he awoke, he wanted to kill someone. What a life."

While there were wrestlers who shied away from fans, and others who loved the action as much as possible, the road managers with Crockett used to warn fans asking Hawk for autographs. Sometimes he'd oblige and be the nicest guy, but at the wrong time, he would hit fans just because he was wound so tight. In wrestling, he broke the nose of Ken Lucas, a veteran Southern star who was brought in to job for the Warriors at a Pro Wrestling USA taping. He didn't like Lucas taking some offense, and punched him in the nose, and it led to Lucas getting out of the business.

He was in many other somewhat famous skirmishes, the most publicized being with Randy Savage. The first took place in Japan, when Savage made either some comments about Hawk's wife, Dale, who Savage knew before she met Hawk (it was Hulk Hogan who introduced Hawk to his wife, who Hogan met when she was working at a gym), or they were arguing over a slice of pizza. Either way, Hawk decked Savage. Years later, Savage got retribution at a Kid Rock concert, throwing a sucker punch to Hawk and knocking him silly, although worse, Savage's girlfriend, Stephanie Bellars, and another woman beat the hell out of Dale. Hawk claimed Savage suckered him, didn't knock him out, but people got between them when he was going to retaliate, and he contemplated filing civil charges against them for the beating his wife took. He was once cut up by a knife-wielding Iranian at a Tokyo night club. Hawk also sucker punched Eddy Guerrero in Japan in 1994 when they were in an argument over who was the better tag team, the Hell

Raisers or Los Gringos Locos. Hawk was beaten up on the New Japan bus by Charles Skaggs (Too Cold Scorpio), which resulted in Skaggs, who was a prelim guy, losing his job, even though Hawk had goaded the fight, because in the hierarchy, prelim guys aren't supposed to be beating up superstars. Because of his size and ability to portray ferocity, most fans believed Hawk to be one of the toughest men in the business.

While he was no longer a major star, the image was ended when he suffered a broken nose in a Brawl-for-All match on television against Darren Drozdov in 1998 where both men looked like they were huge strong guys who didn't know the first thing about actual fighting.

His reputation in Japan for the most part was just the opposite.

"He was the nicest guy," said Fumi Saito, who was one of his best friends in the country. "He was like Terry Funk or Hulk Hogan. They were such big stars that they didn't need to push how big stars they were."

He loved to go out in Japan and socialize with people and party hard. Unlike most American wrestlers who don't really like Japan, it became almost a second home to him. In the '90s, when he went more frequently, he enjoyed it even more because it was largely devoid of the stressful politics of the U.S. companies.

Outside wrestling, his life was stormy until recent years, after his marriage to Dale. His first marriage, in the '80s, was a disaster. He dated numerous women in between, the most high profile being

"HE WAS THE NICEST GUY. HE WAS LIKE TERRY FUNK OR HULK HOGAN. THEY WERE SUCH BIG STARS THAT THEY DIDN'T NEED TO PUSH HOW BIG STARS THEY WERE."

—FRIEND FUMI SAITO ON HAWK

Eleanor Mondale, the daughter of the former Vice President Walter Mondale in the early '90s. In fact, Hawk and Walter Mondale socialized a decent amount, because when Hawk was working full-time for New Japan as half of the Hell Raisers, and Mondale was the U.S. Ambassador to Japan from 1993-97 during the Clinton Administration. He even dated Missy Hyatt in 1993, which caused him a lot of ribbing from wrestlers because of her reputation. He would defend her, and the double standard of the wrestlers, noting she'd been with a lot of guys, but he'd been with plenty of women, so what was the difference? But they had a nasty break up, not all that long before Hogan introduced him to his second wife.

In 1987, the Road Warriors lit Chicago on fire, pacing Crockett Promotions to seven straight sellouts at the UIC Pavilion in their adopted hometown. At the same time, they began negotiating with McMahon. Most consid-ered them Crockett's most valuable act, with the possible exception of Flair. They were also wrestling the best matches of their career, because they were mainly working with the best working heels in the business, like the Horsemen and Midnight Express. In order to keep them, Crockett made an unheard of offer at the time, offering both Hawk and Animal $500,000 per year, which was Japanese-level money at the time, plus Ellering got $275,000, even more unheard of since Ellering really wasn't a very good pro wrestling manager and the babyface manager role in wrestling was almost useless. Crockett was planning on making millions with quarterly PPV events, and when those events didn't generate the money he expected, he fell deeply into debt.

McMahon, who didn't offer them a guaranteed deal, didn't take losing the negotiations well, and created his own team in the image of the Warriors, called

Demolition, consisting of Bill Eadie and Darsow. Eventually, McMahon also signed the Powers of Pain, Warlord and Barbarian, a bigger, stronger, but less talented and far less charismatic version of the Road Warriors, who they were feuding with in Crockett Promotions. Although the Powers of Pain were never big draws with anyone else, they had a program that did surprisingly well stemming from a much-hyped bench-press contest, which saw them attack Animal when he was under 500 pounds. In the ensuing brawl, Animal legitimately suffered a broken orbital bone, and had to come back wearing a hockey mask. It was the first time anyone had seen the Road Warriors gain revenge for an injury, so it worked.

They were building to a series of scaffold matches, but Warlord and Barbarian opted out because they knew they were losing, and at their size, were afraid they'd blow out their knees taking those bumps every night, just as Jim Cornette had at the Night of the Skywalkers. So the Powers of Pain went to WWF, and at first, got huge pops when they showed up in Road Warrior outfits with the same haircuts and face paint, as fans who didn't follow Crockett thought it was the Warriors, just under a new name.

The Warriors were part of the crew that introduced the War Games on July 4, 1987, at the Omni, drawing 13,500 fans paying $250,000. The match had the Warriors and Nikita (now a babyface) and Rhodes and Ellering beating The Four Horsemen (Flair and Arn Anderson and Blanchard and Lex Luger) and manager J.J. Dillon in a match where Dillon legitimately destroyed his shoulder taking the Warriors' doomsday device finisher. While the move looked scary, with many of what appeared to be sick landings, with the exception of that move on Dillon, and a decade later, a broken neck to Mark Canterbury (Henry Godwinn), the move didn't result in a lot of serious injuries. The War Games success led to numerous sellouts around the U.S. with the Warriors on one side and the Horsemen on the other in War Games matches, which became the hottest new gimmick introduced in years. The Chicago sellout streak led to Starrcade being moved out of Greensboro, its traditional home, on November 26, 1987. The Warriors were to challenge Tully Blanchard and Arn Anderson for the elusive NWA tag titles they had yet to win. The fans were banking on a title change, and when they did another Dusty finish, it killed the city dead for the promotion, as Chicago never drew well for the company again for about ten years. Even the famous February 20, 1989, Flair-Ricky Steamboat title change, which included Warriors beating Williams and Kevin Sullivan in an NWA tag title defense, only drew 5,111 paid and had to be papered heavily to make the building look good for PPV.

The Warriors finally won the NWA International tag-team titles from Tsuruta and Tenryu in a one-fall match, via count

OPPOSITE: Road Warrior Hawk looks very different without his makeup and away from the ring. (Dr. Mike Lano)

out on March 12, 1987, at Budokan Hall. They retained it over Tsuruta and Hiroshi Wajima via countout on June 9, 1987, at Budokan Hall. On October 30, 1987, they went to a double countout, keeping the belts, against Choshu and Yatsu. To show the level of negotiations it took for them to drop the titles on June 10, 1988, at Budokan Hall in a match to unify the World and International tag belts as the double tag title that still exists today, consider this scenario. First, the night before the big match, the scheduled card was changed to a non-title match where World tag champs Tsuruta and Yatsu lost cleanly to the Warriors when Animal pinned Yatsu. Then, before 11,800 fans the next night on a show with no undercard, they used an Americanized finish in the unification match. Ref Joe Higuchi was knocked out of the ring by Hawk. A second ref came in as they double-teamed and pinned Tsuruta. However, Higuchi overruled the pin, and instead DQ'd the Warriors, and since titles in those days changed hands via DQ, that is how they lost the International tag titles.

They finally won the NWA belts on October 29, 1988, in New Orleans, from Bobby Eaton and Stan Lane. Blanchard and Anderson had recently quit the promotion and joined WWF, and Rhodes figured the Warriors could fill the void as the heel tag champs, and have a new program with Sting and Lex Luger, as well as give him new opponents. But while the orignial turn was almost flawlessly executed, just as before, the fans wouldn't boo the Warriors. Worse, the company was dying

at this point and on the verge of being sold, and Warriors vs. Sting and Luger was a disappointment at the gate. A deal was made with All Japan, where Tenryu would replace Rhodes on their six-man championship team, and the belts would be recognized and defended in both companies, legitimizing them as world titles. The deal ended up destroying the Crockett/All Japan relationship for good and put All Japan into its isolationist policy.

THE TURN WAS GIVEN UP on in February. At a live Clash of the Champions special in Cleveland on February 15, 1989, the Warriors and Tenryu were scheduled to face Sting and Junkyard Dog and Michael Hayes that would also be taped for airing on NTV in Japan. As they were doing a backstage interview with Sting's team, Kevin Sullivan locked them in the dressing room. The change was made because the TBS hierarchy had decreed Sting to be the new rising star and were scared to death of him getting booed on live television. Instead, heels Sullivan and Mike Rotunda and Steve Williams came out and had a match. Sting and company were eventually unlocked, although it took them forever to hit the ring, and the show ended. It was impossible for Giant Baba, who ran wrestling with the idea it was a legit sport, to explain a match not taking place because a dressing room door was locked, particularly one that was going to air on his television. He didn't want anything more to do with American promotions.

The team suffered its first pinfall loss in nearly four years on April 2, 1989, when it came time to drop the NWA tag titles to Williams and Rotunda on a live Clash in New Orleans. The finish was ref Teddy Long turning heel and refusing to count as the Warriors had the match won, and then fast-counting Hawk when Williams got him from behind. One of the most famous and scariest backstage episodes happened at that same time, between Williams and Hawk. Williams, who many considered the toughest guy in the business, and was a college football and college wrestling standout, was having trouble with Hawk's not selling. But the scary situation was alleviated with neither man getting hurt.

The next year, with their contracts expiring, business was down and they weren't nearly the hot acts they were in 1987. With six months left on their deal, Jim Herd, who was running WCW at the time, offered them $156,000 apiece for a new deal. To say they were insulted would be putting it mildly. Given the finances at the time and that their drawing power was no longer there, a pay cut was going to have to be necessary, although it would have been difficult for the Warriors to understand it at the time. Herd also wanted them to break up the team and start wrestling against each other, feeling it was the one angle left that hadn't been done. Feuding with each other sounded great without thinking, but with any serious thought, it was insane. Fans didn't want to see it, and they would kill their aura when one would job, which no doubt would have been Hawk, since he was almost always the one who would agree since

Animal had always had more problems with being asked to lose. Worse, Herd didn't realize what a disappointment it had been a few years earlier when they experimented with them in some singles matches.

They asked out of their contract early to go to WWF. Herd felt relieved to get out from the under the weight of the $1.275 million per-year deal for the act he inherited from Crockett. So it was off to WWF, which was the beginning of the end. First, McMahon didn't want Ellering. When Ellering saw he was getting in the way of making a deal, he stepped down voluntarily, and that ended the association. Second, because the two had trademarked the Road Warriors name as a wrestling team when they got hot, McMahon didn't want it. He instead called them the Legion of Doom. They were used to calling their own shots and being treated as something special. McMahon always put them over, but it was at the tag-team title level, so they didn't work with the top people, and didn't make the money they were used to making. But they were considered such a hot act that McMahon brought them in, and immediately put them over his creations, Demolition. But that so-called dream feud was disappointing at the gate.

While the team was very popular, it was not the hot act it had been a few years earlier in the NWA. Still, it was a pretty big deal when they beat the Nasty Boys in Madison Square Garden at SummerSlam of 1991, on August 26, to win the tag-team titles. The title loss, on February 7,

1992, to Ted DiBiase and IRS (Rotunda) in Denver, was quite strange. First, it was at a house show. Second, it was clearly not planned in advance, as on all the WWF television shows that aired the next weekend, it was never acknowledged. Third, the DiBiase and IRS tag team, later called Money Inc., had not even debuted on television. Fourth, none of the four knew when they got to the building the title was going to change hands, although it was known DiBiase and IRS were eventually going to beat them before Wrestlemania to win the belts to set up a return at the big show. LOD had to be promised that there would be no film of the match to agree to do the switch, so even though a crew was brought to the show, the switch didn't air on television.

Hawk was then informed that he had failed a steroid test (this was the period when the company was becoming vigilant in cracking down on drug usage) and was suspended for six weeks, which explains why all this happened the way it did. With him out during the Mania build up, the Warriors weren't even on the big show of the year. SummerSlam that year was at Wembley Stadium, and after beating Money Inc. (who had lost the belts, but were set to regain them and feud with the LOD over them), Hawk went wild and disappeared. He had already talked his way out of a second drug suspension, as Dr. Mauro DiPasquale informed him he had tested positive for steroids. Hawk then insisted to DiPasquale that he had been clean. DiPasquale then said he could look into Hawk's eyes and see he was

telling the truth, and rescinded the suspension. Hawk went AWOL in England and missed his flight back home, and basically at the same time both quit and was fired. Animal began teaming with Brian Adams as Crush, as the new LOD, but that didn't last long, as it didn't get over. Very soon after that, Animal suffered a broken tailbone, and claimed he was disabled, enabling him to collect a lucrative Lloyd's of London insurance policy.

Hawk had no interest in working for WCW, and Baba wasn't interested in taking him back. While he was with the WWF, the Road Warriors worked a couple of tours for Super World Sports, a company funded by billionaire Hachiro Tanaka, which was paying McMahon big money for WWF talent. Their biggest match was March 30, 1991, at the Tokyo Dome, when they, wrestling as the Road Warriors instead of LOD, beat Hogan and Tenryu via count out before 36,000 fans. Baba felt that since he had treated them so well, that they should have refused to come to Japan and work what he considered opposition to him.

Hawk called New Japan to see if they would be interested. Masa Saito, who was friends with Hawk dating back to the AWA days, broached an idea to him. Since Animal's career was supposedly over, he asked if they could try something different. The company had been wanting to push Kensuke Sasaki up to the level of Keiji Muto, Shinya Hashimoto and Masahiro Chono, the company's three big stars, but it wasn't clicking with the crowd. While Sasaki was shorter than Animal, he was a stocky powerhouse who could bench 450 and do almost all the same power moves. The concept was to create a new Road Warriors, with Sasaki as Power Warrior, the Japanese Road Warrior. The upside is that Hawk would work every tour in Japan and possibly become a national hero, as there hadn't been a full-time American and Japanese headliner tag team since Giant Baba and The Destroyer in the '70s. On November 23, 1992, before a sellout of 11,500 fans at Tokyo Sumo Hall, the New Road Warriors debuted, beating bookers Choshu and Hiroshi Hase in 3:02, in Road Warrior fashion, doing one power move after another on Hase, who was pinned by Sasaki after a powerslam, and went out on a stretcher to get the team over huge.

There was one big problem. Animal was furious. While the two were like brothers in the early days, and were best friends again later, at this point they were at odds. He complained long and loud about the pairing. Clearly he was not considering his retirement permanent. Hawk was able to pacify him. He agreed they wouldn't use the Road Warrior name, which Animal did partially own the rights to, and that when Animal returned, they would do an angle in New Japan where they would turn on Sasaki (which never happened).

ON THE NEXT TOUR, while Hawk was sitting at a bar in Japan, he started thinking about what would come after a Black Sabbath song. He decided it should be an Ozzy Osbourne solo song. While at a night club in Roppongi in downtown Tokyo, he heard the song "Hellraiser" by Osbourne, and decided that was it, and The Hell Raisers were born on December 14, 1992, when they won the IWGP tag team titles from Scott Norton and Tony Halme before a sellout 6,850 fans at Osaka Furitsu Gym. They had a show-stealing match with the Steiner Brothers on the January 4, 1993, show at the sold out Tokyo Dome (53,500), only with a flat double count out finish as the Steiners refused to do the job. They retained the belts with wins over Halme and Rambo from Austria (Rambo was put over because he had a singles feud with Hawk in Austria, which included a six-month run where Hawk held his only singles world title in Europe), Halme and Bobby Eaton, Chono and Hashimoto and Muto and Hashimoto.

"It was like if Van Halen had a Japanese star," said Saito. "Billy Robinson (in the late '60s) was the first foreigner who lived and worked full time in Japan as a babyface. Baba and Destroyer were the most famous Japanese/U.S. tag team. Hawk sold a lot, and always gave Kensuke the hot tag. That was the role he played with Animal, setting him up to look good. He really put Kensuke over like a superstar."

With the Steiners having signed with WWF, the Hell Raisers lost their main foreign opponents. In August, as part of the G-1 tournament, which had seven straight nights booked in Sumo Hall, one of the themes was "Stop the Hell Raisers," to see who could beat them for the titles and end their unbeaten streak. In one week, they retained their belts over Haku and The Barbarian, The Nasty Boys and Tenryu and Ashura Hara before losing on August 5, 1993, to the Jurassic Powers, Scott Norton and Hercules Hernandez, before 9,000 fans. Power was injured, leaving Hawk against both men. He was double-teamed for several minutes, worn down, and finally pinned by Norton in 13:36 after a powerslam. Even though he was double-teamed, the crowd was stunned seeing Hawk do a job, since he hadn't lost a clean fall in Japan in more than eight years. In a rematch three nights later, before a sellout of 11,500, Hawk got Hernandez's chain and used it on him, and was disqualified.

IN LATE SEPTEMBER, New Japan had its biggest non-Dome house show week in company history, paced by a sellout of 17,000 fans at Yokohama Arena on September 23, 1993, when Hogan and Great Muta beat the Hell Raisers when Hogan pinned Sasaki with an axe bomber in 15:29. Hogan had told Hawk he wanted to do a singles program with him (probably because he was the biggest star of their era that Hogan had never beaten), but it never materialized. The Hell Raisers beat the Jurassic Powers to regain the titles on January 4, 1994, at the Tokyo Dome before 48,000.

The Hell Raisers vs. Steiner Brothers feud restarted on May 1, 1994, at the Fukuoka Dome as the Steiners left WWF. Before an announced 53,500 at the Fukuoka Dome (10,000 less would likely be the accurate number), they handed the Steiners their first loss as a tag team ever in Japan when Scott was pinned after the doomsday device. A rematch saw Scott get pinned again on September 27, 1994, at Osaka Castle Hall in what was a disappointing match. They lost the titles to Muto and Hase on November 25, 1994, in Iwate when Muto pinned Hawk in 25:37 with a Frankensteiner.

Their last big match as a team was on September 20, 1995, when they lost to IWGP tag champs Hashimoto and Junji Hirata when Hawk was pinned by Hirata. Animal returned to Japan on April 29, 1996 teaming with Hawk and Power over The Steiners and Scott Norton at a sold-out Tokyo Dome on the Hashimoto vs. Nobuhiko Takada show.

The Road Warriors reformed, and worked WCW, WWF and New Japan, but they were clearly living off their reps. When Hawk had his chance in 1995 to work as a single in WCW, while Animal was injured and the Hell Raisers had largely run their course, he was not a success. His most memorable feud, and it wasn't all that memorable, was with Manabu Nakanishi, using the name Kurosawa, who supposedly broke his arm at the October 29, 1995, Halloween Havoc PPV with an armbar, allowing him to head back to Japan. His comeback for revenge was even more forgettable, as it went nowhere.

Their last national hurrah would have been when they had many big matches over the tag titles in WWF in 1997-98 challenging both Owen Hart and Davey Boy Smith as well as the New Age Outlaws for the WWF tag-team titles. They won the belts from the Godwinns and lost to the Outlaws, but the highlight of that run was the main event of one of the best shows the company ever put on, the July 6, 1997, Calgary Stampede PPV. As part of Team USA, with Ken Shamrock and Steve Austin and Goldust, they lost one of the company's most heated main events of the era to the Hart Foundation team of Bret and Owen Hart and Davey Boy Smith and Brian Pillman and Jim Neidhart.

The WWF put Drozdov into the group, as a three-man team, but the idea was to phase out Hawk, who was in bad shape by this time. But after getting rid of Hawk with the angle when he tried to commit suicide, and with him acting like he was loaded on television, the Animal and Droz team as LOD 2000 never got off the blocks, and Animal was dropped, as they were considered too hard to work with for their spot on the pecking order.

They bounced around indie groups in the U.S and Japan in recent years. Thanks to Alexander Otsuka, they were put over in a big way in the MMA world. On October 11, 1998, the Battlarts pro wrestler scored one of the great upsets in MMA history when he defeated Brazilian fighting legend Marco Ruas (largely due to Ruas gassing out) at the Tokyo Dome on the undercard of the second Rickson Gracie vs. Takada match. At the post-

match press conference, Otsuka said he was thrilled with the win, but that it wasn't as important to him as his upcoming match the Road Warriors in Battlarts' biggest show ever on November 23, 1998, at Sumo Hall. The foreign MMA reporters laughed, thinking Otsuka was telling a joke, but the Japanese reporters understood that Otsuka grew up as a wrestling fan in a world where MMA and Marco Ruas didn't exist, but the Road Warriors were larger than life. And even though he made a name for himself as a legit guy (which he's since lived down) and was ranked at the top in many top tens among heavyweights in the world, he was only too glad to play stooge for the Warriors' well-known powerhouse spots. But in their first Japan appearance in years, it was clear they weren't the same, and since that time have largely been viewed as a nostalgia act.

Their last high-profile match in Japan was May 2, 1999, on an All Japan show at the Tokyo Dome that drew 55,000 fans as a Memorial to Giant Baba. The Warriors teamed with Animal's brother, Johnny Ace, to beat Kenta Kobashi and Jun Akiyama and Hakushi in the semi-main event underneath the Mitsuharu Misawa Triple Crown title win over Vader. Several groups, including Superstars of Wrestling in Australia and the XWF, with designs on being major players in the U.S. scene, used them as their top tag team.

They were told they would be getting two try-out matches to get back in WWE,

"THERE IS NO WAY THAT I CAN RELATE TO YOU WHAT HAWK HAS MEANT TO ME. ALL I KNOW IS THAT HE IS IRREPLACEABLE."

—SUPERSTAR BILLY GRAHAM

but instead were given a tag title match on a live *Raw* with Rob Van Dam and Kane. They had the Warriors sell most of the way, but Hawk didn't earn many points by popping right up after laying down for Kane's choke slam, and the decision was made not to offer them a deal. They worked two shows for TNA, but were never used again. For the first time since 1990, they were reunited with Ellering (there was a tease on WWE television in the Russo swerve-happy era where Ellering was brought back for a week, but instead turned on them) in Oak Lawn, Illinois for what was billed as the 20th anniversary of the formation of the Road Warriors, an indie show that drew 1,064 fans. Of late they had worked mainly for WJ, where they even put over The Shane Twins in Japan. WJ booked with the idea of building new stars by having them beat established superstars like the Road Warriors, Tenryu and Choshu. Unfortunately, beating the Road Warriors didn't come close to make the Shanes, or anyone else, by that point.

It was not well known that Hawk at one point volunteered to donate a portion of his liver to Graham, who was very bitter about his death. Of course, his liver wasn't in good enough shape to donate. The two had become good friends in recent years. In fact, Graham's wife Valerie always referred to him as "Our Hawk."

"I won't dare ask the question why to anyone, for there is no pastor, priest, rabbi or holy man walking the face of this Earth that can answer that question," he wrote in a letter to Animal to be read at the funeral. "So I bitterly accept the fact that my dear friend is gone from my life. There is no way that I can relate to you what Hawk has meant to me. All I know is that he is irreplaceable."

ABOVE: Former UFC star Dan Severn wrestling Road Warrior Hawk. (Dr. Mike Lano)

CHAPTER 11
WAHOO
McDANIEL

PA ANNOUNCER AT SHEA STADIUM 1964-65: "Tackle by guess who?"

Tens of thousands screaming back: "Wa-hoo! Wa-hoo!"

With all his success on the football field before, and as a pro wrestler later, that was his best memory. McDaniel was an obscure football player with the Denver Broncos, earning about $12,000 per year, and doing a Native American gimmick as a pro wrestler in the off season when he was sent to the Jets as part of a nine-player trade.

Management told him they wanted him as their starting middle linebacker. When he got there, the New York Giants had just traded Sam Huff, a legendary middle linebacker, to the Washington Redskins. Using what he learned from pro wrestling, the first thing he did was talk about Huff's trade, saying, "It's a good thing. This town isn't big enough for Huff and me."

That would have been forgotten immediately had it not been that in the Jets season opener at Shea Stadium in 1964. He had probably his best game ever as a pro, with 23 tackles, in a 30-6 win over the Broncos. The Jets P.A. announcer, after several "Tackle by McDaniel" announcements, sometime in the second quarter said, "Tackle by Wahoo." The crowd popped huge. Later in the game he said, "Tackle by guess who?" The crowd responded, "Wa-hoo! Wa-hoo!"

And a star was born.

OPPOSITE: One of pro wrestling's most colorful characters was Ed "Wahoo" McDaniel. (Dr. Mike Lano)

Again, learning from his stint as a wrestler, the 235-pound McDaniel had his last name taken off his jersey after the game, and showed up the next week as the only player in the AFL with a nickname, "Wahoo," on his jersey. It made him an immediate football cult star. For the rest of the season, the highlight of Jets home games, was when McDaniel would make a tackle, and everyone would wait for the, "Tackle by guess who?"

When the season was over, McDaniel went back to Amarillo for his off-season education in the trade that ended up making him a star for far longer, pro wrestling, under Dory Funk Sr. But Vince McMahon Sr. knew an attraction was ready-made and brought McDaniel to Madison Square Garden on January 25, 1965, where he defeated Boris Malenko in a mid-card match.

He followed it up with third from the top wins over The Golden Terror and Dr. Jerry Graham on two straight sellout shows. Doing business the right way, just before going back to the Jets training camp, McDaniel put the hated Waldo Von Erich over clean. While he was a star in pro wrestling from that point forward, he never returned to New York as a member of the WWWF.

But he went just about everywhere else as a headliner, from all the major regional territories in the NWA, the AWA, Japan, Australia and Puerto Rico. Unlike most football players who turned wrestler, by the end of his career, football had almost turned into his secondary source of income as he became a major wrestling drawing card. And also unlike most, when his football career was over, his career as a wrestler was just starting to take off.

McDaniel is best remembered by wrestling fans in Texas and the old Mid-Atlantic states. After most of Texas had been in a box-office slump, it was McDaniel, Fritz Von Erich, and Johnny Valentine pounding the hell out of each other that brought it back to life, to where it was a territory where some of the top stars could earn $2,000 to $3,000 in a good week. In the Carolinas, several years later, it was the same formula, minus Von Erich.

But in no city was he bigger than Houston. Over a 12-month period for promoter Paul Boesch, in 1970 and 1971, McDaniel headlined eight shows challenging Dory Funk Jr. for the NWA world heavyweight championship, several of which went the full hour to a draw, and all to at or near capacity houses at the Sam Houston Coliseum. It was, and still is, the most successful long-term program in the history of wrestling in that city. Dory Funk Jr. had known the name Wahoo McDaniel long before becoming champion, and in fact, long before McDaniel came to Amarillo to get his Ph.D. in ring psychology from Dory's father.

"I was a freshman in high school," remembered Dory, "and I was reading the paper one morning about this football player from Midland who scored five touchdowns in a game against one of the powerhouse schools in Amarillo named Wahoo McDaniel."

The name Wahoo came long before pro wrestling. It came long before Edward McDaniel was born in 1938. It was actually the nickname of his father, Hugh McDaniel, known as "Big Wahoo," and was passed down to him as a child. And it stuck until his death. "Little Wahoo" was born in Bernice, Oklahoma, a hamlet so small it wasn't even listed on any maps when he was a child. His father, an oil-patch welder, moved his family four times before he was in sixth grade. At that point, they settled in Midland, Texas, where Wahoo's little league coach was former president George Bush.

He was forever getting in trouble, and channelling his energies into sports likely saved his life. At Midland High, he led the state in rushing and was a first-team all-state fullback in both 1954 and 1955. His off-the-field stories started at least that far back. In Wichita Falls, Texas, there is an annual high school all-star football game called the Oil Bowl, and the story of a fight before the 1955 game at the Midwestern College cafeteria between McDaniel and another all-state player who ended up as an Armed Forces Green Beret, was so wild it was a favorite of sports people in that city to recite before the big game for at least the next 30 years.

While recruiting high school football players was nothing like it is today, he was heavily pressured by big-money oil people to attend either Texas or Texas A&M. But he grew up in Southeastern Oklahoma and wanted to play for Bud Wilkinson at Oklahoma, who was probably the most respected coach in the country at the time,

in the midst of the team's legendary 47-game winning streak.

Because he was such a colorful personality, even in college, he was remembered as a better player than he really was. He lost his freshman year due to knee surgery and didn't play much as a sophomore. McDaniel was moved to tight end as a junior. He went both ways, starting most games, as a tight end and defensive back. In the season opener against West Virginia, he blitzed from his defensive back position to block a punt as well as caught an 86-yard touchdown pass from quarterback Bobby Boyd. The Sooners, then ranked No. 1 in the nation, won 47-14.

He also punted (39.5-yard average for the season) and kicked extra points.

During the off season, he got interested in wrestling after fooling around with it. He trained a lot with the wrestling team, a powerhouse squad that won the NCAA tournament in 1957 and placed third the next two years.

AT ONE POINT, a big argument was started between members of the football and wrestling team over which group of athletes trained harder. Bill Watts, who was on both teams, and was a big mouth even then, noted that wrestlers were so tough that coach Port Robertson had once run from Norman (the school's campus) to Chikasha (32 miles) to sweat off the necessary pounds to make weight in a match. McDaniel, who had no training as a distance runner, but was already known for his temper and never turning down a challenge, said he could do that. On a

"HE WAS A REAL INDIAN AND A GREAT TALKER.

HE AND DON EAGLE WOULD HAVE TO RANK AS THE

GREATEST INDIAN WRESTLERS OF ALL TIME, AND

SINCE HE LASTED SO MUCH LONGER, HE'D HAVE

TO BE THE GREATEST."

—JIM BARNETT

$100 bet, McDaniel ran the distance in six hours and became a local folk hero. He was then dared, double-or-nothing on the same bet, that he could drink a quart of motor oil. Most accounts, including his own, had him winning that bet as well. Other accounts had him passing out after drinking half a quart.

Between his drinking, training, and football, he didn't spend a lot of time in class. Punishment for missing class meant running the 62 rows of bleachers at the stadium 25 times. Before his junior year was over, he had already run the bleachers 700 times. As a senior, he was one of the stars of the team, starting both ways and being named second-team all-conference. He was also nearly suspended after being caught drinking after a game. His teammates rallied behind him because he was so popular to prevent him being kicked off the team.

He wanted to get into pro wrestling out of college, but never made the right connections. He ended up working for his father's welding shop in Midland when he wasn't playing football in 1960 and 1961. After the 1961 season, he was recommended by Oklahoma promoter Leroy McGuirk, who knew of his college football exploits and likely by Danny Hodge, who was McGuirk's top star, when Jim Barnett was looking for a new Native American star.

"He was quite an attraction," said Barnett. "We brought him to Australia and he drew very well. He was a real Indian and a great talker. He and Don Eagle would have to rank as the greatest Indian wrestlers of all time, and since he lasted so much longer, he'd have to be the greatest."

McDaniel's New York glory was short lived. But he was there for Joe

Namath's rookie season and made enough of an impression that whenever the name Wahoo would be brought up, Namath loved to tell the story about how some of the players, since Wahoo was always playing jokes on them, knew about a transvestite and somehow were at a bar and got Wahoo to pick up on him. The story was that when Wahoo found out, he beat the hell out of the guy and threw him down the stairs while the players couldn't stop laughing about it for the rest of their lives. Namath conceded in his autobiography that McDaniel scared him to death.

The Miami Dolphins were formed in 1966 and would be filled by an expansion draft of players left unprotected from the other AFL teams. Probably more as a public relations coup because he was a year removed from one of the league's hottest stars and the team was looking for an attention getter and drawing card, he became the first player drafted in the history of the Dolphins. He spent three seasons in Miami before bowing out of football. By this point, he was one of the better paid athletes in the country, earning $42,000 from football and making a similar amount in the off season wrestling.

The Dolphins' P.R. coup was also a coup for local promoter Eddie Graham. The Dolphins were the state's first major sports franchise, and Graham loved anything that would legitimize pro wrestling as real competition. The fact was that the Dolphins' first pick by this point was not just a pro wrestler, but a good one. He also had the Indian gimmick and national fame from New York. It was hardly a surprise that Graham tagged him with another ethnic draw, Jose Lothario, and quickly made them world tag-team champions the summer before his first year with the Dolphins. He wrestled mainly in Florida the next off season as well, always in the main events.

Les Thatcher was in the territory in late 1967, travelling in McDaniel's Cadillac, when McDaniel told him they were going to break the territory's record going the 200 miles from Tampa to Jacksonville. Keep in mind that there was no straight-shot expressway in those days, and they were going on a lot of small roads and through communities much of the way. McDaniel did the trip in two hours, 25 minutes.

"He told me when it was over, that he could have done it better," Thatcher said. "I told him he couldn't do it better with me in the car."

One night in Sarasota, he grabbed a chair, and a fan pulled the chair from him. Even though he had a hot temper, he knew not to break character, because it would make the match secondary, and went right back at his opponent. He went to pick up a chair again, and the fan grabbed it a second time. McDaniel nailed him with a punch, sending him flying five feet, and knocking the man unconscious.

He made an auspicious debut with the Dolphins. Early in his first season, on a trip to New York for a game against his former team, the police were waiting for him for a disturbing the peace warrant from when he lived there. The coaches had to pay a fine to get him released so he could play in the game. He was the most famous player on the team with his "Wahoo" jersey roaming the middle. He was starting middle linebacker and punter, but his punting average of 34.5 yards was among the worst in the league that season and he was replaced in that role the next season.

Jim Kiick and Larry Csonka, the starting backfield for the legendary 17-0 Dolphins Super Bowl winning team of a few years later, started their NFL careers in Miami when Wahoo was finishing his. In their autobiography, they devoted a chapter to the three wildest characters that played for the team. Naturally McDaniel was one of them. They marvelled during the summer when they did their two-a-day practices, that after the morning session, everyone would go their rooms to lay in bed, dead, having to rest up for the afternoon session. Everyone but McDaniel, who by this point was just about the oldest player on the team. He'd routinely play 18 holes of golf, and then return for the afternoon session.

His ending in Miami was a few games into the 1968 season. The night before a game in Denver, McDaniel had gotten into a fight after drinking. The police came, and he put a few of them out with a sleeper hold. Coach George Wilson got the news at 3:30 a.m. and had him traded to San Diego before dawn. As it turned out, the sleeper hold on police officers was his last move as an active pro football player.

He flew out to Hawaii for promoter Ed Francis and started as a full-time wrestler, but after his notoriety in New York and Florida, he nearly quit. He moved into a large apartment with Nick Bockwinkel and Tex McKenzie on Waikiki Beach.

"We took him out the first night to show him all the hot night spots," remembered Bockwinkel. "We took him out again the next night perusing. We were coming back after some action and he said, 'If I don't get laid in this town by tomorrow night, I'm leaving.'"

"He was so big in New York and Miami, so I said, 'You are such a chicken-shit. Maybe the mayor of Miami should have taken the time to tell the mayor of Honolulu that the great Wahoo McDaniel was coming and had him make a public announcement so the women would throw themselves at you.'"

The two nearly came to blows at the moment, right in the car, but cooler heads prevailed. They became friends, and Bockwinkel remembers some great parties at the apartment that year, not knowing at the time that their paths would frequently cross in the ring over the next 15 years.

His glory years in Houston were in the early '70s. His feud with Boris Malenko grew so hot that after a sellout at the Coliseum in a hair vs. hair match that Malenko lost, the two set an all-time city attendance record that stood for nearly two decades when they went to the Astrodome and McDaniel beat Malenko

OPPOSITE: Wahoo McDaniel was a known bleeder in the ring, and his constant companion was his Indian strap. (Dr. Mike Lano)

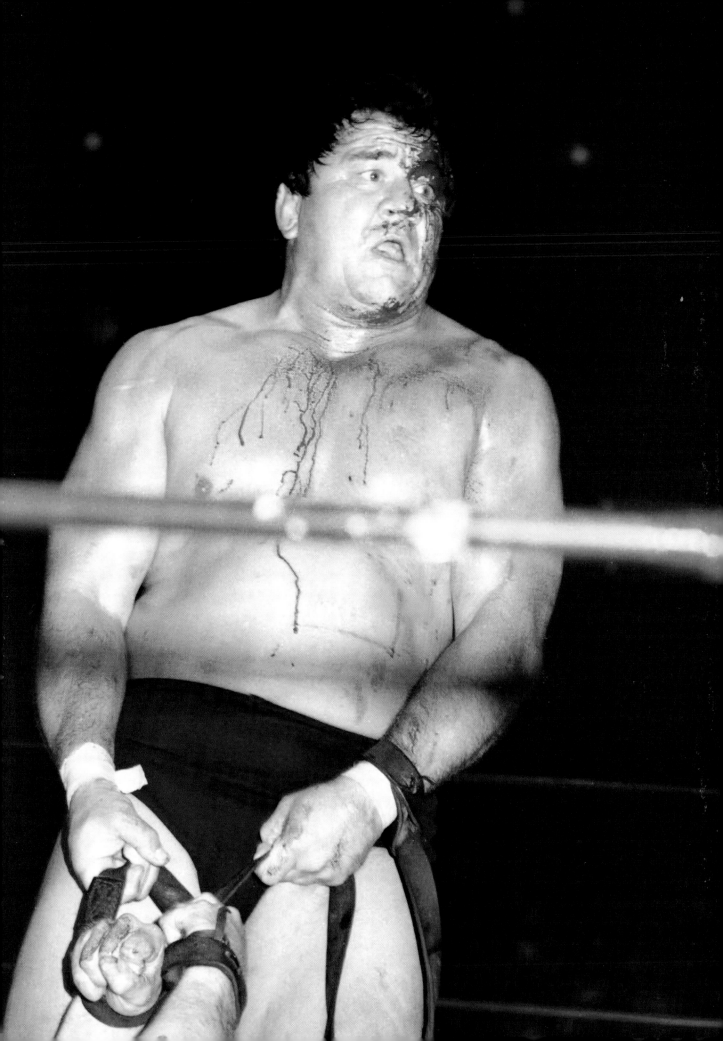

in a loser leaves town match. McDaniel was also responsible for making the most famous wrestling fan in America, former President George Bush, whose original connection with McDaniel was in Midland, Texas, as McDaniel's pony league baseball coach. When Boesch celebrated his 20th anniversary as a promoter, he looked back at his books and said the biggest drawing card ever in the city was McDaniel.

McDaniel used to joke about those days in Texas, making big payoffs most nights, particularly on Fridays, and losing them in bets on the golf course. While McDaniel was a star in two professional sports, as well as being highly competitive in fishing and hunting, many say his best sport, and without question his favorite sport, was actually golf. Unfortunately, his golfing buddy at the time whom he always bet with, was Lee Trevino, one of the greatest in the world at the time. McDaniel would spend day after day constantly trying, and failing, to beat him. Once, after missing a putt with a lot of money on the line in a bet with Trevino, McDaniel smashed his putter against a fence, and the club snapped back right into his mouth, splitting his lip open.

In 1973, he became good friends and a teacher to Ric Flair, a 270-pound chunky powerlifter who was an opening match wrestler in the AWA. In the ring, he set box office records in almost every city on that circuit for his feud with Superstar Billy Graham.

"I didn't know him that well other than the run we had together," remembered Graham. "I never socialized with him because of Verne Gagne's berserk kayfabe mentality. Maybe we met at a Christmas party for wrestlers once, but we couldn't be seen together.

"We had a lot of fun together wrestling. We did big business, especially with the strap matches (which for the next 15 years, was considered the McDaniel specialty match that he almost never lost). It was my first serious angle that turned into a major run, and we set box office records in almost every city in a major territory."

It was a simple angle. Graham spent weeks flexing his massive arms, and bragging that nobody could beat him at either arm wrestling or wrestling. Gagne had him plow through the prelim guys and embarrassing all of them.

Fans were ready for a star to take notice, and it was Wahoo. They had a TV arm wrestling match, and even though McDaniel didn't have the musculature, the people believed in him because of his rep, background and because he was such a confident talker. Plus, wrestling hype had exaggerated his football prowess to where he was a multi-time All-American in college and All-Pro in the AFL who left football by choice. As Graham was on the verge of losing, he turned the table over on McDaniel and left him a bloody mess.

Graham rarely talked to McDaniel during that run, only remembering McDaniel was always interested in the gate when he got to the building, and would make sure to let him know when they set another record.

"THOSE CHOPS WERE FEROCIOUS. THE STUFF HE, FLAIR AND VALENTINE DID WITH EACH OTHER, I HATED IT. THEY'D BEAT ON EACH OTHER UNTIL THEY WERE BLEEDING FROM THE CHEST."

—BILLY GRAHAM

"Out of all the guys I worked against on top, even Bruno and Dusty, he was the most giving as far as making me look good and letting me get heat on him. That man would sell for me. It made it easy for me."

McDaniel only liked selling when it was believable, because he had a tough-guy mentality coming from real sports, and used a physical style. But Graham was such a draw that McDaniel eased up on him. The feud was such a success that Gagne couldn't wait to shoot a second angle, leading to tag matches with McDaniel with various partners, usually The Crusher, facing Graham and Ivan Koloff.

"Those chops were ferocious," Graham said. "The stuff he, Flair and Valentine did with each other, I hated it. They'd beat on each other until they were bleeding from the chest. At first I'd try and block the chop with my shoulder because it hurt so bad. I'd tell him, "Don't hit me so hard. Don't worry, I'll sell it.'

Finally I talked him into where he'd just do the chop to the top of the head instead of the slap to the chest. I'd lay on the ground and flop around like a fish after the chop to the head. So I wasn't the recipient of very many of those chops. They hurt too much. But he never did anything in the ring maliciously. He just wanted it looking good and looking real. He made it easy to sell tickets. We sold out in some major blizzards."

Graham said he considered the business with McDaniel in the AWA as a career highlight. While he drew more money with Bruno Sammartino and others in the WWWF, those were always programs based around a title belt that was over.

"This, we just shot an angle. No belts, and it was just pride. He rates at the top for me. It was my first big angle after learning from Pat Patterson and Ray Stevens in Frisco."

McDaniel moved to Charlotte in early 1974 after Jim Crockett Jr. won a struggle for power from his brother-in-law, John Ringley, after his father passed away. Crockett had ambitions of making the Carolinas the biggest territory in the country, and if you consider popularity and quality of the product and creating new superstars over the period of several years, his territory deserved that honor for much of the next ten plus years. He brought in George Scott as a booker and tried to recapture the realism with McDaniel and Valentine that turned around Texas.

His first meeting with Crockett was legendary in itself. Crockett had a rule that when you wrestled on a major show, such as at the Greensboro Coliseum, the wrestlers, to show they were professionals, were supposed to come to the building in a suit and tie. McDaniel, showed up in nothing of the sort.

Crockett came up to him and told him his attire wasn't acceptable, and not knowing who he was, his first words to Scott were, "Who the f*** is this?" Scott then formally introduced him to his new boss.

Drawing money healed that problem quickly. A few months later, McDaniel got Flair into the Carolinas after Swede Hanson suffered a heart attack and they were looking for a new tag-team partner for Rip Hawk. Scott wanted Flair to copy Buddy Rogers. By early 1975, McDaniel and Paul Jones were headlining against Flair and Valentine. Their first major singles match was July 26, 1975 before 8,547 fans at the Greensboro Coliseum when McDaniel beat Flair for the Mid-Atlantic title. The program actually didn't get going strong, as both went in different directions at that point. Right as they were about to go back to it, Flair was put down for four months in the plane crash that ended Valentine's career on October 4, 1975.

When Flair returned, the feud with McDaniel heated up. Their first match back on February 2, 1976 drew 11,187 fans in Greensboro, and they packed almost all of the smaller buildings. They probably wrestled each other 180 times over the next year before the issue had run its course. During that period in Greensboro, where they wrestled 13 times out of 25 shows in either singles or tags, they never drew less than 7,000 fans. Business was similarly strong in every major Mid-Atlantic market that year. This was the program that established Flair as a major singles superstar and got people thinking about him as a potential future world champion. Their most famous match was October 16, 1976, at the Greensboro Coliseum where Flair regained the Mid-Atlantic title, putting up his hair, before 8,233 fans. In what was a legendary angle at the time, Flair threw him into a table, which broke, and used the table leg to the eye, resulting in heavy juice and supposedly 43 stitches. Wahoo's revenge led to another big business pickup throughout the circuit for the rest of

OPPOSITE: Wahoo McDaniel held championship belts all over the world. (Dr. Mike Lano)

the year, including 11,063 fans for the annual Thanksgiving show.

Although he worked most of the major territories at some point, and even briefly held a version of the world title for the IWE promotion in Japan and Texas, from that point forward he was mostly a Carolinas fixture.

Not that he was exclusive property. He worked in Georgia just as wrestling was becoming huge on the Superstation in 1979, feuding with The Masked Superstar over the Georgia title and teaming with Tommy Rich against Ole Anderson and Koloff for the tag-team titles.

He ended up leaving for Texas, where there was a major promotional shift, which later turned into a war. The Blanchards brought McDaniel in as their top babyface to feud with Tully, popping a struggling San Antonio-based territory. With his feud with Tully Blanchard, or tag matches where he'd take numerous partners like The Funks, Manny Fernandez or Ivan Putski to face the Dynamic Duo, Blanchard and Gino Hernandez, the latter team became one of the country's hottest heel tag-team commodities, business was at a high point. But McDaniel and Tully never got along outside the ring, and while the money was good, particularly in Houston, it was shortlived. In the summer of 1981, Wahoo went back to the Carolinas.

JUST BEFORE McDANIEL LEFT, on April 17, 1981, NWA champion Harley Race was scheduled to defend the title against Tony Atlas, a match so hot they sold out the 12,000-seat Coliseum. Just before the show was about to start, Boesch received a phone call from Race, still in Kansas City, saying he missed his flight. Boesch was so furious, and a world champion no-show in his mind was totally unacceptable for the public, so he announced before the show that he would no longer recognize Race as champion, and was doing a one-night tournament that night to create a champion. McDaniel was put over in the event, which included Atlas, Dory and Terry Funk, Hernandez, Putski, Scott Casey and Tank Patton, and was announced that night as the new world champion. The Race no-show was the straw that broke the camel's back, and Boesch quit the NWA.

However, Boesch decided against the idea of having a local world champion, because he felt it wasn't in the best interest of the business as a whole, plus he knew McDaniel was getting fed up with the situation in San Antonio and was ready to hit the trail. Instead, he began recognizing AWA champ Bockwinkel, which led to a strong Bockwinkel vs. McDaniel program.

He frequently worked for the AWA, during a period when he was something of Hulk Hogan's understudy. Hogan was the top star but was making his biggest money in Japan. While he was absent, McDaniel would be brought in against the top heels and frequently headlined that territory with Bockwinkel as well.

But it was the Carolinas where he spent most of his time. There was the angle where Greg Valentine, the son of his retired rival, broke his leg in 1977 (Wahoo actually toured Japan while selling the injury) that established Valentine as a major singles star. That angle was so successful the WWF used it a few years later with Valentine and Chief Jay Strongbow. Or his feuds with Sgt. Slaughter or Roddy Piper over the U.S. title, or when Piper brought in Abdullah the Butcher, and he and Butcher had their bloodbaths. In 1976, McDaniel endorsed Ricky Steamboat as his protégé, which led to the original Flair-Steamboat matches.

Then there was the 1984 heel turn with Tully Blanchard as his partner. This led to the final Flair-McDaniel major run, this time with Flair as the world champion and McDaniel as the old bitter heel as his career was winding down. He won the U.S. title from Ricky Steamboat in the match where he established his heel turn that had been hinted for weeks. The two had started a babyface program for the belt.

With the touring champ Flair as the top babyface in the territory, whenever he came home, his best drawing opponent was once again McDaniel. On a worldwide basis, McDaniel was Flair's most frequent opponent as champion from July 1984 through February 1985. At that point, McDaniel took a job as booker in Florida and would fly back to lose strap matches to Flair (since the NWA title was at stake) in the major Mid-Atlantic cities.

McDaniel, back as a babyface, became Flair's usual opponent when he would tour Florida, including the match at the first Battle of the Belts in Tampa. The two drew 10,000 fans on July 12,

1985 when Boesch brought McDaniel back to the Sam Houston Coliseum for a match in which they did the Dusty finish. He brought them back two weeks later with no DQ and drew another crowd of 8,000, with Flair using the ropes to score the pin.

There were plenty of wild stories from that period as well. McDaniel got so much heat turning on the Carolina fans, and had such a hot temper, that people remember him coming back from the ring, with fans swarming him to attack him, and him holding them off by literally sending people flying in every direction with his pro wrestling chops. One of wrestling's most famous bleeders, an incident on July 1, 1986 at Veterans Memorial Stadium in Philadelphia played a major role short term in that city's history.

Philadelphia had become a major bragging rights city. By this time, Vince McMahon had gone national, and while he had success with Hulk Hogan in most places, he could never draw in the Carolinas. While Crockett, who followed in his footsteps, was not drawing as well on a national basis, he was stronger in his territory, but in what was a black eye for McMahon at the time, beating him in Philadelphia, even with weaker television and using the secondary arena. The Philadelphia fans loved the blood and violence the Crockett product was giving them, and the NWA crowds kept increasing by the month while WWF levelled off.

Crockett got a little too ambitious with his success, booking baseball stadiums in major cities for a Great American

Bash tour. McDaniel was no longer a headliner, and by this point was back as a babyface working in the middle. The first show of the tour was in Philadelphia, and the promotion wanted to give the people blood. And they did. One wrestler after another. Obviously Wahoo would bleed, and he did. But with all his scar tissue after a quarter-century in the ring, his blade got lodged into his forehead and he couldn't get it out. James Bins, a member of the state athletic commission, seeing this and the pattern of the show, was horrified at the potential health hazards. He wanted the show stopped, which would have been disastrous. He was talked out of it, but only if they promised no more blood for the rest of the show, which made the show a disappointment for fans who had come to believe an NWA main event meant juice.

Bins got a ban on blading passed in the state. While the law remains on the books today making it illegal to blade in a pro wrestling match, it's a law that hasn't been enforced in years. But it was enforced for several years after that point, making Philadelphia the wrestling equivalent of a dry town. While Crockett did have some success in Philadelphia without bloody shows, it was a momentum shifter in the big war for that city.

Early in McDaniel's career, he came upon Watts, and showed him what he was making as a wrestler. To Watts, that was huge money, and he started in Indianapolis eight months after McDaniel. Watts joked about how the two were both drafted into the Armed Forces. Even though both were top wrestlers and two of the toughest guys in a tough man's profession, they failed the physical because the outdated military bodyweight charts listed them obese based on their height.

WHILE EVERYONE SPOKE HIGHLY of him when he was on their side, his temper was legendary, as were his fights outside the ring. There was the night in Atlanta in 1979 when someone called him a fake, and then went after him brandishing either a pipe or a baseball bat (depending upon whose version of the story one wants to believe). He told the guy to settle it outside, and was able to get a gun that he always carried, from his car. He punched the guy first, with the gun, which he thought wasn't loaded. It was, and the force of the blow knocking the man out, caused the weapon to discharge. The bullet went through Dick Slater's thigh. Luckily the bullet didn't go through any bone or muscle. McDaniel ended up paying all of Slater's medical bills and his salary for the six weeks he was out of action, while the Knoxville promotion, where Slater was the top star, had to rebook its territory.

In an incident that made headlines throughout North Carolina, Flair and McDaniel, who at this time were both babyfaces, after a match on August 2, 1981, where they were tag team partners against Gene Anderson and Piper, were out at the VIP Lounge, a new club in Charlotte. According to testimony in that case, Bill Newton, a 29-year-old lawyer went to Flair and complimented him at first, but then said he thought wrestling was fake. He claimed Flair slapped him in the face. Flair admitted slapping him three times and kicking his butt, but only after Newton had insulted him and spun him around. McDaniel jumped in, punching Newton, when others got involved. A woman jumped on McDaniel, and he just shrugged her off. She came back and punched him on his shoulder as hard as she could. It became a major case because the question was, even when attacked first, how much bodily injury should pro wrestlers be allowed to inflict in coming back in fights. Judge P.B. Beachum ended up giving McDaniel an assault conviction and a 30-day suspended sentence, plus fined him $81.

Dory Funk remembered a story in Lubbock when he, Ricky Romero and Wahoo were eating. A man told a Mexican joke, clearly directed at Romero. Wahoo jumped right into the guy's face and told him that he was also part Mexican and shut him up, noting Romero always loved McDaniel after that.

He also remembered being in a hotel when Valentine and McDaniel had legitimate heat and their worked feud suddenly became very real and even more violent than it appeared in the ring.

"I disappeared. I don't know how that one ended up."

Les Thatcher, who has been around wrestling for more than 40 years, recounts the most violent fight he ever saw in his life was in a small dressing room containing McDaniel, and a frequent ring rival, the 6-5, 275-pound Don Jardine, also known as The Masked Spoiler. The two were arguing over a finish at the TV studio in Raleigh, North Carolina.

"Like most of the time, Wahoo got the better of that one," Thatcher recalled, noting the floor ended up covered with blood, and all the wrestlers were afraid to break it up, until finally Swede Hanson stepped between them.

McDaniel's most famous lost fight may have been with his girlfriend at the time, Evelyn Stevens, a woman wrestler in Texas. As the story goes, McDaniel was fooling around on Stevens and was totally lit, when she showed up in the bar, caught him, knocked the bar stool from under him and put the boots to him.

McDaniel came to Japan for the first time in November 1973, to the IWE promotion, which had a working agreement with the AWA. Shozo "Strong" Kobayashi had gone undefeated in Japan for two and a half years as the promotion's International heavyweight champion, stopping virtually every top AWA name in the process. McDaniel was brought in with the idea of becoming his biggest foreign rival, winning the title on November 9, 1973 in Wakayama. He retained it with a 60-minute draw in a rematch five days later, before losing it at Korakuen Hall on November 30, 1973. McDaniel never returned to the promotion, since he left

"PEOPLE CAN BELIEVE WHAT THEY WANT.

BUT WHAT I EXPERIENCED IN THE RING WAS

AS TOUGH OR TOUGHER THAN ANYTHING I

ENCOUNTERED ON A FOOTBALL FIELD."

—WAHOO McDANIEL

the AWA for the Carolinas. When Gagne switched affiliation in 1976 to All Japan, he sent himself, Wahoo, Ray Stevens, Bruiser and Crusher. McDaniel, as a former IWE champ, got a main event on March 8, 1976, with Giant Baba for the PWF title in Nagoya, losing a three-fall match. But because the bout was a disappointment, McDaniel never became the same level star in Japan as he was in the U.S. He did have singles feuds with Abdullah the Butcher and Jumbo Tsuruta.

His final Japan tour was in early 1982, switching to New Japan, where he rekindled his feud with Butcher, and was only pinned once. It was in the final night of the tour in his only singles match ever with Antonio Inoki.

In 1994, he was brought in by the WWF as an extra for an angle on *Raw* where he and Chief Jay Strongbow presented an Indian headdress for Tatanka, with the idea the two legends were endorsing him as the new Native American pro wrestling star, leading to an angle McDaniel often did, where the heel then would ruin the ceremony. In his final years in the ring, he took on a tag team partner, billed as his son, Ricky McDaniel.

"People can believe what they want," McDaniel said in *Sports Illustrated*, "but what I experienced in the ring was as tough or tougher than anything I encountered on a football field." But he also noted that what he experienced outside the ring was tougher than either.

OPPOSITE: One of the biggest matches in wrestling of the '70s was matching Wahoo McDaniel vs. eight-time NWA champion Harley Race. (Dr. Mike Lano)

CHAPTER 12
TIM
WOODS

ALTHOUGH THE TIME HE SPENT as a full-time wrestler in Georgia was relatively short, the legend of Mr. Wrestling, Tim Woods, his greatest successes and most famous matches and feuds were in that state. It was one of those booking ideas that worked to perfection. Leo Garibaldi, the booker in Georgia in 1967, wanted to build the territory around the gimmick of Mr. Wrestling, who had achieved some notoriety when he turned into a drawing card for promoter Joe Dusek's Nebraska promotion.

Dusek came up with the concept of Mr. Wrestling in 1965, with the white trunks, white boots and all-white mask, as the technical wrestling marvel. A few years earlier Dusek had huge success with

another former college wrestler, Big Bill Miller, putting him under the mask as the black-clad Dr. X in 1959 and making him his local world champion. It led to the most successful long-term business period in the history of the city, as the top stars from around the country were brought in to end the winning streak, as well as reveal the identity of the monster heel.

With Mr. Wrestling, Dusek tried the opposite. That was revolutionary, as there had been few masked babyfaces who were major stars outside of Mexico. The gimmick was a success, as Mr. Wrestling became Dusek's biggest star, regularly drawing crowds of more than 4,000 fans per week at the Omaha City Auditorium. After going to a 60-minute draw with

OPPOSITE: As Mr. Wrestling, Tim Woods was the first superstar masked babyface in the United States. (Dr. Mike Lano)

AWA champion Mad Dog Vachon, it was announced that for the no-time-limit rematch, Mr. Wrestling would unmask before the match. Dusek even released that the mystery man had twice won the AAU and Big-10 championships. On January 7, 1966, he unmasked, announcing his name as Tim Woods, and won the match in 33:57 to become the AWA world heavyweight champion. Well, it wasn't all that it sounded. The title change was only recognized in Omaha, and Vachon left the city, belt in hand, to defend it everywhere else on the AWA circuit, where nobody would know of this title change. Two weeks later, Vachon returned, and they did a gimmick where Vachon got a lucky first fall win, and ran away for the rest of the match, which went 60 minutes, escaping with the belt back around his waist.

Woods, who took up pro wrestling rather late, starting at age 29 after a stellar amateur career, had just come in from Texas. He got his first push because promoter Dory Funk Sr. liked to use former amateur wrestlers for their credibility, and also because he thought it gave his sons and him more athletic credibility when they outwrestled them. Woods's major push came when he ended a long winning streak of Dory Funk Jr. in Amarillo in 1965 in a match to determine who would get a shot at NWA champion Lou Thesz the next week.

Known since the age of 11 as Tim Woodin (his real first name was George), he had it shortened to Woods for pro wrestling when he started as a prelim wrestler in the old WWWF territory in late 1962. In his rookie year, he mainly was known for losing television matches to the top heels in the territory and getting an occasional win. He worked low on the cards, working nine times in Madison Square Garden in 1963 before heading to Florida, where he worked most of 1964 before getting his first break in Texas. His Madison Square Garden record included prelim wins over Jose Quinones, Miguel Torres, Tony Nero and Magnificent Maurice, draws with Brute Bernard and Pat Barrett, losses to Johnny Barend (on the famous May 17 show where Bruno Sammartino won the WWWF title from Buddy Rogers) and Klondike Bill and a tag loss to the Kangaroos teaming with Cowboy Ron Reed, who later became one of his biggest rivals in the Southeast under the name Buddy Colt.

His background was very different than most wrestlers of the era. He grew up in a poor family, but was so good at wrestling that local coach Jimmy Miller was able to get him into Wyoming Seminary, a prep school in Pennsylvania where he started applying himself to academics like he did to wrestling. He credited that year with turning his life around.

His first match against the other great American masked wrestler of the era, Dick "Destroyer" Beyer was at an AAU meet in 1952; Woodin was already nationally ranked. Beyer was wrestling for Syracuse while Woodin was a high school senior. Beyer, a senior at the time, won the match, which Woodin denied to everyone in pro wrestling for most of the next 50 years.

HE WAS WELL SPOKEN and had a strong academic background in a business where most of its participants had neither. He had a degree in Agricultural Engineering from Cornell University, where he didn't wrestle collegiately but was a dominant force at the time in the AAU ranks. He went to Oklahoma State University on a wrestling scholarship, and in the 1957 season, he decided to make what may have been a foolhardy move, dropping down from 191 pounds to 177, largely so he could take a shot at unbeatable Dan Hodge of Oklahoma, then in his senior year. But Woodin had problems with coach Myron Roderick, who brought in the national champion from Iraq (Adnan Kaisey, who later became a pro star as Sheik Adnan Al Kaissie, General Adnan and Billy White Wolf), who he wanted to push ahead of Woodin for the same spot. Over Christmas break, before ever wrestling a match for the Cowboys, Woodin quit school and transferred to Michigan State.

It cost him the 1957 season and a shot at Hodge. But it was at Michigan State where he became known as a pinning master. At Michigan State, he got his second degree in mechanical engineering. But his most memorable match as an amateur was one of his two collegiate losses, in the finals of the 1958 NCAA tournament in Laramie, Wyoming. He had finished unbeaten in the regular season, capping it off by winning the Big-10 title at 177 pounds a few weeks earlier, pinning everyone in the tournament, finishing with Iowa's Gary Kurdelmeier. He breezed

through the NCAA tournament that he was heavily favored to win, until meeting, and losing, to Kurdelmeier in the finals on a close decision, which haunted him for decades. He went unbeaten in 1959, moving back to 191 pounds, but once again lost in the NCAA finals to Art Baker of Syracuse. Woodin did gain a measure of revenge in the semifinals by beating Kaisey, the man Roderick picked to take his spot, 8-2.

For months before Woods arrived in Georgia in 1967, Garibaldi would put his photo in the programs and talk about the mysterious man who had to hide his face because if the top stars knew who he was, they'd be afraid to face him. He was billed as a man who nobody could beat in a legitimate match. When he arrived, he went through opponents with a series of different finishing maneuvers that nobody in that part of the country had ever seen, from the "short suplex" (now known as a fisherman suplex), the three-quarter nelson pinning combination, the lateral guillotine pin from amateur wrestling, the O'Connor rolling reverse cradle, as well as his unique standing head cradle. The gimmick is he could pin you from any position, and from more different angles than anyone they had ever seen.

The standing head cradle became one of his long-term trademarks, largely because few wrestlers have ever copied it. It was basically a three-quarter nelson side roll from amateur wrestling where Mr. Wrestling would end up tying up his foe, while at the same time standing on his head. The move was actually legit, developed by accident in a collegiate match when he went for a side roll as a pinning combination, and in rolling and getting the pin, momentarily wound up standing on his head. It popped the crowd big so he brought it back when he got into pro wrestling.

To seal the deal, Garibaldi brought him in, and he'd go to the various weekly cities and use all these moves nobody had ever seen to win his matches, but also he would offer an open challenge of $1,000 to any fan who could last ten minutes with him. Taking on all comers was fraught with risks, and in the case of Woods, one of them reared its ugly head. The belief was that nobody except a top-flight amateur wrestler could hang with him for more than a minute anyway.

But at first it worked like a charm. Mr. Wrestling became the top babyface in Georgia and one of its biggest drawing cards in a long time. Wrestling was a very different beast in those days, as it's ridiculous today to think of any top pro, even those who are legitimately tough guys, doing unscripted matches with fans out of the crowd. There was little in the way of communication. There were wrestling magazines, and lots of fans were aware of them at every magazine counter. But even so, few were aware that Mr. Wrestling had already unmasked in Omaha more than a year earlier.

Probably the most famous incident from that time period wasn't scripted. In Columbus, Georgia, a group of thugs from across the border in Alabama started attending the matches, and the biggest of the guys, a notorious tough guy who knew that wrestling was fake, wanted to have at Mr. Wrestling. This had been building up, and people on both sides were looking for trouble. Several of the wrestlers brought guns to the building. Nobody was really concerned that the 280-pound street fighter, Arnold Spurling, would be able to handle Woods, even with about a 55-pound weight edge, because the only guys who could hang with him in legit wrestling were world-class-level guys. But everyone was concerned about what would happen with his buddies after he didn't.

IT ALL HAPPENED FAST. The wrestlers surrounded the ring, to make sure Spurling's buddies didn't attack. Even though they were supposed to wrestle, Spurling immediately sucker punched Mr. Wrestling, and unmasked him, throwing the mask into the crowd, which got things off on a bad foot, since no pro wrestlers had been able to unmask him for months. Woods had a dual problem, because he couldn't have his face exposed due to his gimmick, but putting his face in his hands to hide his identity would be disastrous in a street fight. Woods buried his face in his hands until his mask was given back to him. He put it on, and immediately took Spurling down. He started playing with him and embarrassing him as he blew him up, punishing and making fun of him instead of attempting to pin him and get it over with. Spurling twice managed to get to the ropes, but would be immediately taken down again. This quieted Spurling's friends immediately. As he took him down a third time, and went for a crossface to really punish him, Spurling bit one of Woods, fingers off at the first joint, and then spit it out. The remaining part of the finger bounced on the canvas, right in front of midget wrestler Lord Littlebrook. Instead of it being stopped, Woods proceeded to hurt the guy quickly and badly, kicking him hard in the face and back, before it was broken up. Woods was then rushed to the hospital where they attempted to sew the finger back on. It became infected, and he had numerous operations. But he was never able to regain use of it. It also largely ended the practice of wrestlers taking on all-comers from the audience (the only practitioners in major circuits after this were Adrian Adonis in Amarillo and perhaps Masa Saito in Georgia).

Which, of course, built to a major wrestling angle. It became well known throughout Georgia about what happened, and it only served to make Mr. Wrestling even more of a legend as the guy who put a major hurting on a cocky thug after the guy had both sucker punched him and later bitten his finger off. He went on a winning streak to culminate with a match with NWA world champion Gene Kiniski at the old Atlanta City Auditorium. The 5,100-seat arena was sold out immediately, reportedly the fastest sellout in the history of the city. After all, by this point the fans thought that nobody could beat Mr. Wrestling, and announcer Ed Capral reminded the fans that Atlanta had never seen an NWA world title change hands, so it was a

chance to be part of history. With Mr. Wrestling getting near falls using his pins from all angles, Kiniski became desperate, and started attacking the finger. Ultimately, the referee stopped the match, ruling that Mr. Wrestling needed medical attention because of fear he would lose the finger, even though he wanted to continue. The promotion was so excited about the success of the bout, and the heat coming off the finish, that they planned to take the rematch to Fulton County Stadium and hoped to set an all-time pro wrestling attendance record. However, after Woods got a $400 payoff for his quick sellout, he demanded more or he wouldn't do the stadium match. The promotion, perhaps foolishly at the time, didn't budge.

Perhaps, in hindsight, this could have been a career difference maker. If they had set a record crowd, Mr. Wrestling would have been viewed on a different level of star on a national basis. With his background as an amateur, and drawing a house of more than 15,000 people in that era in wrestling, had he unmasked, he probably would have been considered as a potential world champion when Kiniski went to the Alliance meeting in late 1968 and basically told the promoters to shove it. But Georgia was not an influential territory and he had never worked strong in St. Louis, the most important NWA city. So he wasn't even under consideration when the NWA Board of Directors, through heavy lobbying from Dory Funk Sr., got the title to his son.

Mr. Wrestling left for the Carolinas, which at the time was a tag-team territory. He joined up with Sammy Steamboat (Hawaiian wrestler Sam Mokuahi, who is the wrestler Ricky Steamboat was years later named after because Ricky was originally billed as Sammy's son when he got his first push), and occasionally huge Kentuckian Luke Brown, to feud with teams like Rip Hawk and Swede Hanson, Gene and Lars Anderson and Hiro Matsuda and Missouri Mauler. He had a memorable Christmas during this period, as they were doing one-night tournaments that week. With two tournaments to win, one in Greenville, SC and the other in Charlotte, he wrestled 11 matches that year on Christmas Day.

He then headed to the major Texas office out of Dallas, where the business was hot and the money was a lot better, feuding with and losing his mask in a match where Johnny Valentine put up his famous hair. As Tim Woods, he spent most of the rest of his stay as tag-team partner of George Scott, including a nine-month reign holding the American tag-team championship. He was brought into Florida with the mask in 1971 (he had worked the Florida territory in 1964 as Tim Woods before going to Amarillo), which was becoming a real hotbed at the time, in a new role, as an almost totally scientific heel. The storyline was that the two top contenders for NWA world champion Dory Funk Jr. were collegiate stars of such equal ability and records that the alliance couldn't decide who was the real top contender between the mysterious Mr. Wrestling, and Jack Brisco. Although the two had never wrestled, they knew each other well. Woods helped Oklahoma promoter Leroy McGuirk recruit Brisco, the 1965 NCAA champion at 191 pounds, who was wrestling for Roderick. Brisco had made it clear his life's goal was to be a pro wrestler like his heroes Thesz and Hodge, and Woods was one of the first guys to teach him the ropes.

The storyline started that they were both great wrestlers going after the same thing. Mr. Wrestling didn't wrestle as a heel, but made subtle heel remarks. Since Brisco was the local star and so popular, it was a unique kind of heel heat for the time period. Brisco would say he respected the man's ability but refused to call the masked man Mr. Wrestling. Wrestling was then offended by the slight. They started out doing supposed amateur wrestling matches, with local promoter and noted area amateur wrestling coach John Heath as referee. They would trade takedowns and keep the score close until Brisco would suddenly get a run of points and Mr. Wrestling would lose his temper. They then went to pro matches, and numerous time limit draws in scientific matches where Wrestling would elbow on the break or do something very subtle to turn heel late in the match as Brisco was outwrestling him, "proving nothing." Eventually, Brisco beat Mr. Wrestling with a figure four leglock, with the gimmick Wrestling tore knee ligaments from waiting so long before submitting to the move.

OPPOSITE: After removing his Mr. Wrestling mask, Tim Woods remained a major star in the Southeast, holding many championships. (Dr. Mike Lano)

Wrestling came back wearing a knee brace, with the gimmick that when Brisco would then apply the figure four, Mr. Wrestling wouldn't feel any pain and would be able to reverse it. At one point, he turned the knee brace around and used it as a foreign object to beat Brisco and heat up their issue. As a heel, he also feuded with a man under a hood as The Grappler, who later became his tag-team partner when he turned face, Johnny Walker. Eddie Graham had been grooming Brisco for years, so he eventually went over in the feud, ending by beating Mr. Wrestling for his mask to set up matches with Funk Jr.

As Tim Woods, he turned babyface and had memorable feuds with Buddy Colt, Bobby Shane, Dusty Rhodes, Valentine and Paul Jones over the different regional titles as well as several world title matches with Dory Funk Jr. over the next few years. His biggest win was in a tag match in 1972, teaming with Johnny Walker to beat Paul Jones and Dory Funk Jr. when he pinned Funk with a three-quarter nelson. This set up numerous title matches in Florida, several of which went to 60-minute draws and others of which were won by Funk Jr.

While he was a regular on the Florida circuit, amends were made in Georgia and he started appearing there once again, still with his mask, but largely only in Atlanta on Fridays since he was working the rest of the week in the major Florida cities. While fans in South Georgia, who could see Florida TV out of either Jacksonville or Tallahassee were aware Mr. Wrestling was

Tim Woods, but in the rest of the state, including the big markets like Atlanta, Columbus, Savannah and Macon, it was only the small percentage of fans who read wrestling magazines who would have known. He had one match with Funk, which ended with the Dusty finish, long before that finish became infamous in the '80s. It was a finish that was great the first time it was used in a territory. In Atlanta, Mr. Wrestling pinned Funk with a three-quarter nelson with a second ref counting the pin after a ref bump. As he celebrated the win, Dory Funk Sr., who was at ringside, grabbed the belt from him (Sr. grabbed the belt and pulled it so hard it legit cut up Woods's hand) and slugged him, which the original ref then saw, and called for a disqualification on Jr., which meant the title didn't change hands. A photo of the brief moment of him holding the NWA title was his prized possession in his wrestling collection. That match led to grudge matches, where Dory Sr., put up the bounty to bring in the top stars from around the country to either beat or injure him to remove him as a title contender, but naturally failed.

Then, one of the nastiest promotional wars ever broke out in Georgia. Ray Gunkel, an amateur star at Purdue, who was part owner of the promotion and one of the state's all time most popular wrestlers dating back to the mid-'50s, had returned to a full-time schedule as the company's top babyface after Mr. Wrestling left. Gunkel dropped dead of a heart attack in the dressing room after an August 1, 1972 match with Ox Baker in

Savannah at the age of 47. His widow, Ann, a much younger, stunning model, had gotten Georgia wrestling strong local television on Saturday nights on Ted Turner's WTCG (which ultimately changed the history of wrestling).

After Ray died, Ann was looking to have a major say in wrestling operations. The other owners of the territory, Paul Jones (not the famous wrestler of that time period but an aging wrestler from the '20s who had been a promoter in Atlanta as far back as anyone could remember), Lester Welch and Buddy Fuller (father of Ron and Robert Fuller, whose last name was really Welch) wanted to pretend she didn't exist, because wrestling was considered a man's business at the time. When she kept making noise, they decided to shut her up by figuratively screwing her. They closed down the company on paper, and then re-opened it under another name without her, basically screwing her out of her percentage.

Where they miscalculated was that Ray was extremely popular among almost everyone in the company, and even in a cutthroat business as wrestling, screwing his widow so shortly after he died left most of the company up in arms.

Suddenly, on Thanksgiving morning, the day of the company's biggest show of the year, an annual tag-team tournament that was an automatic sellout because it took place right after a major downtown celebration, Welch, Jones and Fuller opened up the morning paper, and saw a front-page story that virtually every employee and wrestler in their company was quitting and wouldn't be appearing on their show that night, and would be working for Gunkel in her new promotion, called All South Wrestling.

With the exception of mid-card babyface Bob Armstrong and a referee, everyone was gone. In a panic, the NWA, still a strong organization at the time, saved the day, sending in many of the biggest names from around the country to save the show, and the city. Gunkel even got all of the local promoters to side with her, except Fred Ward, who was on the fence.

Ward ran weekly shows in Macon and Columbus, the latter the company's second best market, and was given 20 percent of the restructured company to keep those markets on the NWA side, and Ward also for his loyalty was named vice president of the NWA.

ATLANTA TURNED INTO A WAR ZONE, with Gunkel running all the Georgia local favorites every Tuesday night, and the NWA running every Friday night, flying in national stars from other territories. Welch and Fuller went to Florida promoter Eddie Graham for help in rebuilding. Through her close friendship with Turner, Gunkel was able to get an hour of wrestling on WTCG, creating the weird situation in a very nasty war. Both shows were taped in the same TV studio on Saturday mornings (the studio that housed Crockett's tapings in the '80s) where wrestlers from both companies shared dressing rooms while their respective bosses wanted to kill each other.

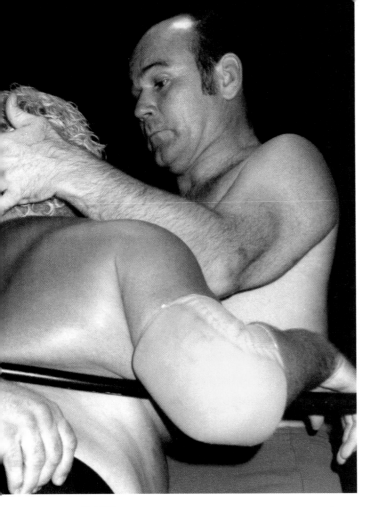

ABOVE: While Mr. Wrestling II was one of the biggest gate attractions of the late '70s, most fans would not have even recognized the man under the mask, Johnny "Rubberman" Walker. (Dr. Mike Lano)

In order to save the Georgia market for the NWA, the various NWA promoters from around the country immediately sent their top talent to Georgia to rebuild the circuit, and would send top talent in every Friday night and Saturday morning for TV studio tapings, to win the wrestling war. It was during this period that Gordon Solie was first brought in as announcer to replace Capral, who sided with Gunkel.

Graham didn't want a piece of the new company, but suggested to the owners to cut the key stars in for small per-centages of the company to keep them from jumping to the opposition. Mr. Wrestling at this point became more valuable than ever as the state's top draw in the middle of a war, so he was cut in for 2.5 percent of the new company. Also cut in were Bill Watts, who was brought in from Oklahoma to be the booker, Buddy Colt, who was the top heel in the South, and Jack Brisco, who was being groomed by the NWA to be its next world champion.

They did a program where the NWA turned Atlanta into the wrestling hotbed. Every Friday night one of the top ten contenders would come into Atlanta to try to knock Mr. Wrestling out of his supposed No. 1 contender slot. They did a string of sellouts the last three weeks with Mr. Wrestling beating Kiniski, Lou Thesz and Jack Brisco in succession to lead to the rematch with Dory Jr. That match had another unique finish, as Mr. Wrestling got a series of near falls and was continually weakening Funk Jr. with the sleeper. At the 47-minute mark, suddenly, in a planned spot, the ring broke as Wrestling hit a turnbuckle and he tumbled to the floor, "injured" and unable to continue. This was pushed on television as the fluke of all flukes. Everyone couldn't wait for Funk Jr. to return, and Atlanta finally would get its world title change.

The name Mr. Wrestling became so strong that the Amarillo circuit in 1972 created an imposter, played by noted shooter Gordon Nelson (the father of Steve Nelson). It was Nelson who went into California in 1973 under the name, working as a heel, mainly in Southern California, but working a few shots in Northern California. A few years later, in a forgettable part of Woods's career, he went into Northern California for six months, working mainly prelim and mid-card matches. He came in with the gimmick of going on television and demonstrating amateur wrestling moves. But in that part of the country, where amateur wrestling was never featured as an important part of pro wrestling as it was elsewhere, the segments, with his calm straightforward interview style came off as bland. It was an unsuccessful run. Because he was a legitimate national star, he was never asked to do jobs until he was on the way out, and even then only to the very top heels.

In his glory years, he started taking advantage of his wrestling popularity by opening up a restaurant in Atlanta as well as an electronics store called Mr. Audio, which he pushed based on a tag line as the place where Mr. Wrestling will get you the best deals on stereo equipment.

While Atlanta was doing well with the national stars, Columbus and Macon were struggling, because the national stars were working their home circuits during the week. With Woods as a regular in Florida and doing so well, Eddie Graham didn't want to give him up. They came up with the idea of Mr. Wrestling II, with the idea he could be the babyface headliner in the other two cities. Walker, his frequent tag partner in Florida, was chosen.

Walker was considered a great worker, who had been a major star in Tennessee for years before coming to Florida, because of his ability to work his amazing flexibility into matches. He was known at the time as Johnny "Rubberman" Walker. But by this point he was in his early 40s, hurt, being bald and haggard, and he looked even older, and because of that his career looked like it was just about over. They did an injury angle in Florida, where Valentine supposedly broke both arms of Walker by smashing them into the ringpost. Then they did an injury angle in Georgia, where Mr. Wrestling couldn't wrestle in the tournament to crown the new Georgia heavyweight champion that was vacant when Roberto Soto left with Gunkel, and he brought in Mr. Wrestling II, who was put over in the tournament and became an instant success.

It ended up being such a success that Wrestling II ended up becoming more popular and a bigger draw then the original. II differed from Mr. Wrestling in that he did fired-up interviews, as opposed to the articulate sports style, and did far more brawling, which was new for a pure babyface in Georgia, and made fiery comebacks, building to his "million-dollar kneelift" as a finisher and the catchy chants of , "2, 2, 2." Times were changing in Southern wrestling. The quiet babyface who was a technician and wrestled a legitimate-looking wrestling match on top like Mr. Wrestling, Brisco and Funk Jr. were losing ground to the wilder-talking, brawling babyfaces who got by more on charisma, squirming their bodies and dancing, like II, Wahoo McDaniel and Dusty Rhodes.

They went for the big payoff on June 1, 1973, at the new Omni in Atlanta, with Dory Funk Jr. vs. Mr. Wrestling. Two weeks earlier, they had run the first Omni wrestling show ever with Bill Watts beating Mr. Wrestling for the Georgia title in the main event, and garnered a ton of media attention by drawing 13,000 fans, the biggest crowd in the history of wrestling in the city. It was a strange result for the show leading up to Mr. Wrestling getting his return shot at Funk Jr.

Six days later in Kansas City, Harley Race ended Funk Jr.'s four-plus year reign as champion. Mr. Wrestling announced on television the Saturday before the show, that before the start of the match the next week at the Omni, he would unmask and reveal his identity. He had beaten Race before in Atlanta, and everyone expected a title change, as a lot of fans believed the NWA would never allow a masked man to hold the title, and his agreeing to unmask must have been a prelude to a title switch. A crowd of 16,000 sold out the building for the first time ever, for a match that went to a 60-minute draw with Race asleep from the sleeper at the bell.

A FEW MONTHS LATER, Welch and Fuller sold their stock in Georgia Championship Wrestling to Jim Barnett, who had been promoting for years and had turned Australia into one of the hottest wrestling markets in the world, and returned stateside after getting into tax problems overseas.

Watts, who never cared for Barnett, quit to become a booker in Florida. Jerry Jarrett came in as a booker, and his big angle was to do the unthinkable. Woods had left Florida since it was time to move on, and it was natural for him to come full time to rebuild Georgia, since he was established as a top draw along with being a minority owner. Jarrett had Mr. Wrestling II turned heel on Mr. Wrestling, claiming he had disgraced the sacred mask by taking it off. While most promoters weren't following what was going on outside their territories in those days, Atlanta was different because of the wrestling war. Vince McMahon Sr. even called Barnett to tell him what a terrible idea it was because two masked men feuding in the main event would never draw.

They had a major and successful feud, including a period of 12 straight sellouts in the City Auditorium, which is credited with winning the promotional war for the NWA. The feud climaxed with II winning a mask vs. hair match through usage of a foreign object, and Woods had his head shaved. Barnett bought out Gunkel, ending the promotional war, and giving Georgia wrestling a full-time schedule as they were able to get into the cities Gunkel controlled. Jarrett returned to Tennessee since his success in Atlanta caused local promoter Nick Gulas to give him the book. Jarrett years later ended up starting and winning a promotional war with Gulas to take the territory. And Georgia Championship Wrestling got two hours every Saturday night on WTCG in Atlanta.

Wrestling I and II got back together as babyfaces when II saved him after an attack by the Anderson Brothers. When II turned back, Wrestling I, as he was becoming known, had passed his drawing power peak, and became the secondary member of the team. Business was hot in Georgia, and television ratings in the local markets were through the roof with the two masked men as the top regular faces and the big stars from around the country coming in for the major events, but it was during this period that Wrestling II clearly became the man. Many would have had bitterness over a guy coming in with the gimmick you've established, and ultimately taking your spot as the king of the territory. If that were the case, Woods sure hid it well. Woods and Walker personally remained close friends, and in recent years even shared rooms together when attending the same old-timers functions.

Mr. Wrestling made his first tour of Japan for the 1974 Champion Carnival under the mask, vowing to unmask if anyone could beat him. To get him over as an American technical wrestling marvel, he was put over Japanese Olympians Thunder Sugiyama (who passed away one week earlier) and Jumbo Tsuruta (who rarely lost in those days) before losing in the finals, and unmasking, against Giant Baba on May 14, 1974, in Maebashi. He was supposed to be the top foreigner on the tour, but he didn't get over as they had hoped for, despite his big wins, as fans were more into the wild bleeders on the tour like Abdullah the Butcher, King Curtis Iaukea and Mark Lewin. Because of his success the year before, he was brought back for the 1975 Carnival and made the final four, losing in round-robin competition to eventual winner Baba, Kiniski and The Destroyer. He was probably also the only active pro wrestler ever to get a sports announcing gig on network television, when he was brought in as a color commentator by *ABC's Wide World of Sports* when they televised an international freestyle wrestling meet in 1974.

He also raced drag cars and motorcycles, and played the piano and saxophone, including as a kid, appearing in a band that played on the popular network *Ted Mack Amateur Hour show*.

The remainder of his career went back and forth between Georgia, and his new full-time home in Charlotte. His Carolinas stint didn't start out that great, with the famous plane crash. In a sense, the crash could have been the destruction of the territory and its lessons of what could have happened led to promoters who hadn't done so previously, and strengthened the resolve of those who had already, banning faces and heels from traveling together.

In a story that will be covered, coincidentally, on the 12/14 edition of *WWE Confidential*, on October 4, 1975,

Carolinas promoter Jim Crockett Jr. and both sets of main eventers for a show that night in Wilmington, North Carolina, at Legion Stadium, which consisted of the territory's two top programs at the time, Wahoo McDaniel vs. Ric Flair for the Mid-Atlantic title and Valentine vs. Woods for the U.S. title, were scheduled to fly in a six-seat Cessna 310 at 5:30 p.m. However, late that day, McDaniel decided to drive to the show, so Bob Bruggers took his place on the plane, and Jim Crockett Jr. at the last minute sent brother David to take his place at the show. To this day, Flair believes had McDaniel not canceled the trip, that the territory would have collapsed for a long time with the revelation that he and McDaniel, who were bitter storyline rivals, were traveling together.

Pilot Joseph Michael Farkas had dumped fuel before taking off because of the weight of the passengers, and the plane ran out of fuel. Farkas, who passed away in the crash that ended the careers of both Valentine and Bruggers and left Valentine crippled, radioed the control tower that his engines had stopped when he was about a mile from the Wilmington Airport.

The plane hit several tree tops on the way down and the wing collapsed, hitting a utility pole before the plane crashed about a half-mile short of its destination on a railroad embankment near the state prison. Flair ended up with a broken back in the crash, although later wrestling reports that he was told he would never wrestle again were exaggerated as he was told shortly after the crash he'd be able to return. Flair was back in the ring four months later.

Woods left the hospital the next day against doctors' orders in order to avoid word getting out that he was George Burrell Woodin and was traveling with Valentine and Flair, and showed up on the next television tapings, despite being barely able to move, to quell rumors that had been started. It probably cost him money in the insurance settlement, but things were very different in those days, as today they all would have had a huge settlement. Farkas, as it turned out, had no insurance, but there was a settlement with Valentine and Bruggers each getting $70,000 and Flair and Crockett getting $38,000. Because Woods left the hospital so quickly, he ended up getting little or nothing.

He was not the star of the circuit, wrestling both with and without the mask, but was always kept in a strong position and worked with the top heels. His identity was not made a mystery, as he was Tim "Mr. Wrestling" Woods, wrestling both with or without the mask. The feeling was that the South Carolina fans, who got the Georgia show from some border city stations, knew his story already. He worked with all the major heels, from Valentine to Mulligan to Flair to Piper, to the Andersons in tag matches. He lost mask vs. title matches to Valentine and later, lost his mask and the U.S. title on April 9, 1978, to Flair, in a match where Flair put up his hair. He would still make runs in Georgia, spending much of

1977 there for the Wrestling I and II vs. Andersons programs over both the World and Georgia tag-team titles.

One of the stories more famous among the wrestlers was the night he and Wahoo McDaniel looked like they were going to go at it. Because the two were babyfaces for most of their respective careers, even though they were headliners and contemporaries, they only wrestled each other twice, once in a tournament in the Carolinas and the second time in a tag match as part of the Real World Tag League tournament in Japan in 1979. In the first meeting, Woods, who would later praise McDaniel as being the best natural athlete he competed against, wasn't in the mood to take McDaniel's chops, having several matches to wrestle in one day. McDaniel said the chops were his trademark and he had to do them. Woods ended up, before going out to the ring, taking his kneepads off and taping them to his chest, and went to the ring wearing a shirt. McDaniel chopped the kneepads. In the dressing room after the match, the quick-tempered McDaniel was boiling. All the wrestlers were staring because McDaniel was known for not hesitating to fight, and Woods had his own reputation. But it never got past the screaming.

When Georgia Championship Wrestling started gaining national exposure with the advent of cable in 1979, Mr. Wrestling I, who was 45 by this time, was in the role of the former superstar who occasionally wrestled. He would do television matches, frequently pushed local amateur events, and do in-ring clinics demonstrating the differences between amateur and legitimate pro moves in the ring. When Wrestling II would do an occasional injury angle or take an out date, he would be plugged into his spot, such as the feud with Masked Superstar including losing a mask vs. mask match. His last major singles program was in 1980, challenging U.S. champion Jimmy Snuka. He and Mr. Wrestling II held their final tag-team title reign that year, and were the team that put over The Fabulous Freebirds when they first arrived in Georgia for the belts. He wrestled sparingly from that point on, and was the rare headliner who was never relegated to jobber or prelim status. His final pro match was on August 14, 1983, in the main event at the Omni, teaming with Wrestling II for the last time, as a legendary team put back together to put over and give legitimacy to the company's new tag-team creation, the Road Warriors.

UNLIKE MANY OF HIS CONTEMPORARIES, who would complain at functions like the Cauliflower Alley Club meetings about how bad wrestling had gotten, he was matter of fact about it and continued to follow it, while remaining close with many of his contemporaries. "'It's business,' he would say," said longtime friend Bill Murdock of Asheville. "He'd say it's different, and not necessarily better or worse. He had no problem with the changes and would say he was just glad to see the current stars were doing so well. He would enjoy himself when he attended WWF shows."

CHAPTER 13
TERRY GORDY

IF THERE ARE LESSONS TO BE LEARNED of the tragic life of Terry Gordy, it may be the typical lessons hammered home so many times in this industry. Too much partying works against you in the long run, even when you have a natural aptitude for the industry. While we marvel at just how talented Gordy really was, main eventing the Superdome at the age of 18 and a national television star a year later, there is some question about an industry where someone has their first pro match at 13 and is on the road working full time in a major promotion before the age of 16.

Gordy passed away at the age of 40 of a heart attack caused by a blood clot. His lasting legacy in wrestling seems to be that no heavyweight wrestler of the modern era was as good in the ring so young and had so much success at an early age in so many different places.

Although his biggest money years working for All Japan followed, Gordy's career in the ring seemed to peak at the age of 25. At that point he held the Universal Wrestling Federation championship, the world title of the No. 3 promotion in the country, headed by Bill Watts. He was the in-ring cornerstone of the Fabulous Freebirds, perhaps the most charismatic trio in pro wrestling history. It was during that period that he blew out his knee, the first of many knee injuries he was to suffer. Rather than take off the six months it would have required to fix the knee ligament problems, he bandaged it

OPPOSITE: Terry Gordy was one of the best big men in wrestling history, even while just a teenager. (Dr. Mike Lano)

up, and kept working hard, night after night, in title matches that on occasion lasted as long as one hour. Although he remained a top performer, the knee never fully recovered and remained a weakness for the rest of his career.

In Japan, Gordy was always a key part of the main event mix, generally considered the most talented of the big foreigners. It was Gordy who was called on to work so many big matches for the company.

"Lots of people have to bump it up (their personalities) for television," said Michael Hayes. "We had to tone it down. We probably owe a lot of apologies to a lot of people. We were taught that in pro wrestling, you live your gimmick.

"I'm really proud of what we accomplished, because it's something they can never take away from us," he said. "You wouldn't believe how much trouble we had as teenagers in a man's business."

GORDY WAS THE KIND OF GUY those in wrestling would tell wild stories about, but in a nice way. He didn't seem to be a bad guy, but he grew up and achieved fame probably too young to handle it. He got caught up in a world that led him to tragedy, when wrestling caught fire in Dallas. Many stories told of times where Gordy would party too much, get wildly out of control, wound up the next day with Gordy not remembering much about it, and sheepishly apologizing for whatever disturbances he caused that he couldn't remember.

There was one story that made the papers in Dallas when, arrested for being intoxicated in public, it took several officers to subdue him, and even when they finally handcuffed him, he head-butted the headlight out and with his head, dented up the police car. The next day when he woke up, he was calm and apologetic, signing autographs for everyone at the jail.

Ted DiBiase, whose career intertwined with Gordy in the Mid South, Georgia and Japan, remembered an incident in the Orient when he and Gordy were invited to dinner by a wealthy pearl dealer who was a big fan and known for being well connected. Being familiar with Japanese customs by this point, they understood the honor of a Japanese inviting them to their house and were on their best behavior. Gordy kept himself from drinking, but the host, who knew Gordy's fondness for Jack Daniels, gave him a bottle as a present. The more Gordy drank, the wilder he became, before DiBiase had to apologize, telling the hosts that they had to get out before this wild bull destroyed their home. On the trip back, Gordy, who passed out in the cab, would wake up and get out of control, with DiBiase continually trying to keep him under wraps until they finally got to the hotel. Once they got to the hotel, DiBiase had to put Gordy in a baggage cart and wheel him up to his room because he was totally out. As DiBiase grabbed Gordy's key to open the door, Gordy awoke, hit DiBiase in the back as he was putting the key in the door, and the key broke in the door.

There was a hilarious scene of three Japanese hotel employees with tweezers and flashlights trying to get the broken part of the key out of the door, before they gave up in despair, and just deposited Gordy in a vacant room. At 1 p.m. the next day, DiBiase got a phone call. It was Gordy, asking Ted, "Did I f*** up really bad last night?"

"Pretty bad, Terry."

"Because I woke up and my room looked different, and all my clothes are gone. I didn't know where I was."

"But he had a heart of gold," DiBiase recalled, "he was a lot like Kerry Von Erich in that way."

Like most who remember The Freebirds from the beginning, there was Hayes, one of the great talkers of all time and one of the great heels of the modern era, but not exactly a wrestler that opponents relished working with. Gordy, who was one of the great workers even as a teenager, was the one carrying the match, almost a Southern version of the Adrian Adonis and Jesse Ventura team which was on top in the AWA at about the same time.

They set attendance records throughout Watts's territory and were the heels responsible for making Junkyard Dog the all-time biggest draw the state of Louisiana ever had. They hooked up with Buddy Roberts, who came in as a single. Watts put them together because while Gordy and Hayes were drawing money, they were very green in other ways. Roberts was an experienced star who was part of one of the '70s best tag teams, The Hollywood Blonds, with partner Jerry Brown and manager Sir Oliver Humperdink. Since some of the wrestlers didn't like working with Hayes at the time, Watts had the idea it would create even more heat if Hayes did all the talking and acted like a manager, hiding behind the veteran wrestler and the huge prodigy.

They created the idea of the three-man team, a staple of Mexican wrestling but pretty much unheard of in the U.S. By the time they got to Georgia in late 1980 and won the tag-team titles, the idea was that any two of the three could defend it. Watts, a stickler for credibility, didn't go for that concept, but that became their trademark when they hit Atlanta and became national superstars on TBS.

"We had to be frustrating to Buck Robley (the booker at the time for Watts)," Hayes recalled. "We were very green, but we were drawing. He thought Buddy could teach us."

Gordy and Hayes were against the idea of adding Roberts to the act when Watts suggested it to them. Hayes told Watts, "What if I don't want to do that?" Watts responded immediately, "Are you guys giving me your notice?"

Gordy and Hayes first thought of Roberts as a veteran office stooge, but on a trip from Jackson, Mississippi to Shreveport, Louisiana, after shaving cream and pissing on each other (literally, as the Freebirds in that era were known for giving people they liked—and sometimes didn't like as well—golden showers) for 220 miles, Roberts was officially a Freebird for life, even if Hayes and Gordy at that time thought it was only temporary. Word in wrestling travelled much slower in those days. The Freebirds could have been doing big business in Louisiana, but nobody outside the territory would know. Dusty Rhodes and Ole Anderson were booked for a major show, and on seeing them, Ole asked them to come to Atlanta.

Gordy actually had his first pro wrestling match at the age of 13 at the WRIP television studio in Rossville, Georgia, his home town, teaming with Eddie Griffin as a tag team called The Masked Scavengers. As a huge kid, he was already a star in baseball and football, but didn't pursue sports as he dropped out of school in the ninth grade to pursue pro wrestling.

Even as a freshman, the combination of his size and speed already made college coaches salivate. His wrestling career was guided by his uncle, known as "Hook," because he only had one arm. His uncle told his high school football coach, Lynn Murdock of Rossville High, that Terry wasn't coming back to school for his sophomore year. The uncle, lured by the prospects of him as a pro wrestler, told Murdock that in one year, he'd make more than the coach and within two years would be making $100,000 per year.

At the time, that sounded ridiculous. He was Terry Mecca, working for Angelo Poffo's ICW with the likes of Randy Savage and Lanny Poffo at 14. There was no money there, but it did pay off later. He was already working main-event programs by his 16th birthday, working as the top babyface and holding the Mississippi title for Gil and George Culkin in 1977 and 1978. He left the territory for Memphis the first time after losing a hair match and came to Memphis for a few weeks.

Those who remember 15-year-old Gordy showing up in Memphis described him as a 260-pound kid, with a short crewcut from losing the hair match, and two left feet, contrary to the legend of him always being a great worker. He met Michael Seitz, who was wrestling under the name Lord Michael Hayes, and they worked in Alabama and Mississippi as a tag team.

"When I met him, I told him, 'You'll make it for sure, and somehow, I'm gonna make it. But if we get together, we'll make it that much quicker,'" Hayes recalled. Hayes convinced the booker to turn Gordy heel and put them together as a tag team. Business picked up with them as the top heels, until a night in Natchez, Mississippi, where the house was up significantly, and Hayes, seeing just a $50 payoff, confronted the office, getting a "If you don't like it, then leave," response. Hayes walked out the door. Sitting in his car, Hayes thought he had just screwed up his career. Contemplating his next move, he was shocked, a few minutes later, when Gordy came into the car. His first words were, "Where are we going?" as he had just gone to the promoters and told them if Hayes left, he was leaving with him.

By 1978, Hayes, now known as "Pretty Boy Michael Hayes," became full-time tag partners with Gordy working for

Nick Gulas out of Nashville, feuding with Gulas's territory-killing son, George, and the great worker carrying him, Bobby Eaton. By this time Gordy was already a polished worker. It was there that Hayes first suggested the idea of coming to the ring to the song "Freebird," which is what the two will always be remembered for.

Hayes said he actually first came up with the idea at the age of 14, when he was working putting rings up in Pensacola and going to Southern rock concerts and would see some of the same faces at both shows and thought the marriage of the two would be a great idea.

He went to Gulas and booker Tom Renesto (after convincing Gordy to go for it), with the idea of dimming the house lights, putting the spotlight on them like what he'd seen at rock concerts, and them coming to the ring to the song "Freebird."

"He (Gulas) looked at Tom Renesto Sr. and told him, 'I think those boys are taking them marijuana pills again,'" Hayes recalled.

AFTER LEAVING THAT TERRITORY and going to Memphis, Jerry Jarrett was the first promoter to allow Hayes to see his vision and The Fabulous Freebirds were born in 1978, when they showed up in Memphis for a three-month run. The first Freebird interview at the WMC-TV studios, and match where the two faced the top two local babyfaces, Jerry Lawler and Bill Dundee, is one of those tape collectors classics of the era. Hayes, quoting from popular music, said the two were "The Hot Childs of the city. He does run

wild. And I do look pretty." Hayes, then 18, was already doing the strut he'd become famous for. By this time Gordy, 16, had improved immensely in the ring, doing amazing bumps reminiscent of Ric Flair, and blowing nearly everyone in the territory away with his work. Their two-of-three fall first television match was memorable, because it was the debut of them under the name the Fabulous Freebirds, and also because during the second fall on live television, Hayes shit in his pants, literally. He had to run to the rest room during the television commercial break between falls.

The Freebirds were booked as the No. 2 heel team, however, behind Wayne Farris (later known as Honky Tonk Man) and Larry Latham (later known as Moondog Spot), known then as the Blond Bombers, even though the Freebirds were already far better in the ring and often stole the shows. Soon the fans were cheering them and Jarrett decided to turn them babyface.

"I'll never forget the look on Lawler's face," Hayes said. "The entire place was standing (when they came down the aisle at the Coliseum and the music played)."

When they got to television the next Saturday word came that they were being turned back heel. Eddie Marlin and Bill Dundee told them that Jarrett saw the tape and thought they hadn't gotten over big enough, so was switching them back. Lawler then came in with a different story, saying they had gotten over so huge, that Jarrett decided to turn them heel for a top program. They knew management was lying to them in some form, which led to their decision to leave for Mid South.

After Mid South, they showed up on *Georgia Championship Wrestling*, the top-rated cable show in the nation, in September of 1980 as a three-man team with the idea that any two of the three could wrestle, although in most cases it was Gordy and Roberts. It was almost always Gordy and someone. They were immediately put on top, winning the tag-team titles in a three-way over the area's top heel team of the '60s, The Masked Assassins (although these weren't the same famous duo, Jody Hamilton was the same, but his new partner was Roger Smith) and the area's all-time top babyface team, Mr. Wrestling (Tim Woodin) and Mr. Wrestling II (Johnny Walker).

Things started out well, even though Anderson didn't quite understand the music and the ring outfits, but let them do it, and they got over remarkably fast. They were in main events in weeks, champs within a month, and in less than two months, Gordy was in a singles main event at the Omni against Jack Brisco. But then, Anderson quit as booker and was replaced by Robert Fuller, who, when it came to logic, was a far cry from either Anderson or Watts. The territory was going down fast with the Freebirds on top feuding with Fuller, Ted DiBiase and six-foot-nine, 430-pound Stan Frazier, a hideous worker and a name that most involved roll their eyes when talking about.

After Fuller was gone and replaced by Robley, they started to recreate old Mid-South angles that had drawn big money. While not the success they were in Louisiana since Junkyard Dog wasn't as over as a babyface in Georgia, they did turn things around somewhat. The most famous angle of that time wasn't a recreation, and it's one that probably everyone who saw it likely still remembers due to its dramatic nature.

In a televised tag match against DiBiase and Junkyard Dog, Gordy pile-drove DiBiase on the floor. In those days, that was an angle and a stretcher job all by itself. But DiBiase, who was being pushed as the super babyface because they were grooming him for the NWA title, somehow got up, and rolled into the ring.

He then kicked out of the pin, which nobody at the time expected, and the shock of it not being the finish made the angle. After two more piledrivers in the ring, DiBiase bit a condom he'd kept in his mouth filled with blood, which made it appear he was internally bleeding as the blood came out of his mouth. They did the stretcher job, and to give it authenticity, DiBiase went to the hospital, working everyone at the hospital that the angle was real and his neck was badly injured.

Announcer Gordon Solie gave the name of the hospital DiBiase had been rushed to, lending authenticity. The hospital was flooded with phone calls from all over the country. Those who called, were, in fact, told, because the hospital employees knew no better, that DiBiase really was

ABOVE: One of Japan's most famous tag teams in history was the second Miracle Power Combination of Steve Williams and Terry Gordy. (Dr. Mike Lano)

in the hospital with a severe neck injury. DiBiase worked the hospital employees for a week regarding neck pain and spent the week in bed, filled with morphine, before getting released. Several weeks later, he returned to a big pop on television, and the feud was back on. They also retold the story of what is to this day the biggest angle ever in New Orleans, when Hayes used the famous secret Freebird cream (that'll take people back a few decades to a time when the Freebirds debuted catch phrases in interviews, talking about grow-

ing up on Badstreet USA, the drug-induced exploits on the so-called Freebird mountain—believed to be actually Lookout Mountain in Georgia, and so many others) to blind JYD, with the idea he was blind the day his first daughter was born. The angle which was blown off before nearly 30,000 fans at the Superdome, is a figure that to this day has never been equalled in that city.

The Freebirds, like the Road Warriors of a few years later, because of the music and the charisma, ended up being half babyfaces in Atlanta. To most of the crowd, particularly the older audience, they were the top heels. But to a lot of males aged 15-25, due to the song and the attitude, they were already getting cheered. They dominated the tag-team scene in Georgia through the summer of 1981. Instead of turning face as a trio, Roberts left, and Hayes and Gordy split. Hayes went babyface for a tag-team feud, with Hayes first teaming with Kevin Von Erich, and later with former Oakland Raiders star Otis Sistrunk, who only lasted a few weeks before finding wrestling wasn't to his liking, against Gordy with new partner Jimmy Snuka.

Gordy, and eventually Hayes, left for Southeastern Championship Wrestling, continuing their feud from national TV. Having been there long enough, Hayes felt it was time for him to return to Atlanta, and gave notice. In his last match in the territory, Gordy beat Hayes in a hair vs. hair match in a cage. Gordy wanted to go to a territory where he could be the top singles star, and Hayes was just happy being able to spend three nights a week at home in Pensacola for the first time in years. They thought it was time to get off national television before they burned out, but knew after a rest they had to return. As the group of heels led by LeDuc and the Sheepherders, were giving the beaten Hayes a beating after he had lost and before cutting his hair, Gordy snapped, saved his former partner from the haircut, and turned himself babyface. A short time later, when Hayes was attacked on Atlanta TV by Buzz Sawyer

and Kevin Sullivan, Gordy returned to make the save, and the tape from Alabama of them getting back together was shown nationally. The team was back together, as full-fledged babyfaces on national TV. The return to Atlanta didn't last long, as Hayes and Anderson had their problems and Hayes was fired, or quit. It was announced on television a few days later that he had suffered a broken leg, to send him the message that he couldn't come back anytime soon.

Next stop was Dallas. At the time, Dallas was a struggling territory. The promotion was really just designed by Fritz to be a vehicle to make stars and eventually NWA world champions out of his three sons, who had become very popular with teenagers. But their big crowds were usually limited to appearances by Ric Flair as world champion defending against one of the sons.

Hayes was only planning on going for a week or two before venturing to a big-money territory. But he was there when they had a big show with Flair in San Antonio, and the kids challenging Flair always did business. Hayes smelled something, called up Gordy that night, and told him to give his notice in Atlanta.

Hayes and Gordy arrived as babyfaces, with the story being that they had befriended David, the wildest of the brothers, when David wrestled in Georgia (David actually never wrestled in Georgia, and Kevin actually was Hayes's tag partner for a few weeks in Atlanta). At the time, The Freebirds, having been successful draws in much hotter territories and coming off national exposure, were seen as far too big stars for an office that wasn't doing much business.

In one of those rare nights where wrestling history changed, December 25, 1982, Flair and Kerry Von Erich wrestled before 12,000 fans, the largest crowd to witness wrestling in that part of the country since Fritz's glory days against the likes of Dory Funk Jr., in a cage match at Reunion Arena for the NWA title, with Hayes as referee, voted on by the fans since referee problems in the past had cost Kerry an earlier title match with Flair. Gordy was appointed by Hayes to watch the door to keep any heels from interfering. Earlier in the show, the promotion created the World six-man titles, which over the next few years, became the biggest drawing belt in the territory and among the hottest titles in all of wrestling.

IT WAS AND STILL REMAINS the only time in a major American promotion where the six-man titles were a bigger drawing title than either the main singles or tag-team titles, largely due to the rivalry. The Freebirds, with Roberts returning, were scheduled against champs Bill Irwin and Great Kabuki and The Mongol. To make the story even better, Roberts "missed the show due to a plane delay." David, being their friend from Georgia, volunteered to take his place, actually scored the winning fall, and then announced he was giving Roberts the third belt, since he figured that would be the right thing to do.

Back to the main event. In one of the classic matches of the '80s, both for ring

work, and more for turning a territory around in one night, Kerry had the match won, but Hayes started subtly heeling as ref. Finally, Gordy slammed the cage door on Kerry's head, causing him to lose, and Freebirds vs. Von Erichs was born.

It was the right program to turn around a territory at the right time. Five guys ranging in age from 22 to 25, all charismatic in their own way, and veteran Roberts, an established ring general. World Class, built around this program, started syndicating the show nationally, and even internationally; it was a particular hit in the Middle East. The Freebirds were such great heels, introducing vignettes (the idea of Keith Mitchell and Dan Bynum) to the world of pro wrestling, such as where they'd be in public with announcer Bill Mercer and be wise-asses such as going to drive-through windows at fast-food places and not paying, or going places and sticking Mercer with the check. It changed television wrestling forever. It was no longer a typical low-rent wrestling TV show, but well-produced television, ironically syndicated by the Christian Broadcasting Network (the Von Erichs did a big Christian gimmick) where wrestling was the product.

The Von Erichs became three of the hottest babyfaces in wrestling, due to having the right heel opposition. While several territories caught fire in 1983, a huge year nationwide for the business, World Class had the hottest program of them all. Various mixes of the feud were drawing 4,500 people every Friday night in Dallas at the decrepit Sportatorium, and the big shows, called "Star Wars," were now selling out Reunion Arena's 18,000 seats. Suddenly David passed away in Japan from a drug overdose, but the territory was so hot they introduced Mike Von Erich as a replacement. The 19-year-old, some would say, was the single least credible main eventer of the time, as he was rushed into the hottest programs in wrestling. Gordy and Roberts were so good as workers that they somehow got Mike over, and the territory didn't miss a beat. It peaked on May 6, 1984, when, underneath the famous Kerry title win over Flair in David's honor, Fritz and Mike and Kevin beat The Freebirds in a Bad Street match for the six-man titles before 32,123 fans at Texas Stadium, one of the largest crowds in the history of pro wrestling until that point in time.

Gordy had debuted for All Japan in August of 1983 when Bruiser Brody saw his potential working several matches against him in Texas, most notably a tag match (Hayes and Gordy losing the American tag titles to Brody and Kerry) on June 17, 1983, at Reunion Arena. Brody recommended him to Giant Baba. On Gordy's first tour, he did so well that Japan ended up being his wrestling home for most of the next decade.

Days before he was supposed to go for what may have been the highest profile match of his career, Gordy wanted to cancel, saying he didn't want to go to Japan or fly that far. Hayes had to talk him into going at the last minute.

Gordy on occasion used the move now known as the power bomb as a piledriver-like finish in the United States, although it didn't have a name. He debuted it on August 25, 1983, in Japan against Genichiro Tenryu, and it got over so big, it eventually became his trademark, and became, by the late '80s, the hot finishing move in Japan.

His success in Japan ultimately broke up the original Freebird team. Hayes in 1989 reformed a Freebird team in WCW with Jimmy Garvin and managers Diamond Dallas Page and Humperdink, a pairing most Freebird fans of the '80s would choose to forget.

"He went from being a guy scared to go out on his own (to Japan) to a guy who flourished on his own," Hayes said. "We would never want to stop another from achieving success."

When Vince McMahon went national in 1984 and tried to lock up the most marketable talent in the country to run against the established regional offices, the Freebirds would seemingly be high on his list of people to take. It's a forgotten chapter in wrestling history. Hayes, who already produced a music video with the help of the crack production crew in Dallas, went to the WWF to become a rock star under the tutelage of Cyndi Lauper's manager, David Wolfe. McMahon's idea was to create a rock band that would wrestle, and Hayes, with his love for music and his charisma in wrestling, was the most obvious choice. To say this was a flop would be an understatement. As wild as the wrestlers of that era were, they weren't ready for the Freebirds, who only lasted a few weeks. Gordy at the

"HE WENT FROM BEING A GUY SCARED TO GO OUT ON HIS OWN (TO JAPAN) TO A GUY WHO FLOURISHED ON HIS OWN. WE WOULD NEVER WANT TO STOP ANOTHER FROM ACHIEVING SUCCESS."

—MICHAEL HAYES

same time got a nearly full-time offer from Giant Baba and was gone.

"We were young and cocky and it was a culture shock," remembered Hayes of the short-lived and forgotten stay. It was the typical WWF attitude. The Freebirds, coming off their success, felt they had nothing to prove going to the WWF as they were already stars. The WWF attitude was that what was done elsewhere didn't count.

"We didn't like it," Hayes recalled. "Terry and Buddy really didn't like it."

Dallas had already peaked. Same people for too long. It was really only designed as a promotional vehicle for the kids, and with the same babyfaces, and many of the same heels, running every Monday and Friday in the same metropolitan area, the territory never regained its 1983-84 peak. Freebirds did their face turns, turns on each other, getting back together again for more Freebirds vs. Von

Erichs, but the glory days were over. They went to Florida when Eddie Graham gave Hayes the book, but then Graham committed suicide, and the territory wasn't doing business.

They had a run in the AWA that led to a pretty hot drawing program with the Road Warriors, including a Comiskey Park show in Chicago that drew more than 20,000 fans, but Freebirds and Verne Gagne ultimately mixed like oil and water and the stay was short-lived.

"We drove everyone crazy," Hayes said. "We even drove ourselves crazy."

The Freebirds suggested doing the natural program with the Road Warriors, since they were, along with the Von Erichs, probably the most established main-event tag teams in the business at the time. Verne Gagne was against it, thinking the Road Warriors were heels (even though almost all the fans were cheering them at the time). But the

Freebirds' programs with the other AWA babyfaces (whose heat was almost all killed by the Road Warriors, as heels, not selling for the other faces) were cold and they hated the weather and got out.

They ended up back in Texas. When Watts decided to follow the lead of McMahon and Jim Crockett and go national, particularly expanding into Texas, he and booker Ken Lusk launched a full-scale raid of the Von Erich territory, taking many of the top stars, including The Freebirds, with popular valet Sunshine (Valerie French) as their manager.

Lawsuits followed, but ultimately, the economy in Watts's territory was weak, and wrestling was past its peak. Going national proved to be too expensive. For whatever reason, probably having worked too long in the same general part of the country and no longer being a fresh act, the Freebirds' drawing power wasn't there this time, although they had numerous great matches.

By this point Gordy was considered one of the best in-ring performers in the business, and when Watts chose his first world champion to base his national company around, Gordy got the nod, beating top face Jim Duggan in the finals of a hot tournament on May 30, 1986, in Houston. Gordy was a tremendous champion in the ring, with classic matches against Duggan, Steve Williams, Ted DiBiase, Terry Taylor and others. At one point, when wrestling started changing and fans were losing patience with slow-building matches, Watts decided to fight the tide, ordering DiBiase, his best pure worker, and Gordy to do 55-minute matches in every city, making the fans believe they were going to see the old 60-minute broadway, and then, when they were sure that was the finish, having Gordy use heel tactics to score a pinfall.

The matches were classics, but the cost of signing all that talent, combined with weak gates partially due to a lack of fresh talent and also because the home base was hit hard by a recession due to the collapse of the oil business, and an expensive national syndication network that was costing big money in the major markets to maintain and wasn't generating enough ad revenue, it wasn't a winning formula. Going with Gordy as champion for most promoters was a decision they wouldn't have made because his Japanese commitments saw him frequently leave. With three of his top wrestlers, Gordy, Williams, and DiBiase, all having heavy and lucrative Japanese deals, it was getting harder to build momentum of championship programs. There were only so many injury angles you could do with DiBiase and Williams before it started to get out of hand. Gordy ended up being injured legitimately in an auto accident that November but was going to end up losing the title anyway, since Watts had a big Superdome show on Thanksgiving and Gordy was booked in Baba's tag-team tournament at the same time. The injury forced Gordy to forfeit the title to One Man Gang at a time when Watts decided to move the heat from what he felt were the more immature Freebirds to the more solid crew led by Scandor Akbar, who, while more professional, totally lacked charisma, and the territory went down the tubes. In early 1987, Watts sold the Universal Wrestling Federation to Jim Crockett.

For the most part, the original Freebirds were finished. When DiBiase signed with WWF to become the Million-Dollar Man, Gordy got his spot as Hansen's regular tag-team partner, including winning the 1988 Real World Tag League tournament over Genichiro Tenryu and Toshiaki Kawada in the match that made Kawada a superstar. Tenryu was injured and Kawada was by himself for several minutes against both the company's top foreigners, kicking out of one big move after another, before finally losing in one of the all-time classic matches.

Gordy's final big run in Texas took place one year earlier, the controversial angle on December 25, 1987—five years to the day of them doing the angle setting the company on fire. By this point, both David and Mike Von Erich had passed away, and an angle was shot where Gordy, Roberts and King Parsons, known as the Blackbirds, turned on Fritz, then 59, and pounded on him until Fritz faked a heart attack and for the next several weeks, depending largely on the gate the previous Friday, pretended to be either getting better (after a sellout) or near death (when the houses started to drop). Even people in wrestling, who already had some major

ABOVE: Terry Gordy in his days in Dallas when he would regularly wrestle against the Von Erich dynasty. (Dr. Mike Lano)

latitude when it came to angles, were repulsed by Fritz playing off the deaths of his two children for what was the last angle that actually drew money for the family as Kevin and Kerry went for revenge in early 1988. But Dallas was by this point just a stop between Japan tours for Gordy.

In 1990, Baba, attempting to duplicate the success of the Hansen and Brody tag team of 1982-85, tried to recreate it with Gordy and Williams. From the start, Baba wanted to build the tag-team division around them and in their first major match on March 6, 1990, at Budokan Hall, they defeated the company's top foreign star, Hansen, and top native star, Tenryu, to win the world tag-team titles.

THEY DOMINATED THE BELTS for the next three years, including in 1990 and 1991 becoming the first tag team to win back-to-back Real World Tag League tournament victories. Although not quite the force inside the ring he had been before the knee problems, Gordy at the time was still probably the best "big man" inside the ring in the business. He was being groomed for the top position in All Japan with the aging Hansen being moved to that veteran gunslinger position, and toward that end, twice held the Triple Crown in 1990. He first won it from Jumbo Tsuruta on June 5 in Chiba, just for a short run to heat up his feud with Hansen, who won the title three days later at Budokan Hall before 14,800 fans. The feud was designed to make fans see the younger Gordy as Hansen's equal while still protecting Hansen's legend, as Gordy was put on the same plane as Hansen six weeks later winning the Triple Crown on June 17, 1990, in Kanazawa.

At the time, this was one of the few times up to that point in the 13 years he had been the most popular foreign wrestler in Japan that Hansen had done a clean job for another foreigner. It was a transition period for All Japan, with Misawa replacing Tsuruta as the focal point of the company with Tsuruta taking the old native gunslinger role that Baba took years earlier when Tsuruta was made the regular main event native, and similarly, Gordy, from the same generation, would take the focal role on the foreigner side from Hansen, with the idea Misawa vs. Gordy would be the legendary singles program of the '90s. But shortly after the win, while partying at Roppongi, a hot nightlife part of Tokyo, he collapsed at a club, suffering from a major overdose. His heart stopped beating. He was revived, survived, and returned to the ring on the next tour with no discernable damage, but unfortunately, the scare didn't teach him the lesson it should have, as his lifestyle never changed.

Baba stripped him of the title and he nearly lost his job in the process. Drugs, both painkillers and otherwise, were commonplace by this point among the foreigners in Japan, both to combat being in Japan for a month straight at times, as well as the pain from the matches. However, Baba, the beloved father figure and boss, came from another era and had little tolerance for them, or at least had adopted a see-no-evil attitude. The overdose forced Baba to see the issue, and it took a lot of pleading for him to allow Gordy back. But he never gave him the Triple Crown again, and never even allowed him to challenge for it until three years later, ironically, in a match that would never take place.

Gordy and Williams were together only three years, but their total time holding the world tag-team titles was longer than all but nine teams in the history of pro wrestling. In Japan, they had classic battles with all the top tag teams of that hot era, including Hansen and Tenryu, Hansen and Danny Spivey, Misawa and Kawada, The Funks, Giant Baba and Andre the Giant, Jumbo Tsuruta and Yoshiaki Yatsu, Tsuruta and Kabuki, Tsuruta and Akira Taue, Doug Furnas and Dan Kroffat, Kawada and Taue, Misawa and Kobashi and Hansen and Gary Albright.

To relieve the pressure on his bad knees, Gordy trimmed down, getting as light as 245 pounds in 1991, which looked positively skinny on his broad frame. As drawing cards, the team peaked during the 1991 tournament, setting television ratings records that still stand in Japan on successive weeks in December of that year. In the 12:30 a.m. to 1:30 a.m. Sunday night time slot, Gordy and Williams's match with Hansen and Spivey was the main event on a show that drew a 7.0 rating, the largest rating in the history of that time slot in Japan. The record lasted only one week, as the tournament final, where they beat Misawa and Kawada, drew an 8.2 (part of this record was also because that was the Dynamite Kid retirement ceremony), both weeks doing better than a 75 audience share.

Watts even brought them back to WCW in 1992, where they held both the WCW and newly created NWA world tag-team titles working programs with both the Steiner Brothers (which was an intriguing feud for Japan, since the Steiners were top draws for New Japan while Gordy and Williams were the top foreigners for All Japan) and Dustin Rhodes and Barry Windham, but ultimately their stay was short due to Japan commitments and neither wanting to give up what in those days was considered one of the prime jobs in wrestling. Those were Gordy's peak earning years, working 26 weeks for Baba at nearly $10,000 per week, plus another $200,000 WCW deal that Jim Ross and Watts put together for them.

They held the All Japan world tag-team titles five times over three years, including also holding both the NWA and WCW tag titles in the United States in 1992. They would have likely remained the dominant foreign team in All Japan for the rest of the decade.

Terry Gordy, pro wrestling superstar, ended on August 18, 1993. At the age of 32, while flying to Japan for a tour, which was to climax with a show at Budokan Hall a few weeks later where he would finally be allowed to main event on his own, challenging Misawa for the Triple Crown on a show that was already sold out, he took 50 somas on the flight. It was generally a known rule that Gordy would come to Japan two days before the tour started, and get so loaded on the long flight, that he'd spend a day sleeping it off in his Tokyo hotel room on arrival, and the wrestlers and his friends knew to just let him be. But this time, when the plane landed, he was out, and turning blue. While on the plane, nobody reacted because he was always like that on the trip over. But this time he wasn't sleeping, he was in a coma. When they couldn't awaken him, EMTs got on the plane to perform CPR to attempt to revive him, and at one point, once again, his heart stopped beating and his brain stopped functioning. He was rushed to the hospital and remained in a coma for five days. He was never the same.

"That was a self-induced problem," Hayes said. "I don't know if he didn't understand the success or couldn't handle the success."

The overdose left him brain damaged and robbed him of his athletic ability. He had to relearn to talk, then relearn to walk, and eventually even relearned to wrestle, up to a point. He could no longer perform at a top level, but he still had a name and bills to pay, and he only knew one thing. He returned to wrestling several months later in the dying days of the Global Wrestling Federation in Texas, joining Hayes and Jimmy Garvin as the Freebirds. With no advertising, advanced publicity, fanfare or pressure, Baba brought him in for a series of mid-card matches starting with the seventh annual Bruiser Brody Memorial show on July 16, 1994 in Nagasaki for a short run, but it was not a success. After finishing the tour

on July 28, 1994 at Budokan Hall, he was never brought back to All Japan.

Over his last six years, he continued to wrestle, as a shadow of himself, mainly working small independent shows in the South or for the IWA in Japan, who tried to use the famous Terry Gordy name from his glory days on network television to sell tickets and booked him strong. He had a few somewhat high-profile appearances, including being Cactus Jack's first-round opponent in the legendary Kawasaki Stadium King of the Death match tournament for IWA on August 20, 1995, before 28,757 fans; and brief forays as champ in promotions on their last legs like the GWF in Dallas and Smoky Mountain Wrestling in Tennessee, desperate that his name might briefly inject some life into their sagging box office. He had later brief runs in ECW and finally, WWF, under a mask as Foley's short-lived tag-team partner.

Hayes said the last few years of Gordy's life were very tough on him. He said Gordy lost a lot of his drive when he realized he couldn't come all the way back.

"In his mind, I think it really bothered him that he'd never be that Terry Gordy again."

ABOVE: During the heyday of Mid South Wrestling, Jim Ross interviews Buddy Roberts, Michael Hayes and Terry Gordy, the most famous incarnation of The Freebirds. (Dr. Mike Lano)

CHAPTER 14

ELIZABETH

THE LOVELY ELIZABETH WAS ONE OF THE MOST atypical characters in the history of pro wrestling. But the demise of the woman playing the role, Elizabeth Hulette, on May 1, 2003, was sadly, far too typical.

Hulette, 42, died at Kennestone Hospital in Marietta, Georgia after emergency personnel responded to a 911 call at about 5:30 a.m. saying that she wasn't breathing. Larry Pfohl, 44, her boyfriend, best known as Lex Luger, was arrested later that day, not in connection with the death, but because police found large quantities of drugs at the $300,000 townhouse the two shared in Cobb County, just outside of Marietta in suburban Atlanta.

The story of two people who from the outside seemed to have it all at different times in their lives, and where it went wrong, is hard to ascertain. Hulette was described universally within wrestling as a sweet and beautiful woman, whose sudden and unplanned stardom in the late 1980s never went to her head. At her

peak, with the possible exception of Rena Mero as Sable, she was the most popular female performer in the history of the business outside of Japan. In her heyday as the shy, demure Elizabeth from 1985 through 1992 in the WWF, she was the idol and role model to virtually every young girl who watched wrestling, and the first crush of a generation of young television wrestling fans. It was a role not planned for her, nor did anyone expect it to take off the way it did.

And ironically, despite the success of the role, no woman in wrestling has ever been put in a similar role, including herself when she returned in a far less effective role with WCW in 1996. Vince McMahon at first tried a similar role for Sable, but that ended up transformed into weekly scenarios to find reasons to get her in as little clothing as possible as a ratings draw, which set the stage for women in pro wrestling since that time.

Hulette, who was let go by WCW from her $156,000 per year job just before

OPPOSITE: Long after they divorced in real life, Elizabeth and former husband Randy Savage still worked together in WCW. (Dr. Mike Lano)

the company closed up, began working at the front desk of Main Event Fitness in Marietta, Georgia, the gym that Pfohl had owned for years after he and Steve Borden (Sting) opened it during their wrestling heyday. The two had become an item in 1998 while both worked for WCW, at a time when both were married to people not affiliated with wrestling.

Luger, who hadn't wrestled since WCW closed in March of 2001, and Elizabeth, who hadn't appeared on a wrestling show even longer than that, were both booked on a December 2002 European tour with World Wrestling All-Stars. It was obvious to those on the tour that things were very wrong.

Elizabeth, even though booked on the tour, never left her hotel room, except to get on the bus or plane to the next show. Those on the tour said she looked bloated and her behavior worried people, but on that tour, there were others, like Luger, who appeared far worse off.

Exactly what the root of their problems were is uncertain. While together in WCW, Hulette became, like Luger, a fitness freak. Those in WCW who spent a lot of time with both said that if Luger had any drug issues outside of the obvious physique drugs, he was able to keep them under wraps in public. When he would travel from Atlanta, he never appeared incoherent on airplanes or anything that would be obvious, even though recreational drug use in that promotion was rampant, shocking even people who came over from ECW. After WCW folded, Luger finally split from wife, Peggy.

Friends of Hulette said the two were planning on getting married before the end of the year. But both had strangely stopped going to the gym. Several wrestlers who knew him speculated that as vain as he was, he was having a hard time with getting older, not getting the adrenaline rush of being in front of crowds, even though it was known he never liked wrestling—it was just a job for him that paid him well for years.

THE FIRST SIGN OF PROBLEMS, at least to police, came in April 2003, when they responded to a call about a fight in the garage of the couple's home. When police arrived, Hulette had two black eyes, knots on her forehead and a split lip. She claimed she had fallen down while trying to control the family dog. Police didn't buy it, and arrested Pfohl for misdemeanor battery, and he was released on $2,500 bond.

Two days later, he was arrested on a DUI charge after his 2002 Porsche rear-ended another car near his home. According to the police report, he had slurred speech, bloodshot eyes and couldn't find his driver's license, and police also found a handgun in his car. Hulette, with him at the time, was sent home by police in a taxi. His license had been suspended in March after failing to appear for a court date on charges of driving with expired tags and no proof of insurance.

After Hulette's death, although police made clear this was not in connection with the death, he was charged with 14 counts of possession of controlled substances, 13 felonies and one misdemeanor.

Among the drugs found were hundreds of bottles of various forms of steroids, including testosterone. He had 210 tablets of Dianabol (a steroid which is illegal even with a prescription in the U.S.). He also had 98 Xanex pills, five Vicodins, 361 carisoprodol tablets (somas) and several other drugs. He was also arrested on a misdemeanor count of possession, sale and distribution of Saizen, a synthetic Growth Hormone.

Hulette's mother, after the death, broke all ties with anyone in the wrestling business, apparently blaming the industry for her daughter's death. Some heard that there wasn't going to be a funeral. Her body was shipped to Kentucky very quickly. Others heard that there was a funeral, but it was being kept secret, and that they specifically didn't want anyone from wrestling knowing about it, or any flowers sent from people in wrestling.

Hulette, originally from Frankfort, Kentucky, was a teenage wrestling fan who developed a crush on Randy Savage (Randy Poffo). Savage was the local world champion for a group called International Championship Wrestling, based in nearby Lexington. Savage was as gifted as any wrestler in the business at the time inside the ring; he had unique intensity, understood ring psychology from growing up in a wrestling family, was a top-notch athlete, and although small, had one of the best physiques in the industry. However, the promotion, run by his father Angelo, a former Midwest headliner whose career dated back to the '50s, was known in the trade as an outlaw promotion. That meant they promoted in cities against a local National Wrestling Alliance affiliate.

While totally illegal, and in the '50s after a Justice Department investigation, the Alliance promoters had to sign a consent decree that they would not monopolize the business or blacklist talent, the fact was, that's exactly what they were still doing. And there were two sides to every story, as the Poffo's television show would feature the wrestlers, Randy usually being the ringleader, doing promos running down the top stars of both the Jarrett company as well as the Nick Gulas and Ron Welch (Fuller) NWA promotions. The war was so nasty they even went so far as to have wrestlers on their show, in particular Bob Roop, a well-spoken former Olympic wrestler, and Savage, talk about when they worked for the rival promotions, that they would be asked to take dives, and then go on to say, nothing like this happens in ICW. On occasion, when the Jarrett promotion would run in Louisville or Lexington, the ICW wrestlers would go to the show and cause a commotion. It got so bad that when the Jarrett wrestlers made the weekly trip to Louisville, most were carrying guns.

Bill Dundee (Bill Crookshanks) was Jarrett's No. 2 babyface, behind Lawler. Savage would routinely make fun of him, because he was about five foot four, on interviews. Savage would go on television and claim he would put up some ridiculous amount of money for a shoot match, three on one, where he'd face Dundee, Jarrett and Yamamoto. There was a confrontation at one point where

Crookshanks pulled a gun after Poffo approached him. During the ensuing struggle, Poffo got the gun and hit Crookshanks with it, breaking his jaw, and putting him out of wrestling for months. That was a major embarrassment for the Jarrett side, because the Poffo side made sure the word got out. As you can imagine, as great a performer as Savage was, and there were few in his league anywhere, no major promotion would touch him. It was this world that Hulette first saw when she got involved with wrestling.

When she first met Poffo, he was with a woman named Debra Szotecki (second-generation woman wrestler Debbie Combs). As the story goes, when he first met her, she was heavy. Feeling she needed to lose weight to get him, she dropped weight, became a knockout, and the two hooked up. In such a small operation, she quickly became part of the family business. She would sell programs at the shows and helped out on office work. By 1983, she was appearing in front of the camera as the pretty face who hosted the local TV shows and introduced the video clips. But the company simply couldn't compete with the popularity of Jarrett's promotion. Elizabeth and Randy were officially married on December 30, 1984.

Eventually, Angelo Poffo called Jerry Jarrett about trying to make money based on what were previously legitimate hostilities. An interpromotional feud of sorts was started by one of the most brilliantly executed angles of the era. It appeared that Savage showed up uninvited and took over the Memphis television show, and it led to a lucrative series of matches with Lawler as the top guns from each company.

While working in the Memphis territory, George Scott, who was the booker for WWF at the time, saw a tape of Savage, and he was brought in, with a major push. While wrestling at a Memphis television taping on a Saturday morning, Savage got a phone call from Jimmy Hart, who by that time had left Memphis for WWF, and went into the parking lot to talk, and was told they were interested. As talented as Savage was, he had never made big money in wrestling working on outlaw shows.

In those days, the heels were brought in largely to be fed to Hulk Hogan. Savage, while as talented as any, was thought by many at first to be too small as a heel to draw against Hogan, but it ended up being perhaps Hogan's all-time most successful rivalry from the early singles matches that generally did among the best business for any of Hogan's programs. All major heels at the time were also hooked up generally with one of the variety of heel managers, but Savage came in without a manager. They did an angle where all the managers in the promotion were bidding for Savage's services, which only served to make him seem more special than any of the larger but less athletic heels. When the angle played out after several weeks, Savage introduced his manager, and everyone was shocked when an unknown 100-pound woman, all decked out, came to the ring, with announcer Bruno Sammartino surmising that "she must be some sort of a movie star."

THE ORIGINAL IDEA OF ELIZABETH was to be a new heel manager. A beautiful woman, but something out of a soap opera, where she would be a hard-nosed business shark. Some will credit Elizabeth with paving the way for the women characters in wrestling, but that would be incorrect. While there were a few women valets in the '50s, including for top heels like Buddy Rogers, Gorgeous George and The Sheik, for some reason the women in wrestling during the '60s and '70s were wrestlers for the most part. There were a few regional exceptions, like Paul Christy's wife, Bunny Love in Indiana or Cowboy Frankie Laine's wife, Linda, or Bobby Shane's wife, Sherri, but the women were not considered stars on their own as much as accouterments.

The modern day role of women in wrestling started when Jimmy Garvin took Valerie French (Sunshine) to Texas in 1983. Just about every act that was in Dallas in that year caught fire, and this was no different. Booker Ken Mantell (no relation to Dutch) booked a feud by bringing Garvin's real wife, Patty Williams, in as Precious, turning Sunshine babyface and she went with Chris Adams. The four feuded, and it caught fire immediately.

It became Mantell's booking trademark, having valets feud, although he did it for so long it ran out of steam. Soon, there were women everywhere working as managers, like Missy Hyatt and Nickla Roberts in Texas, Dark Journey in Mid South, Sherri Martel in the AWA and on a national basis, Roberts went to Crockett on WTBS as Tully Blanchard's "Perfect 10, Baby Doll."

WWF wanted in on the trend, and made the biggest star of them all, largely because she was portrayed as anything but the typical wrestling woman who dressed as revealing as possible and was portrayed as someone who bounced from male wrestler to male wrestler.

Immediately, the original heel plans were dropped. Fans immediately took to her, and the Savage/Elizabeth dynamic changed to her portrayed as the most beautiful, elegant, but totally approachable woman. She was a pro wrestling version of Lady Di, and Savage was her heelish, jealous, obsessive and overbearing boyfriend. There was a famous angle where George Steele, by then late in his career, developed a crush on Elizabeth. While the Savage-Steele matches were hardly masterpieces in the ring, having Steele, whose role at the time was of an ugly simple guy who could barely talk, but had this love for this beautiful woman, only made the dynamic stronger. Most beautiful women would have blown this ugly beast off. But she was nice to him. But even though she was just being nice, and showing no romantic affection, her boyfriend would go crazy with jealousy.

It was that way when the cameras were off as well. Savage's jealousy was legendary in wrestling. When Savage wasn't watching over her, he would have a road agent or referee or older office person that he trusted with her at all times to make sure none of the boys ever got too close. Savage on occasion chased down and hit fans who tried to touch her as she was walking to and from the ring. Lesser stars were let go by the company for lesser actions involving fans.

Her popularity grew, and with the exception of Hogan, the Savage-Elizabeth act was the top full-time act in the company shortly after her 1985 debut. Her character was far more successful than any woman character in wrestling up to that point in time. While Hogan was a superhero that fans were in awe of, she was probably the most liked character in the business at the time. Savage eventually turned babyface by saving Elizabeth, and pro wrestling's royal couple spent a year on top as Savage held the WWF championship from March 27, 1988 through April 2, 1989.

Savage was a babyface through most of that period, before one of the most famous and successful pro wrestling angles ever. Hogan was knocked out of the WWF title tournament with a no contest with Andre The Giant, which Savage won in the finals over Ted DiBiase. Hogan helped in the title win, which ended with Hogan and Savage both hoisting Elizabeth in the air like she was the real champion. The seed for an angle nearly a year later was planted as Hogan was celebrating with Elizabeth, holding her with his hand on her butt, and Savage gave the briefest glare that foreshadowed the Wrestlemania main event a year later.

When Hogan returned after the making of No Holds Barred, Elizabeth put together Hogan and Savage as The Megapowers, a spoof on the name "The Super Powers" that Dusty Rhodes had come up with for his tag team with Nikita Koloff at the time. The angle to hook them up was taped for Saturday Night's Main Event on November 11, 1987 (airing a few weeks later) when Savage had a singles match with Bret Hart. After winning, Savage was attacked by Honky Tonk Man and Jim Neidhart, along with Hart. Elizabeth ran to the back, and basically dragged Hogan out to make the save and the two shook hands.

At the first ever SummerSlam on August 29, 1988, in Madison Square Garden, the two teamed against Andre the Giant and DiBiase, with heel announcer Jesse Ventura as referee. Most of the pre-match build-up centered around Elizabeth, who by this time was at her peak of popularity. While Elizabeth did pose with Savage doing a bikini poster that was a big seller, she was always dressed up like she was going to a prom whenever she was on television. She was the ultimate homecoming queen who wasn't stuck up, and was nice to the boys who weren't popular. The tease for the match was that if things got bad, Elizabeth, billed as the secret weapon of the Megapowers, under her fancy clothes, was going to wear a bikini.

As it turned out, whether she didn't want to go that far, or Savage didn't want it, with the heels in control, Elizabeth got up on the apron, took off her skirt, and

OPPOSITE: Lex Luger and Elizabeth as a unit in WCW. (Dr. Mike Lano)

the heels were mesmerized by her bikini bottom. Hogan and Savage shook hands like in a cartoon, which wrestling was more like in those days, made their comeback, and of course, won the match.

BUT WHEN 1989 STARTED, to build for the Hogan vs. Savage match, Savage started heeling again, acting more jealous of Hogan's "business" relationship with Elizabeth. The big angle was shot on February 3, 1989 in Milwaukee, during a live primetime special on NBC. The show drew an 11.6 rating, the second most watched pro wrestling television show ever in the U.S. The Megapowers, actually in only their second major match, wrestled Big Bossman, who Hogan had been working a program with, and Akeem, who Savage had been defending his title against. It wasn't so much of a match as a few key spots. Spot No. 1 was Akeem throwing Savage through the ropes, and he dove out almost like a tope, wiping out Elizabeth. Elizabeth had never been involved physically in action, and took a wild bump from a 235-pound man flying out like a missile. She was "out cold," and Hogan picked her up and carried her to the back. The next scene was her in this makeshift hospital room. Most of the next 15 minutes on television consisted of Savage being pounded by both men while Elizabeth was unconscious, with the idea that she was seriously injured, and Hogan was crying, in the room, begging the doctors to save her life. The skit had one of the most unintentionally funny spots ever, as Elizabeth was no actress, even by

wrestling standards, and Hogan was campy on his best days. And this was shot live, which WWE never did in those days except for PPV shows. When they came back from a commercial, and Hogan didn't know they were back, and asked for a "tizime (time) countdown before they would go on," with the whole country watching, and then reverting into the worst overacting, crying and saying, "Doc, please don't let her die," and "Randy didn't mean to do it." Finally, in a scene right out of the *Rocky* movies, Liz woke up, and her first words were, "Go help Randy." Hogan ran back to the ring to save Savage. Savage saw him, thinking he had taken Elizabeth and they both deserted him, and slapped Hogan, and then walked out on Hogan. He wound up in the "hospital room," while Hogan was in the ring with both huge heels. While the cameras barely showed any of the match during the 15 minutes where Hogan and Liz were backstage, they did show Hogan left with both men. He made his superman comeback, pinned Akeem after a legdrop, and then handcuffed Bossman to manager Slick and ran back to the hospital room.

While the acting up to this point had been beyond horrible, Savage saved it from there. Savage accused Hogan of being jealous that he was champion and said that Hogan had lusted after Elizabeth. Savage ended up hitting Hogan from behind with the title belt. Elizabeth, now somewhat recovered, screamed and hovered over Hogan to comfort him. Then, in what was a shocking remark at the time, Savage told Elizabeth to get up or he'd splatter her all over the floor, just like Hogan, turning him in one sentence into an incredibly hot heel. They teased that Savage was going to hit Elizabeth with the belt, but they didn't need to do anything close to that. Instead, he grabbed her and threw her hard and went after Hogan.

Brutus Beefcake, Hogan's best friend and tag partner at the time, came for the save, but Savage laid him out as well, before storming out. Hogan regained the title from Savage at Wrestlemania V on April 2, 1989, in Atlantic City, in a match that because ticket prices were jacked up at Trump Plaza, drew the largest live gate up to that point in the history of U.S. wrestling. Because more homes had PPV than in 1987 for the Hogan-Andre match, it also broke the all-time record for PPV buys with more than 600,000, and that's with a free TV special on TBS going head to head. The estimated $18.9 total revenue gross was the largest wrestling show in history up until that point.

The gimmick was that Elizabeth would be at ringside, but in a neutral corner, and would make her decision of which guy she was going with at the end of the match. Even though everyone saw Savage as the company's top heel once again, she still saw the good in him. Savage took a bad bump on the outside, but Elizabeth went to help him, but he yelled at her. Later Hogan tried to post Savage, but Elizabeth got in the way. This allowed Savage to post Hogan, but

Elizabeth then stopped Savage from attacking Hogan. Savage then ordered Elizabeth to leave ringside, and Hogan came back to win with his foot to the face and legdrop. Elizabeth managed Hogan for a while after Mania, but that dynamic couldn't last for a lot of reasons, and she disappeared from wrestling.

In another of those great soap opera moments in wrestling, she returned, unadvertised, on March 23, 1991, at Wrestlemania VII at the Los Angeles Sports Arena. Savage was wrestling Ultimate Warrior underneath the Hogan-Sgt. Slaughter main event, in a loser must retire match. Savage was actually talking about retiring, and both talked about starting a family, something she desperately wanted and never had. Savage, who by this time was being managed by Sherri Martel, had been a heel for years, but it was clear he was going out sympathetically from the start, since he came out wearing a white cowboy hat. Savage put on a show, stealing the card, as he often did, even with it being his first match back after major thumb surgery. Elizabeth was shown at ringside several times during the match, and after Savage lost, Sherri attacked him and put the boots to him. Elizabeth hit the ring for the save, leading to the big closing hug and kiss spot. This was so well done that probably more people were in tears watching this moment than any moment scripted in company history.

As a babyface, Savage, McMahon and Roddy Piper were the three-man announcing team, and most of the summer was spent with McMahon and Piper urging Savage to ask Elizabeth to marry him in the storyline. Savage kept getting cold feet to build the angle, but finally asked. The wedding, billed as "The Match Made in Heaven," was actually put in the main event position on the SummerSlam PPV on August 26, 1991 in Madison Square Garden. It was a weird deal, as a lot of the live crowd left, and most of the guys in the crowd didn't care. For women wrestling fans, this was like the event of all events, and again, a lot of women fans in the audience were crying like it was a real wedding. The big angle shot was that Elizabeth after the ceremony opened a wedding present, and a snake came out and scared her to death. This led to Savage coming out of retirement for a feud with Jake Roberts.

Later, she was the focal point of her last WWF angle at Wrestlemania VIII on April 5, 1992. Ric Flair by this time was WWF champion, and the angle was that he bragged that he was dating Elizabeth before Savage met her. Flair did his incredible promo work, with the repeated tag line, "She was mine before she was yours." Flair and manager Curt Hennig bragged they were going to show a nude photo of Elizabeth on the screen at Wrestlemania, which was one of the ultimate bait-and-switch angles, since it was never even followed up on during the show after being hyped big. Savage regained the title and the royal couple was back on top. But not for long.

Stories of Savage being possessive of her were legendary. In the WCW days, Bobby Heenan used to sing the song, "How do you handle a hungry man," from a TV dinner theme song, whenever she'd come to talk with him. She had confided to him that when Randy was on the road, he'd buy a TV dinner for every night he was gone, because he never wanted her leaving the house. Another story was in her heyday, when she, Savage, Davey Boy Smith and his then-wife Diana were out at a hotel swimming pool on the road, two very obviously gay men came up to talk to the two women. They just saw her and asked if she was the Elizabeth from television and she said yes and started talking with them. Savage, who was in the pool, saw it, and gave her a look and said, "Liz, in the pool." She told stories about owning a convertible, but Randy would never let her drive with the top down because he didn't want guys whistling at her.

REAL LIFE GOT IN THE WAY. Hulette walked out of the relationship that summer, and when she did, with no fanfare, she was gone from the WWF, for good. It also caused the real-life rift between Hogan and Savage, which continued for years. Although it settled once when both had the chance to make money with each other in WCW, it is still apparent from Savage's side to this day. Savage blamed Hogan and his wife, Linda, for urging Elizabeth to leave him, whether true or not. She ended up spending time at their home hiding out when she finally left him. She quickly hooked up with Miami attorney Cary Lubetsky, who she met at about the same time Hogan was doing the movie Mr. Nanny, in South Florida, and moved there.

She went from superstar to nobody in a long relationship, and kept contact with almost nobody in wrestling. Just months after being a major television show, she was working at a retail clothes store as a salesperson at the Aventura Mall, in South Florida. Somehow, she got the bug in 1995, and made contact with Zane Bresloff, the WCW house show promoter who she, Savage and Gene Okerlund had often traveled with when touring the Rocky Mountain states in the WWF heyday. Bresloff told her to come to Jacksonville to meet the people in charge at WCW. She was then turned down for a job because they thought she was older, didn't look good enough, and there was no place for her. It should be noted that Kevin Sullivan, who was booker, was at the time trying to get his then-wife, Nancy, back into the company, and there wasn't room for more than one woman by the thought pattern of the time. In fact, one of the ideas floating around was for Nancy to manage Savage and be called

"The New Elizabeth." However, only a few weeks later, Eric Bischoff decided her return would mean something for ratings, not to mention the various angles that could be done with Savage.

Her return on the Clash of Champions on January 23, 1996, her first appearance on television in nearly four years, drew a 4.5 rating, which ranked as one of the three most-watched television wrestling shows in the history of TBS up to that point in time. Her return also gave WCW another piece of bragging rights for signing an ex-WWF superstar. She worked angles with Savage, which she confided to friends were very difficult.

She ended up as a heel with Ric Flair, and later in the NWO with Eric Bischoff. The Flair vs. Savage program in early 1996 with Elizabeth as part of the program was the first sign of life of WCW house shows, just before the company's major business turnaround later in that year. Aside from a match where she botched a finish where she was going to use her high heel shoe as a weapon, which was the laughingstock of wrestling for a week, she was largely just another pretty face in the crowd.

CHAPTER 15
LOU
THESZ

PICKING THE GREATEST PRO WRESTLER OF all-time is an impossible task. Lou Thesz was not the most influential. That would probably be either Frank Gotch, Hulk Hogan, Antonio Inoki or Rikidozan. He was not the greatest worker. That honor would probably go to Ric Flair. In mythology, he was certainly among the greatest shooters, and in reality, even among the other legends of wrestling in his class, like Billy Robinson or Danny Hodge or Dick Hutton, they all ranked him right at the top, but even he would concede he was probably not the best. He was not the biggest drawing card. But, because of changes in the business and

because he himself was a physical freak who until the last few months of his life defied all laws of aging, nobody will ever match his longevity at the top. It's hard to see another wrestler matching his seven-consecutive-year tenure as the world champion.

"I thought that Lou was the ultimate combination of a wrestler and a worker," said announcing legend Lance Russell, who began watching Thesz as a fan when he was one of the highest paid athletes in the country during the advent of television. "He was a great wrestler, but he could capture the imagination of the public even though he was as straight (gim-

OPPOSITE: Lou Thesz was still lean and ready to go at the age of 60. (Dr. Mike Lano)

"LOU WAS THE GUY THAT ALL THE FANS KNEW WAS A REAL CHAMPION. HE LOOKED LIKE A CHAMPION. HE DRESSED LIKE A CHAMPION. HE BEHAVED AT ALL TIMES LIKE A CHAMPION."

—DORY FUNK

mick free) as he was. When people ask me the best wrestler I ever saw, it's always been Lou Thesz and Jack Brisco, in that order."

"Lou was the guy that all the fans knew was a real champion," said Dory Funk. "He looked like a champion. He dressed like a champion. He behaved at all times like a champion. He's the one that really laid the foundation (as NWA champion) that allowed the rest of us to have our success. He just represented what everyone thought a world champion wrestler should be."

"He was charming, articulate and a wonderful human being," said former rival Tim Woodin (Tim "Mr. Wrestling" Woods), a former national amateur champion who became a major pro star in the '60s and '70s. "He was the best wrestler I ever knew."

But he was very different than the champions who followed him. Compared with Dory Funk and Flair, generally regarded along with him as the greatest of the NWA champions, their philosophies about the title weren't the same, nor were the philosophies of the promoters. With the NWA champions that followed, the idea was to make every challenger look like they could beat him while at the same time protecting the aura of the champion. It isn't that Thesz didn't put people over. He made several careers. The people he let go to a draw with him were instant stars. The few that beat him had the keys handed to them to superstardom. But Thesz, at least during his prime when he had the power, only waved that magic wand of stardom on occasion and for those who he personally believed deserved it. A believer in wrestling ability as paramount until he died, he refused when he was champion to make what he considered subpar wrestlers look good, even if they were drawing big money at the time.

Stories of Thesz as champion shutting people down completely are legendary. Although he drew some huge crowds with him, Thesz shut down Antonino Rocca, the biggest drawing card of the day, when they wrestled in the 1950s. When Hans Schmidt was the hottest heel in the business as a post-World War II Nazi, to Thesz, he was still Guy LaRose from Montreal and no wrestler. Thesz guzzled him in a mid-'50s television match, and in fact, hurt his neck with his Greco-roman backdrop finisher.

Perhaps the most famous of these situations was in the match Thesz considered in some ways the biggest, but certainly not the best match, of his career.

It was on May 21, 1952, when Thesz, the NWA champion, wrestled Baron Michele Leone, who was recognized in California as world champion, which meant a lot because the Hollywood wrestling that created Gorgeous George had tremendous national penetration. The unification match was the biggest match of that decade, selling out Gilmore Field, a minor league baseball stadium in Los Angeles.

Thesz won the three-fall match in 41:44, but from all accounts, the match was a disaster. Within the business, the story was that Thesz didn't like the colorful Baron gimmick, and had no respect for Leone's wrestling or his billing as world champion, and like he was wont to do, shut him down and gave him a spanking. Thesz's version is that Leone refused to cooperate. At the time, Thesz thought it was because Leone was mad he was losing, but later Leone told him it was over the payoff. Thesz said what happened in the ring that night was the last thing he wanted, because the hype of the first match was so strong that they could have done big business in rematches everywhere. As the match went on, he saw all that rematch money slipping away. Thesz said he whacked the hell out of him to wake him up and do something to save the match, but he couldn't get Leone to do a thing. Either way, it was an ugly sight, ending with Leone's lips swollen, one of his cheeks cut, and one of his eyes swollen shut.

His aura among the wrestlers was so great that opponents, particularly those who had never worked with him before, often froze in the ring with him. Many people had stories of wrestlers who had ability, almost going blank at first when put in the ring with him, to where they forgot what they knew.

Thesz used to tell people his biggest thrill was the first time he won the world title, at age 21, from Everett Marshall in St. Louis, becoming the youngest man in history to do so. Privately, his favorite match was in October 1955 in Pittsburgh, against Dick Hutton, an amateur wrestling legend who Thesz believed could have beaten anyone in a legitimate match, himself included. An overzealous athletic commissioner, an amateur wrestling official upset because the match was billed as for the world heavyweight championship, told the two that he wasn't going to have any fake pro wrestling shenanigans, and if he saw any fakery, he'd shut the match down immediately. Thesz and Hutton worked a three-fall match for 50 minutes, before Thesz won to retain the title. Apparently both men were able to work it to look enough like a shoot that the commissioner couldn't find any evidence they weren't doing an athletic contest. Thesz picked Hutton when he finally decided to give up the NWA title for good.

Thesz-Marshall was Thesz's first big drawing program. Thesz won the title with a count out finish when Marshall fell out of the ring after an airplane spin. Marshall got his foot tangled into the ropes and couldn't get back in the ring by the 20 count. Thesz dropped the title to Bronko Nagurski on June 23, 1939 in Houston and nearly ended a promising career.

Thesz personally liked Nagurski, who was the NFL's biggest star at the time he quit the Chicago Bears. Nagurski could draw off his football name at a time when business generally wasn't strong and was badly in need of a new superstar. But he had very little wrestling training and was not a good worker. About the only thing he could do was his football tackles, and it was up to his opponent to sell them to get it over. When he hit the tackle, Thesz flew over the top rope, lost control taking the bump, and came down on his hands and knees onto the floor, fracturing his left kneecap. After crawling back into the ring, was pinned for the second fall. Thesz recalled that his leg was numb, so limped out for a third fall, even though he was barely mobile and Nagurski pinned him quickly.

It took five years for the knee to fully recover; he adapted his style so his right leg would take most of the stress in the ring. This led to him needing a right hip replacement for the years of taking the punishment too heavily on that side. His doctors told him that was a blessing in disguise, because anyone else wrestling that long and not favoring one side would have likely needed both hips done. He had all the usual injuries, including broken ribs in 1964 when he believed Karl Gotch double-crossed him, blocking his Greco-roman backdrop finisher that was the planned ending.

When he returned from the fractured kneecap, he started wrestling in Eastern Canada, first capturing their version of the World title from Leo Numa. His feud with local hero Yvon Robert over the title, both before being drafted into World War II and after the completion of the war, was his most successful consistent run as a main event draw outside of his enduring success in St. Louis.

Thesz was stationed in Texas during the war, and actually lost the Texas title to Buddy Rogers on May 10, 1946, in Houston, which may have been the only time Thesz ever put Rogers over. It was in that year, when the two were traveling to Louisville for a main event match, when Rogers complained to Thesz that the promoter had brought in Lewis as referee, not realizing that Lewis was Thesz's childhood idol.

Thesz remembered Rogers telling him, "Why do we need that fat old bastard? The money they're paying him should be going in our pockets."

Thesz in his book admitted that since he was still in the army at the time, logical business would have dictated Rogers win the match, but Thesz refused to do anything better than a draw and never put him over in a match again.

The two were considered by many as the two biggest stars of their era and drew huge houses together for years. Their careers will always be linked, and just before Rogers's death in 1992, that the two made peace with each other.

When he returned to St. Louis after the war, the biggest star was "Wild" Bill Longson, the first true heel brawler to win a major recognized World title. But despite a booming wrestling business, promoter Tom Packs was having financial problems due to gambling debts and stock market losses and wanted to sell. Thesz wanted to buy in, and felt the $360,000 asking price for Packs's territory was a bargain.

Thesz couldn't afford that kind of money, but put together a group including himself, Montreal promoter Eddie Quinn, Toronto promoter Frank Tunney, Longson and Managoff. To the public, it was announced that Martin Thesz, Lou's father, had purchased the company from Packs with no mention of the other names, which made sense, since Thesz, Managoff and Longson were doing huge business against each other.

Thesz challenged Longson for the title in January, 1947, with Longson retaining. In booking that became the St. Louis hallmark, they stretched out the program, trying to keep Thesz's elusive title win over Longson himself from happening for as long as possible. Longson dropped the title to Whipper Billy Watson, Tunney's top star. Thesz eventually took the title from Watson, then Longson beat Thesz for the title. Thesz finally beat Longson on July 20, 1948, in Indianapolis in a famous finish where Longson took a bump outside the ring and caught his ankle in a small bucket, suffering an "injury" and being unable to continue. What made it famous, particularly among the wrestlers, is that there was little margin of error in pulling off that finish.

BUT BY 1948, Sam Muchnick started becoming strong competition in St. Louis with Rogers as his top star. In early 1949, the two sides merged, although again, kept that fact secret from the public. Muchnick was one of the founding fathers of the new National Wrestling Alliance. For the new promotion, Thesz drew strong crowds for title defenses against the likes of Enrique Torres, Gorgeous George, and Rocca. The planned "Shootout in St. Louis" to unify the belts with Orville Brown, the other side's world champion, never happened due to Brown's auto accident a few weeks before the match. Instead, after an emergency meeting of promoters, now nearly two dozen strong in the rapidly growing Alliance, Thesz was given unanimous backing as new world champion and told he could keep the title for one year, as long as he drew money.

His deal was renewed annually for the next eight years.

Muchnick became even more of a power broker with his elusive goal being to only have one world champion, Thesz, feeling a real shooter who could work and talk and handle himself well with the media and was gimmick free was the best thing for the business. It didn't hurt that in cities with promotional wars, Thesz would call out the rival's champion, who in almost every case would ignore it, thus coming across to the general public as backing down. Thesz defeated AWA champion Gorgeous George in 1950 in Chicago. George's title wasn't at stake, but the win solidified the NWA as the real championship.

There was a famous incident in Buffalo in 1950, which ended up being Thesz's introduction to someone who later became one of his closest friends. He's now Don Curtis, but was then known under his real name, Don Beitelman.

Thesz was defending his title at the arena, and was asked if he and his manager, Lewis, wanted to come to the local college and train, since they had a great heavyweight. Thesz went there, and as it turned out, there were a lot of onlookers as well as a photographer.

Beitelman then took Thesz down and put him on his back. Lewis quickly got in the way of the photographers, sensing the embarrassment if the wire services were to get a photo of the world champion, on his back at the hands of a college wrestler. As the story went, Thesz quickly reacted by putting Beitelman in a submission move and ended the workout. When the wrestling officials brought up he used an illegal move to beat their guy, his response was, "Maybe under your rules, but not mine."

With wrestling a huge hit on television, business boomed. In one poll in California, Thesz was voted one year the most popular athlete in the country. With the exception of the highest-paid boxing champions, Thesz, whose take was ten percent of the after-tax gate, and George (who often got an even higher percentage because he was such a television star) were probably the highest paid athletes of this era, earning well over the $100,000 mark that Joe DiMaggio, the highest paid salaried major sports star, earned.

Thesz debuted in Madison Square Garden in 1952. Although he was the most recognized world champion, he was not advertised as champion in his debut. His second appearance did draw a sellout, where he beat Gene Stanlee underneath a Rocca vs. Lu Kim main event. This set up Thesz vs. Rocca as a main event, again not billed as a title match, with Thesz winning via DQ. Thesz came back to headline with Pat O'Connor, going to a time limit draw before a horrible crowd, which turned out to be Thesz's last show ever in the building.

But 1953 turned into a monumental year for a number of reasons. His biggest feud was in San Francisco against future Hall of Fame football star Leo Nomellini.

Although Thesz drew some of his biggest crowds when football stars were brought in to challenge him for the title, he had little regard for any of them, with the exception of Nomellini, who was a college heavyweight wrestler at the University of Minnesota.

But for his long-term career, his biggest match was on December 6, 1953, in Honolulu. Rikidozan was a former sumo wrestler getting a big push in Hawaii. Rikidozan was put over in a tournament a week earlier to determine who would get a crack at Thesz. At the time, it was not a major match, with Thesz winning cleanly with his Greco-roman backdrop. But it ended up changing wrestling all over the world.

Rikidozan opened up pro wrestling in Japan in 1954, and was an immediate hit. Rikidozan never lost a match in Japan, drawing huge crowds and even larger television audiences as he defended Japan's honor, chopping down one huge American after another. The people thought he was unbeatable, but there loomed a shadow, Lou Thesz, the world champion, who they had never seen, but who everyone knew had pinned him clean. The longer he didn't come to Japan, the longer Riki's winning streak lasted, the larger the legend grew.

IN THE STATES, Thesz was having more and more problems with Muchnick and the NWA. The schedule as NWA champ was a killer, working two dozen or more territories. Every champ, with the exception of Dory Funk, Harley Race and Ric Flair, all eventually tapped out to the schedule demands, even though they made far more money than they could possibly make without it. Thesz felt the champion shouldn't be working in small cities, but Muchnick booked him as much as possible. Thesz hated most of the promoters, particularly when at an NWA convention, they brought up, in front of him, changing the bylaws to save money and having him fly coach instead of first class. He also demanded that if the NWA champion was on the show, there could be no women wrestlers, midget wrestlers, or wrestling bears, as he considered those acts a freak show. Thesz had a showdown when Al Haft "mistakenly" booked Thesz and women on the same bill. Thesz showed up at the building and went on a tirade. The two called up Muchnick to settle the problem. Muchnick felt since it was already advertised that way, Thesz should work the show. Thesz was irate, because he had put up such a fuss in the dressing room about it, and when Muchnick didn't back him, he lost face with the wrestlers.

In the magazines and programs of the time, his aura grew with his nearly eight-year unbeaten streak, ending with the DQ loss to Nomellini on March 22, 1955, which led to a several-month title dispute. In a situation that got a lot of mainstream press at the time and was important historically, the NWA ruled Thesz was still the champion because of the disqualification. It was this match where the rule about a title not being able to change hands on a disqualification first came into play as a hard and fast NWA rule.

But after fracturing his ankle while skiing, and continuing to wrestle on it for several weeks while using novocaine just to get in the ring, he decided to give up the title, as well as take a rest after nearly eight consecutive years on the road as champion. He dropped the title to Watson. He wanted to drop it to George Gordienko, who he believed was an elite level wrestler and one of the forgotten tough-guys in history, but they weren't able to get Gordienko into the U.S. from Canada because the government thought he was a communist. Because he'd done so much damage continually wrestling on the bad ankle, it took him several months for it to heal. Thesz regained the from Watson in 1956. There was a second quickie title change in 1957 with Edouard Carpentier in a strange match that was also used to create a lot of wrestling history.

On June 14, 1957, in Chicago, Carpentier beat Thesz when Thesz claimed a back injury and failed to come out for the third fall of their title match due to a worked back-injury finish. Carpentier was awarded the title, which was to be a short-term deal. Thesz regained the title in Montreal, but both title changes were ignored in later NWA history even though, at the time, they were recognized by Muchnick, and in every wrestling magazine. But Carpentier still was billed as world champion in some cities, and dropped the title in 1958 to Verne Gagne in Omaha (which later was used as Gagne's storyline claim for a few years later when he billed himself as world champion when his Minneapolis promotion withdrew from the NWA and created the AWA in 1960); and again in 1961 to Fred Blassie in Los Angeles to create the WWA title.

Lou Thesz was already a legend when he arrived in Japan on October 2, 1957, the final spot in a tour that included title defenses in Australia and Singapore, the first time the NWA championship had been defended outside North America. He had two matches scheduled with Rikidozan. From a mainstream stand-point, the biggest match of all time took place on October 7, 1957, at Tokyo's Korakuen Baseball Stadium, on the grounds that now house the Tokyo Dome. The match went 61 minutes, with neither man winning a fall. More importantly, everyone in the country watched the match on television. The company that was handling ratings at the time measured it as an 87.5 rating, making it, by far, the highest-rated television show ever in Japan, and blowing away any television show in history ever in the United States. Six days later, the two had a rematch in Osaka, ending in a double count out in the third fall after splitting the first two.

The impact of these matches can't be overstated. Thesz ended up going to Japan 48 times, and was always paid well and treated as royalty in that country for the

OPPOSITE: Lou Thesz held more world championship belts in his career than anyone except Ric Flair. (Dr. Mike Lano)

next four decades largely based on the impact of these matches.

Sensing the money he could make overseas and with American wrestling going into something of a tailspin, Thesz returned to the U.S., and gave Muchnick the word he was quitting the NWA. The NWA came up with Rogers as his successor, and he turned them down. Their second choice was Hutton.

He had no problems with that, and put Hutton over as strong as he possibly could. He lost it clean in 35:15 when he conceded to an abdominal stretch. With all the things said about Thesz over the years, not a lot really got to him. But something that happened after losing the title continually bothered him. After dropping the title, Thesz first went on a European tour. He billed himself World champion as he and everyone in Europe simply ignored the Hutton match. He looked to wrestle Dara Singh, a movie star in his native India. In their first match before a packed house at Royal Albert Hall, there was a major commotion. The police surrounded a short, stocky man and were trying to take him out of the building. After completing a 60-minute draw, Thesz first heard about the legend of Bert Assirati. He was the man who caused a disturbance, and when Thesz asked about him, he was told that he was the toughest man any of them had ever seen. Although only five foot six, he was a man of freakish strength, able to do a gymnastics iron cross at a weight of 240 pounds. Assirati was genuinely feared in the ring,

because when he was in a bad mood, he really did hurt people, and there was nobody who could do anything to stop him, which is why the big companies wanted nothing to do with him.

Word rarely travelled fast in those days about things overseas, but because it was Thesz, quickly the word got to the States that Assirati's reputation was so fearsome that even Thesz backed down from his challenge. Thesz had been successful enough that he bred jealousy among many wrestlers.

Thesz always claimed, that, sensing business opportunities, he sent word through the wrestlers that he wanted a private meeting, to set up a series of matches, and never heard back. When Thesz left Europe, Assirati stayed, and proclaimed for the rest of his life that he made Thesz back down, even though it was clearly a grandstand challenge, and the promoters Thesz was working for wanted nothing to do with Assirati anyway. That stuck in Thesz's craw for years.

Thesz wrestled all over North America and Europe as the World International heavyweight champion. The idea was to give the belt as much publicity as possible, before dropping it in controversial fashion to Rikidozan, who thought it would be better to win it outside of Japan, and build for rematches in Japan. After defending the title for several months, including in England, Spain, France and Belgium, Rikidozan won the belt at the Olympic Auditorium in Los Angeles on August 27, 1958, leading to probably the most lucrative matches of Thesz's career when he went back to Japan to challenge.

Thesz was living in Phoenix at this point and mainly wrestling in Southern California, but was still being brought in to many cities as a headliner. He was wrestling when he wanted to, as well as raising horses, for the next several years, when he, surprisingly, got the call from Muchnick in 1962 to come back as champion.

Thesz was scheduled to win the title from Rogers in Toronto, but shortly before the match, Rogers was attacked in the dressing room by Karl Gotch and Bill Miller in Columbus, OH and suffered a broken hand. This injury and backstage brawl was legit, including the filing of police reports. He was then scheduled to win it on November 22, 1962, in Houston. However, the day before that match, in a title defense in Montreal, Rogers suffered a broken ankle about two minutes into the first fall of a match with Killer Kowalski, which was then stopped, and he was out of action for several weeks, a scenario that for obvious reasons is questioned to this day for its coincidental nature. Kowalski had not been voted on by the board, so even though that should have been a title switch, they simply billed Kowalski as a title claimant while Rogers was injured. When Rogers returned, they set up a match in Madison Square Garden and Rogers won on January 21, 1963. Thesz caught up with Rogers three nights later in Toronto.

THE NORTHEAST PROMOTERS, Vince Sr. in particular, refused to acknowledge it as a title change, claiming it was only a one-fall match. In those days, all Toronto main events were one fall, and the NWA had several title changes in Toronto under those rules even though two out of three was the norm in most cities at that time. But they were just searching for a public reason because they had their own plans for the title. Rogers was a great draw as champion in New York, and Thesz never drew there. But to shut down that public excuse, Muchnick got Thesz and Rogers booked again for February 7, 1963, in a two-out-of-three fall match in Toronto, which drew 11,000 fans, and Thesz won with a clean pin in the third fall (Rogers did lose the first fall via DQ).

With the exception of the famed title win, his most talked about match from that period most remembered historically was actually a match that wasn't a huge deal at the time. Thesz defended against Bruno Sammartino and pinned him in less than 15 minutes. As silly as this sounds today, when Sammartino then won the WWWF title against Rogers on May 17, 1963, many people looked back at this match as proof that the NWA title was the real deal, and that Thesz was better than Sammartino.

As champion, in supposed mixed matches, Thesz beat former heavyweight boxing world champion Jersey Joe Walcott in Memphis and beat him again in several cities, among them Houston and Jacksonville. Although publicly the first match was always proclaimed as a shoot, the truth was Walcott had done two jobs earlier for Rogers, and it was a worked match.

Dory Funk had only been wrestling for about a year when he had his first match with Thesz, in Amarillo. It was by far the biggest match up to that point in his career. Funk remembers his father telling him how important this match was. When Dory told his father about all the friends and relatives who were coming his father told him, just for this show, have them buy tickets. It was that important to his future career that the word got around wrestling that he drew as big a house as possible when he got the shot after the big build up. The two wrestled each other maybe a half-dozen times over the next few years, with Dory's biggest career match once again in his climb being on March 1, 1968, in St. Louis, when Thesz pinned him.

After a Sammartino unification match never came about, Thesz's days with the belt were over, and after the suggestion being made at the NWA Convention that maybe they needed a younger champion, he agreed to lose it for the final time to Gene Kiniski. Thesz used this opportunity to return to Japan.

He wrestled Giant Baba for the International title, losing a best-of-three-falls match in 44:28. He had a short run as WWA world champion in California. He went to Bombay, India, for his famous rematch with Dara Singh before 50,000 fans, drawing off the legend Singh had created from their match in England ten years earlier.

Thesz became a wrestling outlaw, so to speak, shortly thereafter. Thesz and Toronto promoter Frank Tunney and Great Togo put together an opposition group to the established Baba-led JWP. Isao Yoshihara was the financial backer. The group was called the Trans Worldwide Wrestling Association, and Thesz was made its world champion. TWWA had money problems from the start and soon folded. Thesz and Togo tried to start yet another group with help from the Fuji Network, in 1969, but that also failed. He continued to work regularly in St. Louis, at or near the top, including many sellouts.

Thesz's last St. Louis main event was when he defeated Terry Funk. Clearly that win was to set up Thesz vs. Dory, since Thesz also held a high-profile win over Dory before he won the title. It's not clear why it didn't happen, although Muchnick wasn't happy Thesz would continually work for outlaw promotions.

Thesz did put over Dory in Atlanta. In early 1970, there was talk of building that program again. The storyline at the time was that Thesz was making a comeback, hoping to win his seventh world title.

Thesz largely retired at that point, and was living in Phoenix and working importing carpet from around the world through connections he had made in various countries as a wrestler. Thesz lost so much money in that business, that in

1973, at the age of 56, he went back to wrestling, working mainly for Nick Gulas in Tennessee for $100 per night. It was there he met his third wife, Charlie, who was 31 years his junior, and had several matches challenging Jack Brisco, who as a young child growing up as a wrestling fan in the '50s idolized Thesz, for the NWA title.

HIS MOST FAMOUS MATCH of that period was on October 14, 1973, at the old Tokyo Sumo Hall. Thesz and Karl Gotch wreslted as a tag team against Antonio Inoki and Seiji Sakaguchi, with the Japanese team going over in 47:37, the biggest success up to that point in New Japan's history. The match was remembered as a legendary classic.

Charlie's first trip to Japan was two years later, when Thesz challenged for Inoki's NWF World title on October 9, 1975, at Sumo Hall with Rocca as referee. This was not well received in the Japanese media, the idea that Inoki would defend his title against a 59-year-old man. Thesz's name had remained so strong that they drew another sellout crowd and a 20 rating for Inoki's win, but it was not the match that the tag match was two years earlier.

For the record, Thesz's last match in St. Louis was on November 15, 1974, but it wasn't supposed to happen. Thesz was booked to referee a Brisco title defense against Dory. At the last minute, Muchnick got word that Carpentier, scheduled to face George Steele, had broken his hand while wrestling in California. It was too late to find a sub,

and Thesz volunteered. It was a night Steele never forgot. He was just starting in St. Louis. He realized immediately, that there was no way he could to his "Animal" gimmick with Thesz, and had to do straight wrestling. Once he did a straight wrestling match, there was no way he could go back to his more famous gimmick, and he never got over strong in the city.

While Muchnick and Thesz ended up as close friends, and grew closer as the years went on, they had numerous business clashes. Muchnick thought Thesz, because of his status, should have been the elder statesman of the NWA. But Thesz continually worked for outlaw groups, rubbing the NWA cartel the wrong way. The Japanese stuff in the late '60s was bad enough, but the NWA relations in Japan weren't as big as they would later become.

But in 1975, when Eddie Einhorn formed the IWA, the first attempt to get national syndication and challenge the established offices, and Thesz went with them. Muchnick, as the head of the establishment, was furious on both a business and friendship level. Muchnick was getting out as NWA president, and thought for the credibility of the group, Thesz would make the perfect figurehead long-term successor. But once this happened, there is no way it could have been considered. From 1975 through 1980, Muchnick never even used Thesz as a guest referee. He finally returned on August 8, 1980, for a Harley Race vs. Ken Patera title match.

Thesz wrestled a lot in Mexico during the late '70s, while winding down his career in Japan, and still working in Tennessee. The legend of Thesz in Mexico was such that on July 26, 1975, he was brought in to challenge Mil Mascaras for the IWA title. This was the title Mascaras was given by Einhorn's group to be their flagship star in their national expansion attempt, which failed miserably. The show was booked outdoors at Plaza Mexico, a building holding nearly 50,000 for wrestling and the belief was it would set the all-time recorded attendance record for pro wrestling. But in Mexico today, nearly all the business is walk up. It was even more so in those days. There was a huge rainstorm that day and the show was a financial flop. The match was a mess, with the ring slippery with puddles and wet hair (from a few hair matches underneath). Thesz himself couldn't believe that of the fans who came, nobody left until the end of his match even with the downpour. He worked the elements into the finish, slipping on a puddle when doing his finishing double wristlock, and getting pinned.

He spent the summers from 1977-79 working for the UWA. Thesz came in billed as world heavyweight champion, and held the title for one year before dropping it to Canek in their famous match at the Palacio de los Desportes. He was 62 years old. He was defending the world title. He was so respected in Mexico, that even among the younger fans, Canek's win over "the best wrestler in the world" made him the new "best wrestler in the world."

He did some wrestling in Japan, but mainly worked as a referee for the IWE promotion. His last serious main event was in late 1979, teaming with Nick Bockwinkel over Rusher Kimura and Great Kusatsu.

After the IWE went out of business, Baba gave him work as a referee and trainer. He wrestled a one-week tour for Baba in April of 1982, and wrestled both Mitsuharu Misawa, then a promising rookie, and Shiro Koshinaka in prelim matches. He went on later tours, working as both a referee and training the younger wrestlers. His tenure with the promotion ended after a dispute with the president of All Japan.

As soon as word got out that he was done with All Japan, Joe Daigo of New Japan recruited him to join their side. He came to New Japan regularly for the next six years, including refereeing the company's first two Tokyo Dome shows on April 24, 1989—his 73rd birthday, and February 10, 1990.

In 1985, Eddy Mansfield and Jim Wilson went public on ABC's *20/20* and exposed pro wrestling, saying how it was worked, with Mansfield even blading on the air. This led to a nasty confrontation on a national talk show with Thesz arguing with both of them. He calmly challenged either of the two to a real wrestling match to see if wrestling was fake to prove if either of these guys could really wrestle. Mansfield freaked out, saying he wanted no part of shooter Lou Thesz. Wilson, a former NFL star who was nearly 30 years younger than Thesz, wouldn't oblige

either. While many would have been skeptical of Thesz at that age, one incident at that same point in time indicated Mansfield was not overreacting.

Bruiser Brody was feuding with Inoki in Japan at the same time, and to hype an upcoming feud, the Japanese decided on a storyline where Brody would be trained by Thesz to learn the technical wrestling to go along with his brawling. So they flew Thesz into Belleville, Illinois, for a training session.

Thesz was having fun showing Brody, who knew virtually no wrestling, some basic stuff. After a while, Thesz was feeling frisky and it started to get competitive. Thesz kept doing takedowns, and there was nothing Brody could do to stop him.

"I can remember when it was over, Brody coming to me and saying, 'That old son of a bitch could still beat me today. He could beat almost everybody in the business today,'" remembered St. Louis promoter Larry Matysik. "And Brody wasn't someone who was overwhelmed with anyone's legendary status in wrestling."

In 1990 New Japan came up with the idea for a live television special where they would bring some old-timers out of retirement to wrestle current stars, and asked Thesz, then 74, if he'd wrestle one last match. Thesz agreed without any hesitation, even though his doctor thought he was nuts. The idea was for Thesz, who coached Masahiro Chono the previous year in Virginia, and taught him the STF finisher as a way to give him more credibility for his new push as a top star, to put Chono over with that move. Kind of like the old teacher showing that the pupil learned his lessons well.

THE MATCH WAS A DISASTER, with Thesz's artificial hip giving away early when he tried a piledriver. They struggled through a 5:10 match before going to the finish.

It was that match where he finally had to face the fact he wasn't still 45 years old. But he was eternally grateful the next day, when Tokyo Sports came out, and they put the Thesz vs. Chono match on the front page, with three color photos, something they rarely did for pro wrestling in those days. Thesz called the three photos the only three seconds during the match where he looked like he was still a wrestler.

Thesz never took any solace in that performance or was proud of the fact that that match allowed him to be the only man in history to wrestle professionally in seven different decades.

Thesz was a major part of the Japanese wrestling scene in the early '90s as the figurehead commissioner of UWFI, a shoot group that sprang from the UWF. It was a position he took very seriously, maybe even too seriously. Thesz, Robinson, and Danny Hodge were brought in as coaches and figureheads to give the group credibility to the hardcore fans. In 1992, a period Thesz later said was the second most enjoyable period of his life in wrestling (behind only the period he was learning his craft as an enthusiastic teenager), he went back in time for a grandstand challenge.

Thesz had done them before. Joe Blanchard owned Southwest Championship Wrestling and hired Thesz as his commissioner. Thesz announced that he was inviting all the top champions from around the world to compete in a tournament to declare an undisputed world champion. The winner would get his prized world heavyweight title belt that he wore in the 1950s, and that in the hype, was supposedly the same belt people like Strangler Lewis wore. Because the company had the second most television exposure in the country, trailing only Georgia Championship Wrestling, it was a huge deal at the time.

Eventually a tournament was held in Houston, won by Adrian Adonis. But the show was a flop, drawing only 1,700 fans to the Summit even with names like Terry Funk, Wahoo McDaniel, Abdullah the Butcher, Gino Hernandez, Tully Blanchard and other top Texas draws appearing. Blanchard soon had financial problems and couldn't pay USA for the time, and lost the slot to Vince McMahon Jr. in late 1983, who used his first cable network exposure to springboard his company into going national.

Thesz did basically the same angle in Japan that he had done nine years earlier in Texas, but this time got far more publicity for it and it had major long-term repercussions. With Gary Albright as UWFI champ, a 340-pounder who had strong wrestling credentials, Thesz issued the grandstand challenge, ironically to Chono. While Chono was the focal point, he also challenged champs from the WWF, WCW, All Japan and New Japan. Once again, he said he'd present his title belt that he wore in the '50s as a prize to the winner. When Takada beat Albright, he presented him the belt, and that credibility was part of the reason Takada became such a huge draw. It was a public chess game. Thesz, who believed in a shoot Takada could beat Chono having worked out with both, said New Japan

could name the time and the place for the match and that Takada would do it for free.

Chono, after winning the NWA title tournament, said he wanted to take on all champions in a wrestling magazine interview, which was just something wrestlers in those days would say, not meaning anything by it. Thesz pounced on the article, saying they accepted Chono's challenge. Thesz then took two dozen reporters with him to the New Japan office, to demand the match take place. While something like this would normally be laughed off, and people inside wrestling were sad Thesz was involving himself in such games at his age, because of his name and the weight it carried in the press, this was turning into a huge story.

The status of UWFI, and Takada as a real world champion in Japan, benefitted greatly from the exposure. The next year, Thesz got his final major exposure in the U.S. UWFI, at the time doing huge business in Japan, convinced boxing promoter Joe Hand to market them as a new sport in the United States, called Shootfighting. The promotional campaign directly attacked pro wrestling as fake. The first PPV on October 6, 1993, drew an 0.48 buy rate, a gigantic success for a new product with no television exposure in the country. Thesz did the announcing and served as the company's spokesperson in the U.S. He went, on the broadcast and in all interviews, specifically talking about pro wrestling as being fake and what they were promoting being the real deal. This made many in the pro wrestling community furious.

Whether the American public believed it was real or not turned out to be immaterial. It didn't have the unbridled violence or freak show color of the primitive UFC, which debuted a month later to slightly lower numbers. But UFC garnered far more publicity after its first show five weeks later, as football great Jim Brown, who they used as their spokesperson, carried far more media weight than Thesz, and UFC grew in popularity. By 1995, UWFI was in financial trouble. Thesz left after not being paid, taking his belt with him.

For all the obvious reasons, there was no love lost between Thesz and Vince McMahon. Thesz praised McMahon for the production of his shows, but hated the content and direction. They were two people, very passionate about a business with diametrically opposing views of what that business was.

Still, they did business a few times. When St. Louis wasn't drawing well, McMahon used Thesz as a referee for a Roddy Piper vs. Jimmy Snuka match. In 1987, in an attempt to bring get back the older fan base, he put on a legends Battle Royal at the Meadowlands, and in one of Thesz's last matches in the U.S., and his last high-profile match, he was put over, left in the ring with O'Connor, and they demonstrated a few minutes of old style. But the show tanked at the box office.

Thesz did his own grandstand challenge of Hogan when Hogan had become a huge star in the mid-'80s. As funny as this sounds, one of his backers in the idea was Muchnick, by then retired from wrestling, but not liking McMahon's direction either. They pooled ideas on how to garner publicity to make this happen, apparently neither acknowledging Thesz was roughly 70 years old while they were talking about a shoot match with a 320-pound man who was in his early 30s.

Thesz started as a man from a different era in a totally different business. He was the only link from Strangler Lewis to Kurt Angle. He trained with Joe Stecher and Kiyoshi Tamura. For what the promoters of wrestling wanted in the 1950s as a world champion, he not only fit the bill, but he was the bill. Every champion for the next generation was compared to him.

OPPOSITE: Lou Thesz (second from right), at 84 years of age, meets with his favorite of the current group of wrestlers, Olympian Kurt Angle (far right), while Pat Patterson (far left) looks on. (Dr. Mike Lano)

Celebrate the Heroes of American Sports
in These Other Releases from Sports Publishing!

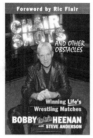

Chair Shots and Other Obstacles: Winning Life's Wrestling Matches
by Bobby Heenan
with Steve Anderson
Foreword by Ric Flair

• 6 x 9 hardcover • 192 pages
• illustrations throughout
• photo section • $24.95
• 2004 release!

King of the Ring: The Harley Race Story
by Harley Race
with Gerry Tritz

• 6 x 9 hardcover
• 250 pages
• 8-page color-photo section
• $24.95
• 2004 release!

The Ageless Warrior: The Life of Boxing Legend Archie Moore
by Mike Fitzgerald
Foreword by Jake LaMotta

• 6 x 9 hardcover • 275 pages
• photos throughout • $24.95
• 2004 release!

Like a Rose: A Celebration of Football
by Rick Telander

• 5.25 x 7.75 hardcover
• 160 pages
• photos throughout • $19.95
• Includes a bonus "Beyond the Book" DVD!
• 2004 release!

Riddell Presents The Gridiron's Greatest Linebackers
by Jonathan Rand

• 8.5 x 11 hardcover • 140 pages
• color photos throughout
• $24.95 • 2004 release!

Dick Enberg: Oh My! 50 Years of Rubbing Shoulders with Greatness
by Dick Enberg with Jim Perry

• 6 x 9 hardcover • 250 pages
• 16-page color-photo section
• $24.95 • Includes a bonus "Beyond the Book" DVD!
• 2004 release!

The Golden Voices of Football
by Ted Patterson

• 10.25 x 10.25 hardcover
• 200 pages
• photos throughout
• Includes an audio CD!
• 2004 release! • $29.95

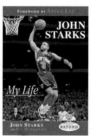

John Starks: My Life
by John Starks
with Dan Markowitz
Foreword by Spike Lee

• 6 x 9 hardcover • 250 pages
• 16-page color-photo insert
• $24.95 • 2004 release!
• Includes a bonus "Beyond the Book" DVD!

Ken Norton: Going the Distance
by Ken Norton with Marshall Terrill and Mike Fitzgerald
Foreword by Joe Frazier

• 6 x 9 hardcover
• 256 pages
• eight-page photo section
• $22.95

Earnie Shavers: Welcome to the Big Time
by Earnie Shavers with Mike Fitzgerald and Marshall Terrill
Foreword by Bert Randolph Sugar

• 6 x 9 hardcover • 245 pages
• eight-page color-photo section
• $22.95